HTML 4 For Dummies®, 4th Edition

D0465947

Golden Rules of HTML

- Always nest correctly.
- Always include ending tags in tag pair elements.
- Always quote attribute values.
- Always begin HTML documents with a DOCTYPE declaration.
- Always include the `<html>`, `<head>`, `<title>`, and `<body>` elements in your document.

Layout and Structure Elements

Element	Name	Function
`<!DOCTYPE>`	Document type	Specifies the version of HTML used in the document
`<address>` - `</address>`	Attribution information	Lists author contact information
`<body>` - `</body>`	Body	Defines or indicates a document's body
`<div>` - `</div>`	Logical divisions	Marks divisions in a document
`<h1>` - `</h1>` - `<h6>` - `</h6>`	Headings	Identifies first-level through sixth-level headings
`<head>` - `</head>`	Head	Indicates a document's head
`<html>` - `</html>`	HTML document	Identifies an HTML document
`<meta>`	Meta-information	Describes aspects of the page's information structure, contents, or relationships to other documents
`<span>` - `</span>`	Localized style formatting	Applies style to subparts of a paragraph
`<title>` - `</title>`	Document title	Briefly describes document information
`<!- - ->`	Comments	Inserts comments are not displayed by browsers

Layout Elements

Element	Name	Function
`<dd>` - `</dd>`	Definition description	Marks the definition for a term in a glossary list
`<dir>` - `</dir>`	Directory list	Marks an unbulleted list of short elements
`<dl>` - `</dl>`	Definition list	Marks a special format for terms and their definitions
`<dt>` - `</dt>`	Definition term	Marks the term being defined in a glossary list
`<li>` - `</li>`	List item	Marks a member item within a list of any type
`<menu>` - `</menu>`	Menu list	Marks a pickable list of elements
`<ol>` - `</ol>`	Ordered list	Marks a numbered list of elements
`<ul>` - `</ul>`	Unordered list	Marks a bulleted list of elements

For Dummies: Bestselling Book Series for Beginners

HTML 4 For Dummies®, 4th Edition

Cheat Sheet

BESTSELLING BOOK SERIES

Text Layout Elements

Element	Name	Function
`<abbr> - </abbr>`	Abbreviation	Identifies expansion for an acronym
`<acronym> - </acronym>`	Acronym	Indicates an acronym
`<blockquote> -</blockquote>`	Quote style	Sets off long quotations or citations
` `	Force line break	Forces a line break in the on-screen text flow
`<cite> - </cite>`	Citation markup	Marks distinctive text for citations
`<code> - </code>`	Program code text	Used for code samples
`<del> - </del>`	Deleted text	Identifies sections of a Web page deleted in revision
`<dfn> - </dfn>`	Defined term	Emphasizes a term about to be defined in the text
`<em> - </em>`	Emphasis	Emphasizes enclosed text
`<ins> - </ins>`	Inserted text	Identifies Web page sections inserted in revision
`<kbd> - </kbd>`	Keyboard text	Marks text entered by the user at the keyboard
`<p> - </p>`	Paragraph	Breaks text into content blocks
`<pre> - </pre>`	Preformatted text	Keeps spacing and layout of original text in monospaced font
`<q> - </q>`	Quotation markup	Marks a short quotation within a sentence
`<samp> - </samp>`	Sample output	Indicates sample output from a program or script
`<strong> - </strong>`	Strong emphasis	Provides maximum emphasis to enclosed text
`<sub> - </sub>`	Subscript	Renders text smaller and slightly lowered
`<sup> - </sup>`	Superscript	Renders text smaller and slightly raised
`<var> - </var>`	Variable text	Marks variable or substitution for some other value

Copyright © 2003 Wiley Publishing, Inc.
All rights reserved.

Item 1995-6.

For more information about Wiley Publishing, call 1-800-762-2974.

For Dummies: Bestselling Book Series for Beginners

HTML 4

FOR

DUMMIES®

4TH EDITION

HTML 4
FOR
DUMMIES®
4TH EDITION

by Ed Tittel & Natanya Pitts

WILEY

Wiley Publishing, Inc.

HTML 4 For Dummies®, 4th Edition

Published by
Wiley Publishing, Inc.
909 Third Avenue
New York, NY 10022
www.wiley.com

Copyright © 2003 by Wiley Publishing, Inc., Indianapolis, Indiana

Published by Wiley Publishing, Inc., Indianapolis, Indiana

Published simultaneously in Canada

For general information on our other products and services or to obtain technical support, please contact our Customer Care Department within the U.S. at 800-762-2974, outside the U.S. at 317-572-3993, or fax 317-572-4002.

Wiley also publishes its books in a variety of electronic formats. Some content that appears in print may not be available in electronic books.

Library of Congress Control Number: 2002114830

ISBN: 0-7645-1995-6

Manufactured in the United States of America

10 9 8 7 6 5 4 3 2 1

4O/TR/QR/QT/IN

About the Authors

Ed Tittel is a full-time writer-trainer who manages a small gang of technoids at LANWrights, his company in Austin, TX. Ed has been writing for the trade press since 1986 and has worked on more than 100 books. In addition to this title, Ed has worked on more than 30 books for Wiley, including *Networking Windows NT Server For Dummies, XML For Dummies,* and *Networking with NetWare For Dummies*.

Ed teaches NetWorld + Interop and for private clients on demand. He also writes regularly for *Certification* magazine, Cramsession.com, and a variety of Web sites. When he's not busy doing all that work stuff, Ed likes to travel, shoot pool, spend time with his family, and wrestle with his indefatigable Labrador retriever, Blackie.

You can contact Ed Tittel by e-mail at etittel@lanw.com.

Natanya Pitts is a writer, trainer, and Web guru in Austin, TX. She has extensive experience in the technical training realm, including overseeing the development of the materials for in-class and Web-based training offerings. She also helped establish the Austin Community College Webmaster Certification program and taught in the program for two years. Natanya has authored, coauthored, or contributed to more than a dozen Web- and Internet-related titles, including *XML For Dummies* (1st, 2nd, and 3rd Editions), *The XML Black Book,* and *XML In Record Time*. Natanya has also taught classes on HTML, Dynamic HTML, and XML at several national conferences (including MacWorld, Networld + Interop, and HP World), as well as at the NASA Ames Research Center.

You can contact Natanya Pitts at natanya@io.com.

Authors' Acknowledgments

Because this is the eighth iteration of *HTML For Dummies,* we'd like to start by thanking our many readers for making this book a continued success. We'd also like to thank them and the Wiley editorial team for the feedback that drives the continuing improvement of this book's content. Please, don't stop now — tell us what you want to do with HTML, and what you do and don't like about this book.

Let me go on by thanking my sterling coauthor, Natanya Pitts, for her efforts on this revision. I am eternally grateful for your ideas, your hard work, and your experience in reaching an audience of budding Web experts.

Next, I'd like to thank the great teams at LANWrights and Wiley for their efforts on this title. At LANWrights, my fervent thanks go to Mary Burmeister, for her services and the time spent on this book. Because Mary herself revised quite a bit of copy, she gets "nodding credit" for her more substantive contributions, too. Thanks Mary! At Wiley, I must thank Bob Woerner and Nicole Haims for their outstanding efforts, and Barry Childs-Helton for his marvelous ways with our words. Other folks we need to thank include the folks in Composition Services for their artful page layouts, and the Media Development team for their assistance with the HTML For Dummies Web site on Dummies.com.

I'd like to thank and welcome my lovely wife, Dina Kutueva-Tittel, for signing up with me all the way from Kyrgyzstan, and for making the big move from central Asia to central Texas. Welcome to my home, my heart, and my house, honey! Finally, I'd like to thank my parents, Al and Ceil, for all the great things they did for me. I must also thank my faithful sidekick, Blackie, who's always ready to pull me away from the keyboard — sometimes literally — to explore the great outdoors.

— Ed Tittel

First and foremost I'd like to thank my coauthor, Ed Tittel, for giving me the opportunity to work on this book again. It's been fun! In addition to being a great coauthor, you've been a great friend. This book wouldn't have been possible without the editorial and managerial efforts of Mary Burmeister. Thank you so much for keeping me on track and keeping me sane. Special thanks to my beloved husband, Robby, and my beautiful daughter, Alanna. All things are easier because you are a part of my life. Thanks to my parents, Charles and Swanya, for always believing in me and supporting me.

— Natanya Pitts

Publisher's Acknowledgments

We're proud of this book; please send us your comments through our online registration form located at www.dummies.com/register/.

Some of the people who helped bring this book to market include the following:

Acquisitions, Editorial, and Media Development

Senior Project Editor: Nicole Haims

Acquisitions Editor: Bob Woerner

Senior Copy Editor: Barry Childs-Helton

Technical Editor: Matthew Haughey

Editorial Manager: Leah Cameron

Permissions Editor: Carmen Krikorian

Media Development Specialist: Megan Decraene

Media Development Manager: Laura VanWinkle

Media Development Supervisor: Richard Graves

Editorial Assistant: Amanda Foxworth

Cartoons: Rich Tennant, www.the5thwave.com

Production

Project Coordinator: Dale White

Layout and Graphics: Michael Kruzil, Kristin McMullan, Tiffany Muth

Proofreaders: Tyler Connoley, John Greenough, Susan Moritz, TECHBOOKS Production Services

Indexer: TECHBOOKS Production Services

Special Help
Diana Conover

Publishing and Editorial for Technology Dummies

Richard Swadley, Vice President and Executive Group Publisher

Andy Cummings, Vice President and Publisher

Mary C. Corder, Editorial Director

Publishing for Consumer Dummies

Diane Graves Steele, Vice President and Publisher

Joyce Pepple, Acquisitions Director

Composition Services

Gerry Fahey, Vice President of Production Services

Debbie Stailey, Director of Composition Services

Contents at a Glance

Table of Contents

Introduction

• •

*W*elcome to the wild, wacky, and wonderful possibilities inherent on the World Wide Web, simply referred to as the Web. In this book, we introduce you to the mysteries of the Hypertext Markup Language (HTML), which is used to build Web pages, and initiate you into the still-select, but rapidly growing, community of Web authors.

If you've tried to build your own Web pages before but found it too forbidding, now you can relax. If you can dial a telephone or find your keys in the morning, you too can become an HTML author. (No kidding!)

When we first wrote this book, we took a straightforward approach to the basics of authoring documents for the Web. In this edition, for the latest generation of Web page designers, we mix the best of old and new approaches. As always, we keep the amount of technobabble to a minimum and stick with plain English whenever possible. Besides plain talk about hypertext, HTML, and the Web, we include lots of examples, plus tag-by-tag instructions to help you build your very own Web pages with minimum muss and fuss. We also provide more examples about what to do with your Web pages once created, so you can share them with the world. We also explain the differences between HTML 4 and XHTML, so you can decide if you want to stick with the most widely used and popular Web markup language (HTML) or the latest and greatest Web markup language (XHTML).

We also have a companion Web site for this book that contains HTML examples from the chapters in usable form — plus a number of pointers to interesting widgets that you can use to embellish your own documents and astound your friends.

About This Book

Think of this book as a friendly, approachable guide to taking up the tools of HTML and building readable, attractive pages for the Web. Although HTML isn't hard to learn, it does pack a plethora of details. You need to wrestle with these details some while you build your Web pages. Some sample topics you find in this book include

↳ Designing and building Web pages
↳ Uploading and publishing Web pages for the world to see

> ✔ Creating interesting page layouts
> ✔ Testing and debugging your Web pages

Although, at first glance, building Web pages may seem to require years of arduous training, advanced aesthetic capabilities, and ritual ablutions in ice-cold streams, take heart: It just ain't so. If you can tell somebody how to drive across town to your house, you can certainly build a Web document that does what you want it to. The purpose of this book isn't to turn you into a rocket scientist (or, for that matter, a rocket scientist into a Web site). The purpose is to show you all the design and technical elements you need to build a good-looking, readable Web page, and to give you the know-how and confidence to do it!

How to Use This Book

This book tells you how to use HTML 4 to get your page up and running on the World Wide Web. We tell you what's involved in designing and building effective Web documents that can bring your ideas and information to the whole online world — if that's what you want to do — and maybe have some high-tech fun communicating them.

All HTML code appears in monospaced type such as this:

```
<head><title>What's in a Title?</title></head>...
```

When you type HTML tags or other related information, be sure to copy the information exactly as you see it between the angle brackets (< and >), including the angle brackets, because that's part of the magic that makes HTML work. Other than that, you find out how to marshal and manage the content that makes your pages special, and we tell you exactly what you need to do to mix the elements of HTML with your own work.

The margins of a book don't give us the same room as the vast reaches of cyberspace. Therefore, some long lines of HTML markup, or designations of Web sites (called *URLs,* for *Uniform Resource Locators*), may wrap to the next line after we present them here. Remember that your computer shows such wrapped lines as a *single line of HTML,* or as a single URL — so if you're typing that hunk of code, keep it as one line. Don't insert a hard return if you see one of these wrapped lines. We clue you in that the HTML markup is supposed to be all one line by breaking the line at a slash, or other appropriate character, (to imply "but wait, there's more!") and slightly indenting the overage, as in the following silly example:

```
http://www.infocadabra.transylvania.com/nexus/plexus/lexus/
        praxis/okay/this/is/a/make-
        believe/URL/but/some/real/
        ones/are/SERIOUSLY/long.html
```

HTML doesn't care if you type tag text in uppercase, lowercase, or both (except for character entities, also known as character codes, which must be typed exactly as indicated in Appendix B of this book). To make your own work look like ours as much as possible, enter all HTML tag text in lowercase only. Those of you who own previous editions of the book may see this as a complete reversal of earlier instructions. That it is! But the keepers of the eternal and ever-magnanimous standard of HTML, the World Wide Web Consortium (W3C), have changed the rules of this game, so we changed our instructions to follow their lead. We may not make the rules, but we *do* know how to play the game!

Three Presumptuous Assumptions

They say that making assumptions makes a fool out of the person who makes them and the person who is subject to those assumptions (and just who are *They,* anyway? We *assume* we know, but . . . never mind). Even so, practicality demands that we make a few assumptions about you, our gentle reader:

- ✔ You can turn your computer on and off.
- ✔ You know how to use a mouse and a keyboard.
- ✔ You want to build your own Web pages for fun, for profit, or for your job.

In addition, we assume you already have a working connection to the Internet, and one of the many fine Web browsers available by hook, by crook, or by download from that same Internet. You don't need to be a master logician or a wizard in the arcane arts of programming, nor do you need a Ph.D. in computer science. You don't even need a detailed sense of what's going on in the innards of your computer to deal with the material in this book.

If you can write a sentence and know the difference between a heading and a paragraph, you're better off than nine out of ten playground bullies — *and* you can build and publish your own documents on the Web. If you have an active imagination and the ability to communicate what's important to you, even better — you've already mastered the key ingredients necessary to build useful, attractive Web pages. The rest consists of details, and we help you with those!

How This Book Is Organized

This book contains seven major parts, arranged like Russian *Matrioshka,* otherwise known as nesting dolls: All these parts contain three or more chapters, and each chapter contains several modular sections. Any time you need help or information, pick up the book and start anywhere you like, or use the Table of Contents or Index to locate specific topics or keywords.

Here is a breakdown of the parts and what you find in each one.

Part I: Meeting HTML in Its Natural Environment

This part sets the stage and includes an overview of and introduction to the Web and the software that people use to mine its treasures. This section also explains how the Web works, including the HTML to which this book is devoted, and the server-side software and services that deliver information to end-users (as all of us are when we're not doing battle with the logical innards of our systems).

HTML documents, also called *Web pages,* are the fundamental units of information organization and delivery on the Web. Here, you also discover what HTML is about and how hypertext can enrich ordinary text. Next, you take a walk on the Web side and build your very first HTML document.

Part II: Getting Started with HTML

HTML mixes ordinary text with special strings of characters, called *markup,* used to instruct browsers how to display HTML documents. In this part of the book, you find out about markup in general and HTML in particular. We start with a fascinating discussion of HTML document organization and structure (well . . . *we* think it's fascinating, and hope you do, too). Next, we tackle how the hyperlinks that put the H into HTML work. After that we discuss how you can find and use graphical images in your Web pages, and make some fancy formatting maneuvers to spruce up those pages.

Throughout this part of the book, we include discussion of HTML markup elements (also known as *tags*) and how they work. Thus, at the same time you learn how to lay out and design Web pages, you'll also learn about the not-so-mysterious markup that really makes HTML work.

By the time you finish Part II, expect to have a good overall idea of what HTML is, what it can do, and how you can use it yourself.

Part III: Taking HTML to the Next Level

Part III takes the same approach used in Part II and kicks it up a notch. That is, it covers the ins and outs of more complex collections of markup —

specifically tables, frames, and forms — and explores and explains them in detail, with lots of examples, to help you design and build commercial-grade HTML documents. You can get started working with related HTML tag syntax and structures that you need to know so you can build complex Web pages. By the time you knock off this section, you'll be ready to create some pretty and sophisticated Web pages of your own.

Part IV: Extending HTML with Other Technologies

By itself, HTML is good at handling text and graphics. But HTML's not terribly good at snazzing up the way such text and graphics look when they're on display, and HTML really can't *do* too much by itself. Because modern, savvy Web designers want to build interactive, dynamic Web pages, other add-ins and technologies help provide such characteristics within an HTML framework.

Thus, in this part of the book you learn about the Cascading Style Sheets (CSS) markup language that can really add color and pizzazz to Web pages. You also learn about scripting languages that enable Web pages to interact with users in interesting ways, and that also provide ways to respond to user input or actions and to grab and massage data along the way. Next, we cover what's involved in adding audio, video, or animations to your Web pages to bring them to life, as we explore various multimedia options that work well on the Web. After that, we explore various ways you can grab data from a database and import it into a Web page, and explain how HTML relates to other, more modern markup languages like the Extensible Markup Language (XML) and a recasting of HTML into XML form called the Extensible Hypertext Markup Language (XHTML).

Throughout this part of the book, we combine examples, advice, and details to help you see and understand how these extra components can enhance and improve your Web site's capabilities — and your users' experiences when visiting your pages.

Part V: From Web Page to Web Site

In this part, we expand your view on what's involved in working with HTML. By themselves, Web pages provide the focus for most real activity and development work when using HTML. But without some sense of how the sets of interlinked and interlocking Web pages known as Web sites work together, or a notion of how to design and manage collections of Web pages on a bigger scale, we wouldn't really be showing you how to make the most of HTML.

Thus, in this part of the book we explain how to manage collections of Web pages and work with entire Web sites. We begin this adventure with a discussion of typical and useful HTML tools, and exploring the contents of a typical Web professional's toolbox. We also explain what's involved in setting up a Web site online, and in arranging to share the fruits of your labors with the world. Finally, we explain what's involved in designing an entire Web site so that all its parts work together well, and so that users can understand how to find their way around and get things done within your HTML documents. As always, we provide ample examples and illustrations to show you what to do, and how to make things work.

Part VI: The Part of Tens

In the concluding part of the book, we sum up and distill the very essence of what you now know about the mystic secrets of HTML. Here, you review how to catch and kill potential bugs and errors in your pages before anybody else sees them, get a second chance to review top do's and don'ts for HTML markup, and can peruse our compendium of top HTML resources available online.

Part VII: Appendixes

The last part of this book ends with a set of appendixes designed to sum up and further expand on the book's contents. Appendix A is an alphabetical list of HTML tags, designed for easy access and reference. Appendix B contains a set of tables that document the various kinds of character codes that you can use to cause all kinds of special and interesting characters to appear within your Web pages. And finally, Appendix C provides a Glossary for the technical terms that appear in this book.

By the time you make it through all the materials in the book, you'll be pretty well equipped to build your own Web documents and perhaps even ready to roll out your own Web site!

Icons Used in This Book

This icon signals technical details that are informative and interesting, but not critical to writing HTML. Skip these if you want (but please, come back and read them later).

This icon flags useful information that makes HTML markup, Web page design, or other important stuff even less complicated than you feared it might be.

This icon points out information you shouldn't pass by — don't overlook these gentle reminders (the life, sanity, or page you save could be your own).

Be cautious when you see this icon. It warns you of things you shouldn't do; consequences can be severe if you ignore the accompanying bit of wisdom.

Text marked with this icon contains information about something that can be found on this book's companion Web site. You can find all the code examples in this book, for starters. Simply visit the Extras section of Dummies.com (`www.dummies.com/extras`) and click the link for this book. We also use this icon to point out great Web resources we think you'll find useful.

The information highlighted with this icon gives best practices — advice that we wish we'd had when we first started out! The techniques here can save you time and money on migraine medication.

Where to Go from Here

This is the part where you pick a direction and hit the road! *HTML 4 For Dummies,* 4th Edition, is a lot like the parable of the six blind men and the elephant: Where you start out doesn't matter; you'll look at lots of different parts as you prepare yourself to build your own Web pages — and each part has a distinctive nature, but the whole is something else again. Don't worry. You can handle it. Who cares if anybody else thinks you're just goofing around? We know you're getting ready to have the time of your life.

Enjoy!

Part I
Meeting HTML in Its Natural Environment

The 5th Wave   By Rich Tennant

"What you want to do is balance the image of the pick-up truck sittin' behind your home page with a busted washing machine in the foreground."

In this part . . .

This part introduces you to the Hypertext Markup Language, a.k.a. HTML. It explains the basic principles behind the way HTML works, including the markup to which this book is primarily devoted. It covers how HTML makes Web pages work, surveys how full-scale Web sites work, and offers pointers for taking best advantage of HTML's many capabilities. We conclude this part with some thrilling hands-on exposure to HTML, as you design, build, save, and view your very own first Web page.

Chapter 1

The Least You Need to Know about HTML and the Web

In This Chapter

▶ Creating HTML in text files

▶ Serving and browsing Web pages

▶ Understanding links and URLs

▶ Understanding basic HTML syntax

*W*elcome to the wonderful world of the Web and HTML. With just a little bit of knowledge, some practice, and, of course, something to say, you too can build your own little piece of cyberspace or expand on work you've already done. This book is your down-and-dirty guide to putting together your first Web page, sprucing up an existing Web page, or creating complex and exciting pages that integrate intricate designs, multimedia, scripting, and more.

The best way to get started working with HTML is to jump right in, so that's what this chapter does: It brings you up to speed on the basics of how HTML works behind the scenes of Web pages, introducing you to HTML's building blocks. When you're done here, you'll have a good idea of just how HTML works so you can start creating Web pages right away.

Introducing Web Pages in Their Natural Habitat

Web pages can contain many different kinds of content:

 Text

▸ Graphics

▸ Forms

> ✔ Audio and video files
>
> ✔ Interactive games

And that's just a partial list. Browse the Web for just a little while, and you'll come across a veritable smorgasbord of information and content displayed in various ways. And although every Web site is different, each has one thing in common: Hypertext Markup Language (HTML).

That's right, no matter what information a Web page may contain, every single Web page is created using HTML. Consider HTML to be the mortar that creates a Web page's structure; the graphics, content, and other information are the bricks. But what exactly is HTML and how does it work? Read on to find out.

Using hypertext to add structure to Web pages

Web pages are nothing more than text documents. In fact, that's what makes the Web work as well as it does. Text is the universal language of computers, which means that any text file (including a Web page) that you create on a Windows computer works equally well on a system running the Mac OS, Linux, Unix, or any other operating system.

Okay, so Web pages aren't *merely* text documents. They're documents made with text of a special, attention-deprived, sugar-loaded kind. HTML is a collection of instructions you include along with your content in a plain-text file that specifies how your page should look and behave. If this doesn't make sense to you right now — well, it will.

Hypertext or not, a Web page's status as a text file means you can create and edit it in any application that creates plain text (such as Notepad or SimpleText). In fact, when you're getting started with HTML, a text editor is the best tool to start with. Just break out Notepad, and you're ready to go. There are, of course, a wide variety of software tools with fancy options and applications (which we discuss in Chapter 16) designed to help you create Web pages, but essentially, they generate text files just as plain-text editors do.

Web browsers were created specifically for the purpose of reading HTML instructions and displaying the resulting page accordingly. For example, take a look at the Web page shown in Figure 1-1 and make a quick mental list of everything you see.

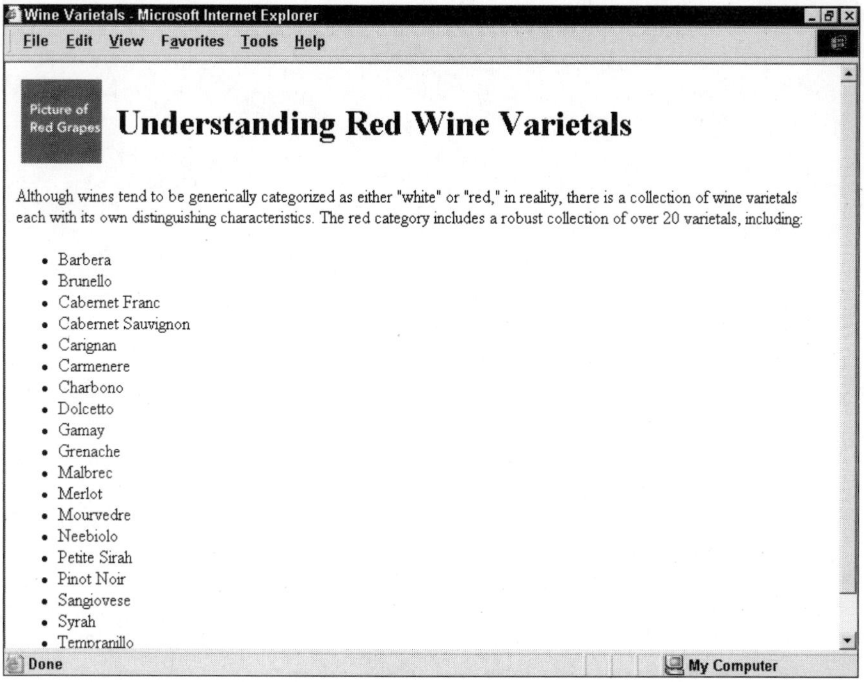

Figure 1-1:
This Web
page has
several
different
components.

The components on this page include an image, a heading that describes the information on the page, a paragraph of text about red wine, and a list of common varietals. Notice, however, that different components of the page have different formatting. The heading at the top of the page is larger than the text in the paragraph, and the items in the list have bullet points before them. The browser knows to display these different components of the page in specific ways thanks to the HTML, which looks like Listing 1-1.

Listing 1-1: Sample HTML Markup

```
<html>
  <head>
    <title>Wine Varietals</title>
  </head>


  <body>
    <h1><img src="red_grapes.jpg" width="75" height="100"
        alt="Red Grapes" align="middle" hspace="5">
        Understanding Red Wine Varietals
    </h1>
    <p>Although wines tend to be generically categorized as
        either "white" or "red," in reality, there is a
        collection of wine varietals each with its own
```

(continued)

Listing 1-1 *(continued)*

```
      distinguishing characteristics. The red category
      includes a robust collection of over 20 varietals,
      including:
  </p>
  <ul>
    <li>Barbera</li>
    <li>Brunello</li>
    <li>Cabernet Franc</li>
    <li>Cabernet Sauvignon</li>
    <li>Carignan</li>
    <li>Carmenere</li>
    <li>Charbono</li>
    <li>Dolcetto</li>
    <li>Gamay</li>
    <li>Grenache</li>
    <li>Malbrec</li>
    <li>Merlot</li>
    <li>Mourvedre</li>
    <li>Neebiolo</li>
    <li>Petite Sirah</li>
    <li>Pinot Noir</li>
    <li>Sangiovese</li>
    <li>Syrah</li>
    <li>Tempranillo</li>
    <li>Zinfandel</li>
  </ul>
  </body>
</html>
```

The text enclosed in the less-than and greater-than signs (< >) is the HTML (often referred to as the *markup*). For example, the <p>...</p> markup identifies the text about red varietals as a paragraph, and the <li>...</li> markup identifies each item in the list of varietals. And that's really all there is to it. You embed the markup in a text file along with your text to let the browser know how to display your Web page.

We delve into the basic syntax of markup a bit later in the chapter in the section "Introducing HTML Syntax and Rules." For now, what's important is that you understand that markup lives inside of a text file along with your content to give instructions to a browser.

Using a server to host your pages

Your HTML pages wouldn't be much good if you couldn't share them with the rest of the world, and Web servers make that possible. A *Web server* is a computer that's connected to the Internet, has Web server software installed, and can respond to requests for particular pages from Web browsers.

Just about any computer can be a Web server, including your home computer; however, Web servers are generally computers dedicated to the task. Although you don't have to be an Internet or computer guru to put your Web pages out so anyone can access them, you do have to find a Web server for your Web pages. If you're building pages for a company Web site, you may already have a Web server to put them on; you just have to ask your IT guru for the information. However, if you're starting a new site for fun or for profit, you'll need to find a host for your pages.

Web hosting is a big business these days, so finding an inexpensive host is easy. We lay out all of the details on figuring out what your hosting needs are and finding the perfect provider in Chapter 17.

Understanding basic browser technology

The last piece of the Web puzzle is a Web browser. Web browsers take instructions written in HTML and use these instructions to display a Web page's content on your screen. Think of it this way: Microsoft Word documents are best viewed using Microsoft Word. You can use other word-processing programs (or even different versions of Word) to view Word documents, and for the most part, the documents look pretty much the same. This concept applies to HTML documents. You should always write your HTML with the idea that people will be viewing the content using a Web browser. Just remember that there's more than one kind of browser out there, and each one comes in several versions.

Usually, Web browsers request and display Web pages available via the Internet from a Web server, but you can also display HTML pages you've saved on your own computer before making them available on a Web server on the Internet. When you're developing your own HTML pages, you view these pages (called *local* pages), in your browser. You can use local pages to get a good idea of what people see when the page goes live on the Internet.

The most important thing to remember about Web browsers is that *each browser interprets HTML in its own way*. The same HTML doesn't look exactly the same from one browser to another. When you're working with basic HTML, the variances aren't significant, but when you start integrating other elements (such as scripting and multimedia), things get a little hairy. The bottom line is that the browser has the ultimate control over how your Web pages look, so you should concentrate on creating solid HTML and let the browser do the rest.

A bevy of browsers

The Web world is full of browsers of many shapes and sizes — or rather versions and feature-sets. The two most popular browsers available today are Microsoft Internet Explorer and Netscape Navigator (sometimes called Mozilla), but there are others like Opera and Amaya in use as well. As a user, you have probably chosen a browser you like best, but as an HTML developer you have to think beyond your own browser needs. Every user has his or her own browser preference and browser settings.

To make things even more complicated (or challenging if you choose to see the glass as half-full), each browser renders your HTML just a bit differently. In addition, every browser handles JavaScript, multimedia, style sheets, and other HTML add-ins just a bit differently. When you throw in different operating systems (Mac or Windows), things get really fun. Most of the time, the differences in the way two browsers display the same HTML will be negligible, but other times, a particular combination of HTML, text, and media may bring a particular browser to its knees.

The bottom line is as you begin to work more with HTML, you'll need to test your pages on as many different browsers as you can manage. You should install two or three different browsers on your own system (we recommend the latest versions of Internet Explorer, Netscape, and Opera) for testing purposes. To access a fairly complete list of the browser's available, visit Yahoo!'s Web browser category (http://dir.yahoo.com/Computers_ and_Internet/Software/Internet/ World_Wide_Web/Browsers/).

In Chapter 3, you find out how to use a Web browser to view a local copy of your first Web page. You can choose from one of several Web browsers to view your pages, but we suggest that you start with the browser you use now to surf the Web. That way you don't have to get used to a new browser *and* get comfortable with HTML all at the same time.

Most people view the Web with graphical browsers (such as Netscape or Internet Explorer) that display images, text formatting, complex layouts, and more. However, some people prefer to use text-only browsers (such as Lynx) because they're visually impaired and can't take advantage of a graphical display or because they like a lean, mean Web server that just displays content. Even if you choose to view the Web with a graphical browser, you should always be sensitive to the fact that at least some of the viewers of your page will only see your page in text. Chapter 18 includes more information on how to make your Web page accessible to everyone regardless of the type of browser they choose to use.

Understanding how hyperlinks make the Web the Web

The World Wide Web comes by its name honestly. It's quite literally a Web of HTML pages hosted on Web servers around the world, connected in a million different ways. Of course, those connections aren't made with spider webbing, but are instead created by *hyperlinks* that connect one page to the next. Without those links (as they're called for short), the Web could still exist, but rather than being a collection of interrelated pages that users can easily traverse, it would just be a group of standalone pages.

In fact, a healthy portion of the Web's value is its ability to link to pages and other resources (such as images, downloadable files, and media presentations) on the same Web site or on another one. For example, FirstGov (`www.firstgov.gov`) is a *gateway* Web site — its sole function is to provide access to other Web sites. If you aren't sure which government agency handles first-time loans for homebuyers, or want to know how to arrange a tour of the Capital, you can visit this site (shown in Figure 1-2) to find out.

TECHNICAL STUFF

Introducing Internet protocols

Interactions between browsers and servers are made possible by a set of computer-communication instructions called the Hypertext Transfer Protocol (HTTP) protocol. This protocol defines all the rules about how browsers should request Web pages and how Web servers should respond to those requests.

HTTP isn't the only protocol at work on the Internet. The Simple Mail Transfer Protocol (SMTP) and Post Office Protocol (POP) protocols make e-mail exchange possible, and the File Transfer Protocol (FTP) allows you to upload, download, move, copy, and delete files and folders across the Internet. The good news

is that Web browsers and servers do all of the HTTP work for you, so you don't have to do anything more than put your pages on a server or type a Web address into a browser to take advantage of this protocol.

If you're interested in how HTTP works, we recommend Webmonkey's article "HTTP Transactions and You" at

```
http://hotwired.lycos.com/
    webmonkey/geektalk/97/06/
    index4a.html
```

for a good overview.

Figure 1-2:
FirstGov is a
gateway
that uses
hyperlinks
to help
visitors find
government
information
on the Web.

Introducing URLs

The Web is made up of millions of resources, each of them linkable. Knowing a page's (or some other resource's) exact location is the key to creating a successful hyperlink to it. Also, without the exact address (called a *Uniform Resource Locator* or URL), you can't use the Address bar in a Web browser to visit a Web site or Web page directly.

URLs provide the standard addressing system for resources on the Web. Each resource (whether Web page, site, or individual file) has a unique URL. URLs work a lot like your postal address. For example, your address includes some general information, such as the state and city you live in, but then it narrows to specify what street you live on, and then what building, and maybe which apartment in that building. And if that isn't specific enough, when you add your name to the address, you have a very precise definition of to whom a piece of mail is supposed to go.

A URL uses a similar approach to zero in on its destination: It begins with generic information and includes increasingly specific information until it points to a single, unique file on the Web. Figure 1-3 identifies the components of a URL.

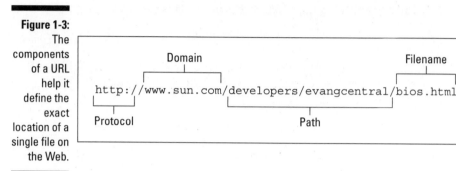

Each component of a URL plays a particular role in defining the location of a Web page or other Web resource:

- ✔ **Protocol:** This portion of the link specifies which protocol the browser should follow when it requests the file. The protocol for Web pages is `http://` (the familiar precursor to most Web URLs).

- ✔ **Domain:** This part of the link points to the general Web site (such as `www.sun.com`) where the file resides. A single domain may host a few files (as does a personal Web site) or millions (as does a corporate site like `www.sun.com`).

- ✔ **Path:** This part of the link names the sequence of folders through which you have to navigate before you get to a particular file. For example, to get to a file in the `evangcentral` folder that resides in the `developers` folder, you would use the `/developers/evangcentral/` path.

- ✔ **Filename:** The name of the file specifies exactly which file in a directory path the browser should access.

The URL shown in Figure 1-3 points to the Sun domain and offers a path that leads to a specific file named `bios.html`:

```
http://www.sun.com/developers/evangcentral/bios.html
```

Chapter 5 provides the complete details on how you use HTML and URLs to add hyperlinks to your Web pages, and Chapter 17 discusses how to obtain a URL for your own Web site after you're ready move it to a Web server.

Introducing HTML Syntax and Rules

All things considered, HTML is a very straightforward language for describing the contents of a Web page. Its components are easy to use — and when you know how to use a little bit of HTML, the rest follows naturally. HTML has three main components:

- ✔ **Elements:** Identify different pieces and parts of an HTML page.
- ✔ **Attributes:** Provide additional information about an instance of an element.
- ✔ **Entities:** Represent non-ASCII text characters such as copyright symbols (©) and accented letters (É). (See Appendix B for more details.)

Every bit of HTML markup that you used to describe a Web page's content includes some combination of elements, attributes, and entities.

The following sections cover the basic form and syntax for elements, attributes, and entities. All the chapters in Parts II and III of the book include details on how to use elements and attributes to do the following:

- ✔ Describe particular kinds of text (such as paragraphs or tables)
- ✔ Create a particular effect on the page (such as changing a font style)
- ✔ Add images and links to a page

Elements

Elements are at the core of HTML, and you use them to describe every piece of text on your page. Elements are made up of *tags,* and an element may have either a start and end tag, or just a start tag. Here's how you know which kind of tag or tags to use:

- ✔ **Elements that describe content use a tag pair:** Content like paragraphs, headings, tables, and lists always use a tag pair that follows the same syntax:

```
<tag>...</tag>
```

For example, the red wine varietal page in Listing 1-1 used the paragraph element (`<p>`) to describe a paragraph:

```
<p>Although wines tend to be generically categorized as either "white"
    or "red," in reality, there is a collection of wine varietals
        each with
    its own distinguishing characteristics. The red category includes a
    robust collection of over 20 varietals, including:
</p>
```

The paragraph element uses a *tag pair* (that is, two tags, one at the start and the other at the end) to surround the text of the paragraph. Think of the start tag as an *on* switch that says to the browser, "The paragraph begins here" — and the end tag as an *off* switch that says, "The paragraph ends here."

✔ **Elements that insert something into the page use one tag:** Content like an image or a line break always uses a single tag:

```
<tag>
```

Listing 1-1 also uses the image element (`<img>`) to include an image on the page:

```
<img src="red_grapes.jpg" width="75" height="100" alt="Red Grapes"
     align="middle" hspace="5">
```

The `<img>` element uses a *single* tag (called an *empty element*) to reference an image. When the browser displays the page, it replaces the `<img>` element with the file that it points to (it uses an attribute to do the pointing, which we discuss next).

You can't go around making up your own HTML elements. The elements that are legal in HTML form a very specific set — if you try to use elements that aren't part of the HTML set, every browser in the universe will ignore them. The actual set of elements you *can* use is defined in the HTML 4.01 specification, discussed later in this chapter.

Many page structures (like the list of red wines you saw earlier) use combinations of elements to describe part of your page. In the case of a bulleted list, for example, the `<ul>` element specifies that the list is unordered (bulleted), and `<li>` elements mark each item in the list.

When you combine elements by this method (called *nesting*), be sure you close the inside element completely before you close the outside element:

```
<ul>
  <li>Barbera</li>
  <li>Brunello</li>
</ul>
```

Think of your elements as suitcases that fit neatly within one another, and you can't go wrong.

Attributes

Attributes allow variety in the way an element describes content or works on the page. Think of attributes as extending an element so you can use it differently depending on the circumstances. For example, the `<img>` element uses the `src` attribute to specify the location of the image you want to include at a particular spot on your page:

```
<img src="red_grapes.jpg" width="75" height="100" alt="Red Grapes"
     align="middle" hspace="5">
```

In this bit of HTML, the `<img>` element itself is a general flag to the browser that you want to include an image; the `src` attribute provides the specifics on the image you want to include, `red_grapes.jpg` in this instance. Other attributes (such as `width`, `height`, `align`, and `hspace`) provide information about how to display the image, and the `alt` attribute provides a text alternative to the image if the browser doesn't display the image.

Chapter 6 discusses the `<img>` element and its attributes in detail.

You always include attributes within the start tag of the element you want them to go with — after the element name but before the closing greater-than sign, like this:

```
<tag attribute="value" attribute="value">
```

Attribute values must always appear in quotation marks, but you can include the attributes and their values in any order *within the start tag.*

Every HTML element has a collection of attributes that can be used with it, and you can't mix and match attributes and elements. Some attributes can take any text as a value because the value could be anything, like the location of an image or a page you want to link to. Others have a specific list of values the attribute can take, such as your options for aligning text in a table cell. The HTML 4.01 specification defines exactly which attributes you can use with any given element and which values (if explicitly defined) each attribute can take.

Each chapter in Parts II and III of the book covers which attributes you can use with each HTML element.

Entities

Although text makes the Web possible, it does have its limitations. There are characters that basic ASCII text doesn't include, such as trademark symbols, fractions, and accented characters. For example, the list of white wine varietals shown in Figure 1-4 includes two accented *e* characters (é) and two *u* characters with umlauts (ü).

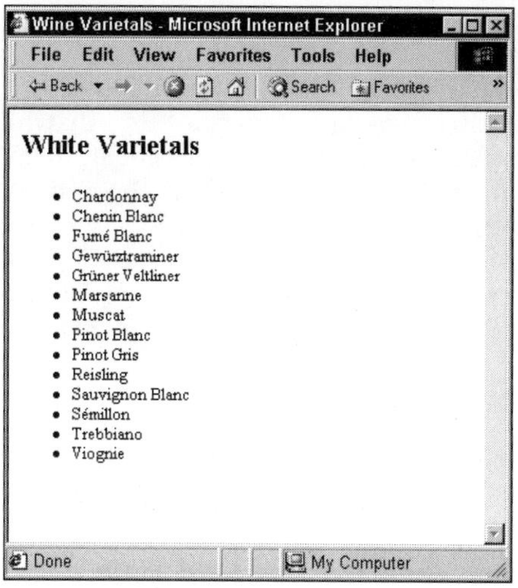

Figure 1-4:
ASCII text
can't
represent
all text
characters
so HTML
entities do
instead.

Because ASCII text doesn't include either the accented *e* or the umlauted *u*, the HTML uses *entities* to represent them instead. When the browser comes across the entity, it replaces it with the character it references. Every entity begins with an ampersand (&) and ends with a semicolon (;). The following markup shows the entities in bold:

```
<html>
<head>
<title>Wine Varietals</title>
</head>

<body bgcolor="#FFFFFF">
  <h2>White Varietals</h2>
  <ul>
    <li> Chardonnay</li>
    <li>Chenin Blanc</li>
    <li>Fum&eacute; Blanc</li>
    <li>Gew&uuml;rztraminer</li>
    <li>Gr&uuml;ner Veltliner</li>
    <li>Marsanne</li>
    <li>Muscat</li>
    <li>Pinot Blanc</li>
    <li>Pinot Gris</li>
    <li>Reisling</li>
    <li>Sauvignon Blanc</li>
    <li>S&eacute;millon</li>
    <li>Trebbiano</li>
    <li>Viognie</li>
</ul>
</body>
</html>
```

The entity that represents the *e* with the acute accent is é and the entity that represents the umlauted u is ü.

As you might expect, the HTML specification lays out exactly which entity you use to replace every non-ASCII character the specification supports. Appendix B includes a complete list of characters and the entities you use to represent them in your HTML.

In addition to non-ASCII characters, you also use entities to represent the characters that HTML uses to differentiate itself from the text around it:

- ✔ **less-than sign (<):** <
- ✔ **greater-than sign (>):** >
- ✔ **ampersand (&):** &

As you may have noticed, the < and > signs are used all the time as part of the markup, but these symbols are *instructions to the browser* and won't actually show up on the page. So if you ever need these symbols to appear on the Web page, you have to include the entities for them in your page, like this:

```
<p>The paragraph element identifies some text as a paragraph:</p>
<p>&lt;p&gt;This is a paragraph.&lt;/p&gt;</p>
```

In the first line of the following markup, we use tags to describe a simple paragraph. The second line shows how to use entities to describe the < and > symbols. Figure 1-5 shows how the browser converts these entities to characters to show the results of your markup in a browser window.

Figure 1-5:
Always use entities when you want to display a less-than sign, greater-than sign, or ampersand in the browser window.

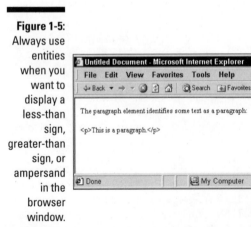

The HTML 4.01 Specification

The HTML 4.01 specification is the rulebook of HTML — it tells you exactly which elements you can use, which attributes go with those elements, and how you use elements in combinations to create lists, forms, tables frames, and other page structures.

The HTML specification uses *Document Type Definitions* (DTDs) written in the Standard Generalized Markup Language (SGML) — the granddaddy of all markup — to define the details of HTML. In its earlier versions, HTML used elements for formatting; over time, developers realized that formatting needed its own language (now called *Cascading Style Sheets,* or CSS) and that HTML elements should just describe a page's structure. That's how the three flavors of HTML that the specification includes came to be:

- ✔ **HTML Transitional:** A version of HTML that includes elements to describe font faces and page colors. HTML Transitional represents a version that accounts for formatting elements in older versions of HTML. Formatting elements in HTML Transitional are *deprecated* (considered obsolete) because the W3C would like to see HTML developers move away from them and to a combination of HTML Strict and CSS.

- ✔ **HTML Strict:** A version of HTML that doesn't include any elements that describe formatting. This version is designed to work with CSS driving the page formatting.

  The CSS-with-HTML Strict approach is an ambitious way to build Web pages, but in practice it has its pros and cons. CSS provides more control over your page formatting, but creating style sheets that work well in all browsers can be tricky. Chapter 11 discusses style sheets and the issues around using them in more detail.

- ✔ **HTML Frameset:** A version of HTML that includes *frames,* which is markup that allows you to display more than one Web page or resource at a time in the same browser window.

All Web browsers support all elements in HTML Transitional; thus you can choose to use elements from it or stick with HTML Strict instead. If you use frames, you'll technically be working with HTML Frameset, but all of the elements work in the same way.

In this book, we cover all HTML tags in all versions, lumping them into a single category (aptly called HTML) because all real-world Web browsers support these three flavors — and they're extremely unlikely to withdraw support for HTML Transitional or HTML Frameset any time soon. What this means is you have a large assortment of elements to choose from when you create your HTML, so you can build the best possible Web page.

Of course, you'll find all the details of the HTML elements, their attributes, and their usage here in this very book — so you don't have to struggle with reading DTDs or arcane technical specifications if you want to learn HTML. Even so, if you ever want to go to the source, it's good to know where the horse's mouth is and what it says. You can review the HTML 4.01 specification and the HTML DTDs at www.w3.org/TR/html4.

Chapter 2

HTML at Work on the Web

*H*TML is rather straightforward, and it's pretty simple to create a tag or two and throw some text in — which is great if you want to create a one-line Web page. However, there's much more to building a Web page than just creating a couple of tags and adding some text. Even the simplest Web page is a well-planned collection of elements and text with images thrown in for good measure.

In the end, your goal is to use HTML to put information on the Web. Whether you want to sell a product, tell potential clients more about your services, or share Christmas pictures, be sure you have a clear idea of what you want HTML to do for you. When you have that firmly in mind, it's just a matter of using the right HTML to get the result you're looking for (which is what the majority of this book is about, of course).

This chapter looks at what others are doing with HTML on the Web — it may spark your imagination if you don't have a Web page goal in mind just yet, or help you refine your ideas if you do. Then we take a look at how you might want to use different elements such as images, multimedia, and even (gasp) programming in your page so you can bring your Web-page plan closer to its final form.

You don't have to know exactly how your page will behave or how it will look before you start creating HTML. In fact, you'll soon discover that Web pages are constantly evolving entities that take on a life of their own. Even so, if you have a basic plan in mind, you'll be able to better direct your HTML work and focus first on those elements and attributes that you need most. You can pick up other elements as your page requires.

What Others Are Doing with HTML

Spend a few moments surfing the Web and you'll quickly see how others are using HTML. From news sites to online stores to personal home pages, HTML helps people around the world share information of incalculable variety.

Building Web pages and Web sites

At its heart, the Web is a collection of Web pages, all built with HTML. Although Web technologies have greatly evolved to include complex programming, streaming multimedia, and intricate interfaces, every Web site starts with a single Web page, and every Web page starts with HTML. The complexity of a Web page has everything to do with both its content as well as the message its creator needs to convey. (Often, these are two sides of the same coin.)

For example, the Impact Online Web page (www.impactonline.com), shown in Figure 2-1, serves as a simple marketing tool for a consultant to let potential clients know what services he offers.

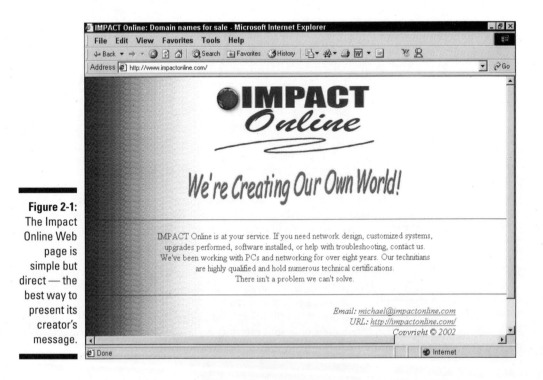

Figure 2-1: The Impact Online Web page is simple but direct — the best way to present its creator's message.

In contrast, the World Wide Web Consortium (W3C) home page (www.w3.org), shown in Figure 2-2, is much more complex and contains more content (hence more HTML) because the page serves as a portal to the vast resources of the W3C.

Even though these two pages are vastly different, they use the same collection of HTML elements and attributes to make content appear in a Web browser. The W3C page has more markup and may use different HTML constructs (such as complex tables) than the Impact Online page does. In the end, they're both just Web pages built with HTML.

If you're thinking that you *have* to do something different with your HTML to build a Web site, think again. A Web site is nothing more than a collection of Web pages. You'll most likely use hyperlinks (discussed in detail in Chapter 5) to connect pages so visitors can easily navigate your site, but all you're really doing is connecting several pages into a cohesive collection of related information.

With the right tools, a hosting provider, and a good interface, you can grow a single Web page into a larger Web site. Check out Chapters 16 through 18 in Part V of this book for the basics.

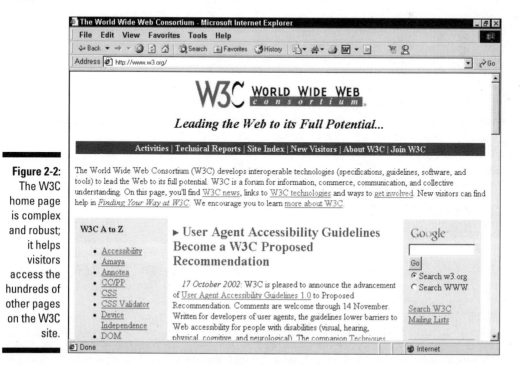

Figure 2-2: The W3C home page is complex and robust; it helps visitors access the hundreds of other pages on the W3C site.

Creating programming- and database-driven sites

Many Web sites these days go beyond plain HTML to include programming code that makes the sites interactive and responsive to individual user needs and preferences. For example, when you visit an online store and add items to your shopping cart, the Web pages you see are different from the ones other visitors see. Each visitor's shopping cart is unique; everyone's view of the shopping cart in a Web browser is unique.

HTML is designed only to help you *display* information. If you want that information to provide a smart response for different viewers (such as varying the display automatically to fit the person viewing it), you'll need some other technologies in addition to HTML.

For example, sites that offer advanced features — such as shopping carts, bill payment, customized news, and personalized displays — use both programming code and databases to make these features work.

Don't let the words *programming* and *database* intimidate you. Neither is required to put together a solid Web site of well-designed and robust pages. There are entire Web sites that meet their goals beautifully without using a lick of programming code (the W3C is a great example). Fortunately, if you find that the only way to meet your page's goals is with programming (selling products online is a typical example), the Web is chock-full of resources to help you.

Chapters 10, 12, and 14 look more closely at what it takes to add programming and database functionality to your Web page or site.

Deciding What You Want to Use HTML For

You've looked around the Web a bit and know what others are dong with their pages, and you have an idea of what you want your page to do, but now it's time to solidify that idea into a more concrete plan. (Okay, we admit that your plan will probably change along the way, but you have to start somewhere.)

To help formulate that plan, answer the four questions that head the upcoming sections as best you can now; revisit them from time to time as your Web page evolves. You can consult the resulting design for your page as you write your HTML.

What do you want your page to do for you?

Why are you building a Web page? Is it for fun, for profit, for some of both? The most important thing you need to know about your page is *what you want it to do for you.* Everything else about your page, from the way it looks to the information and HTML you use to build it, grows out of that one idea.

For example, if you decide to build a Web version of your résumé to give to potential employers or to help drum up some consulting business, you can make some good assumptions about how that page should look and decide what information absolutely must be on it:

- The design should be professional.
- Graphics won't play a large role because the meat of the page should be your work history and other relevant information.
- You will use a combination of headings, paragraphs, lists, and other text elements to build the page.
- The page may link to the Web sites of companies you've worked on in the past.
- You might want to include downloadable versions of your résumé in text, PDF, or Microsoft Word format for easy printing.

Although you may decide to expand your résumé page later into a site that includes examples of your work or references, initially your presence will be just a single page.

If, however, you're planning to put together a digital scrapbook that chronicles your growing family's adventures, you will make a completely different set of assumptions, such as these:

- The design can be fun, playful, and a reflection of your family's personality.
- Graphics, digital video, and even audio clips will play a significant role in the site because images are what digital scrapbook is all about.
- The markup you use may very well run the entire HTML gamut because your page will include everything from text to images to media.
- You may want to link to other family members' Web sites, to your kid's favorite toy stores, or to maps that show the places you visited on vacation.
- You might want to set up a family mailing list or a guest book so visitors to your site can play an active role in the site.

Your site may begin with a single page, but chances are it will rapidly grow into an entire Web site.

When you lay out the assumptions for your page along the same general lines shown here, you catch a glimpse of how your page will evolve from an idea to a Web creation — and what it will take to get you there.

How do you want your page to look?

The way your page looks is critical to how effectively it does its job. Don't believe us? Read the following list and imagine what you might think if you saw pages that matched these descriptions:

- ✔ **Plain = uninteresting:** If the site is too plain, people won't be interested and may not stick around long enough to get to the important information.
- ✔ **Busy = disorienting:** If the page is a riot of images and colors, people may be overwhelmed and visit another site just to give their eyes a rest.
- ✔ **Theme doesn't match content = a joke:** Visitors won't take you or your information seriously if your design doesn't match the information on the page. (A Hawaiian luau, for example, really isn't an appropriate theme for a résumé page unless you cater luaus for a living.)

Although you can continually tweak and update the look and feel of your page, it's a good idea to set aside some time *before* you build the page to decide what you want it to look like. Some quick and easy routes to an initial design idea include these:

- ✔ Bookmark or print pages from other Web sites whose designs are similar to what you want to use.
- ✔ Sketch a design on paper or even a napkin at a restaurant. Just don't smear ketchup on the design.
- ✔ Clip ads and other layouts from magazines if they spark your interest.

The goal here isn't to become a graphic designer or to finalize every detail of your page's appearance. Rather, you want to begin to build an overall *idea* of what you want your HTML to do for you so you can construct it accordingly.

Do you need multimedia, scripts, or other advanced features?

You need to decide whether the overall plan for your page requires that you use multimedia, a shopping cart, a guest book, or any other features that go beyond what HTML can do for you. For example, if you plan to build an online store, you'll need a shopping cart and some form of online payment system. However, a site that just lists your consulting services may not need these features at all.

Table 2-1 shows you different kinds of features you might consider, what kind of effort and skills you might need to do the work yourself, and where you can find information on these skills.

Table 2-1	Adding Advanced Features to a Page	
Feature	*Degree of Difficulty*	*See*
Forms to gather information from visitors	Although many of your Web pages will be designed to present users with information, you may want to gather information from users as well. Suggestion forms, a guest book, and a request for more information page are just a few examples of how you can use forms to interact with your users. Creating HTML isn't difficult, but you'll need to have a script or other application running in the background to work with the form data. Luckily, many such scripts are available on the Web for free.	Chapter 10
Image rollovers, drop-down menus, and other dynamic features	To make your Web page do interesting things such as dynamically swap images, display menus that appear and disappear, and hide and show content with the click of a button, you'll need to use JavaScript or VBScript. Neither is difficult to learn, and the Web is full of example scripts you can leverage.	Chapter 12
Multimedia	Actually adding audio, video, and multimedia to your Web page is easy. Digitizing and editing the multimedia presentations however requires a bit of knowledge and the right equipment.	Chapter 13
Shopping cart	Without any programming knowledge, creating a shopping cart from scratch is not easy. However, many Web site hosting providers have shopping cart tools you can easily integrate into your site for a small fee.	Chapter 14

If your page needs advanced features to meet its goal, you'll need to plan for those at the beginning of your page-building fun — especially if you plan to have someone (such as a consultant or even a friend with the right skills) help you. Think carefully about how you want your advanced features to behave. Consider whether (and then decide how) they will fit with the other elements on your page. Then write everything down so you have a guide for the person helping you put the features together.

If you're not sold on using advanced features now but you think they may be nice to have later on, you can always make a few notes about how you might integrate them into your page, and then set a time frame for either learning how to build them, or for working with someone to have them built.

Do you plan to create a Web site?

If you intend for your Web page to grow into a larger site, start thinking about that larger site as you build the page. Sketch some ideas of other pages your site might include, and how those pages relate to the first page you plan to build. Don't worry too much about those future pages themselves just yet; often an overall page design is different when there are more pages to follow.

Planning ahead for a complete site later can save you a lot of rework on the page you build now. Chapters 17 and 18 provide you the basics about planning and building a site that is easy for visitors to use and that achieves your site goals.

If you aren't sure whether you want your page to grow into a larger site later on, don't sweat it. The great thing about HTML is that you can quickly update it and place a new version of your page on the Web immediately for all to see. When you take advantage of HTML's organic nature, every markup, design, and content decision you make is reversible.

Chapter 3

Creating Your First HTML Page

· ·

In This Chapter

▶ Planning your Web page

▶ Writing some HTML

▶ Saving your page

▶ Viewing your page offline and online

▶ Editing your page

· ·

*C*reating your very first Web page can seem a little daunting, but it's definitely fun, and our experience tells us the best way to get started is to jump right in with both feet. You might splash around a bit at first, but you'll keep your head above water without too much thrashing.

This chapter walks you through four simple steps to creating a Web page. We won't stop and explain every nuance of the markup you're using — we save that for other chapters. Instead, we just want you to get comfortable working with markup and content to create and view a Web page.

Before You Get Started

Creating HTML documents is a little different from creating word-processing documents in an application like Microsoft Word because you have to use two applications: You do the work in one (your text or HTML editor) and view the results in the other (your Web browser). Well, okay, it is a bit unwieldy to edit in one application and switch to another in order to look at your work, but you'll be switching like a pro from text editor to browser and back in (almost) no time.

To get started on your first Web page, you need two things:

✔ A text editor such as Notepad or SimpleText

✔ A Web browser

All figures in this chapter show HTML created with TextPad, a shareware plain-text editor available from `www.textpad.com`.

We discuss these basic tools in a little more detail in Chapter 6. Also, if you plan to use an HTML editor such as FrontPage or Dreamweaver to do your HTML work, put it away for now and whip out good ol' Notepad instead. More advanced HTML editors often hide your HTML from you, and for the purposes of your first page, you want to see your HTML in all of its glory. You'll be able to make a smooth transition to a more advanced editor later.

Although you might be tempted to use Microsoft Word or some other word processor instead of Notepad or a plain-text editor to work with HTML, we strongly recommend that you don't. Word processors tend to store a lot of extra information behind the scenes of the files they create (for example, formatting instructions your computer needs to display or print said files) that you can't see or change, but that will interfere with your HTML.

Creating a Page from Scratch

Using HTML to create a Web page from scratch involves four straightforward steps:

1. **Plan your page design.**
2. **Combine HTML and text in a text editor to make that design a reality.**
3. **Save your page.**
4. **View your page in a Web browser.**

So break out your text editor and Web browser and roll up your sleeves.

Step 1: Planning a simple design

Although you *can* just start writing HTML without a final goal in mind, we've discovered (painfully) over time that a few minutes spent planning your general approach to a page at the beginning of your work will make the whole page creation process much easier. You don't have to create a complicated diagram or elaborate graphical display in this step; just jot down some ideas for what you want on the page and how you want it arranged.

You don't even have to be at your desk to plan your simple design. Take a notepad and pencil outside and design in the sun, or scribble on a napkin while you're having lunch. Remember, this is supposed to be fun.

The example in this chapter is our take on the traditional "Hello World" exercise used as the most basic example for just about every existing programming language. Customarily, you learn how to use a programming language to display the phrase `Hello World` on-screen. In our example, we create a short letter to the world instead, so the page is a bit more substantial and gives you more to work with. Figure 3-1 shows our basic design for this page.

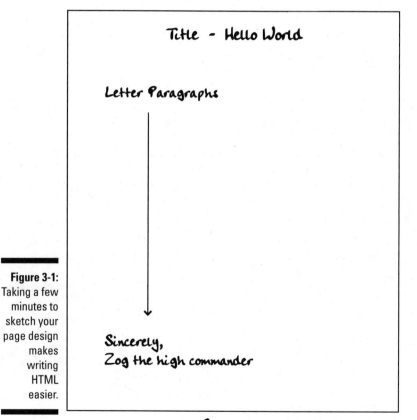

Figure 3-1: Taking a few minutes to sketch your page design makes writing HTML easier.

The basic design for the page includes four basic components:

- A serviceable title: "Hello World".
- A few paragraphs explaining how the page's author plans to help the Earth meet its yearly quota of Znufengerbs.
- A salutation of "Sincerely".
- A signature.

Don't forget to jot down some notes about that color scheme you want to use on the page. For effect, we decided that our example page should have a black background and white text, and the title should be "Greetings From Your Future Znufengerb Minister."

When you know what kind of information you want on the page, you can move on to Step 2 — writing the markup.

Step 2: Writing some HTML

You have a couple of different options when you're ready to create your HTML. If you already have some content that you just want to describe with HTML, you can save that content as a plain-text file and add text around it. Alternately, you can start creating markup and add the content in as you go. In the end, you'll probably use some combination of both.

In our example, we already had some text to start with that was originally in a Word document format; we just saved the content as a text file and added markup around it.

To save a Word file as a text document, choose File➪Save As. In the dialog box that appears, choose Text Only (*.txt) from the Save As Type drop-down list.

Figure 3-2 shows how our draft letter appears in Microsoft Word before we convert it to text for our page.

"Hello World" in HTML

The complete HTML page looks like Listing 3-1:

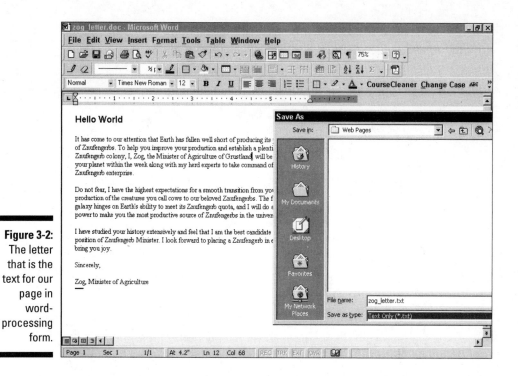

Figure 3-2:
The letter
that is the
text for our
page in
word-
processing
form.

Listing 3-1:   The Complete HTML Page for the Zog Letter

```
<!DOCTYPE HTML PUBLIC "-//W3C//DTD HTML 4.0 Transitional//EN"
        "http://www.w3.org/TR/REC-html40/loose.dtd">

<html>
  <head>
    <title>Greetings From Your Future Znufengerb Minister</title>
  </head>

  <body bgcolor="black" text="white">

  <h1>Hello World</h1>

  <p>It has come to our attention that Earth has fallen well short of
     producing its yearly quota of Znufengerbs. To help you improve your
     production and establish a plentiful Znufengerb colony, I, Zog, the
     Minister of Agriculture of Grustland, will be arriving on your planet
     within the week along with my herd experts to take command of your
     Znufengerb enterprise.
  </p>
```

(continued)

Listing 3-1 *(continued)*

```
<p>Do not fear. I have the highest expectations for a smooth transition
    from your current production of the creatures you call cows to our beloved
    Znufengerbs. The future of the galaxy hinges on Earth's ability to meet
    its Znufengerb quota, and I will do all in my power to make you the most
    productive source of Znufengerbs in the universe.
</p>

<p>I have studied your history extensively and feel that I am the best
    candidate for the position of Znufengerb Minister. I look forward to
    placing a Znufengerb in every home to bring you joy.
</p>

<p>Sincerely,</br>
    Zog, Minister of Agriculture
</p>

</body>
</html>
```

What the markup is doing

The HTML includes a collection of markup elements and attributes that describe the letter's contents:

- ✔ The `<html>` element defines the document as an HTML document.

- ✔ The `<head>` element creates a header section for the document, and the `<title>` element inside of it defines a document title that will be displayed in the browser's title bar.

- ✔ The `<body>` element holds the actual text that will display in the browser window. The `bgcolor` and `text` attributes work with the `<body>` element to set the background color to black and the text color to white.

- ✔ The `<h1>` element marks the Hello World text as a first-level heading.

- ✔ The `<p>` elements identify each of the paragraphs in the document.

- ✔ The `<br>` element adds a manual line break after the word Sincerely in the salutation.

Don't worry about the ins and outs of how all of these elements work. They are covered in detail in Chapters 4 and 7.

After you create a complete HTML page, or at least the first chunk of it that you want to review, you must save it before you can view your work in a browser.

Step 3: Saving your page

Remember that you use a text editor to create your HTML documents and a Web browser to view them, but before you can let your browser loose on your HTML page, you have to save that page. When you're just building a page, you should save a copy of it to your local hard drive and view it locally with your browser.

Choosing a location and name for your file

When you save your file to your hard drive, keep two things in mind:

- ✔ You need to be able to find it again soon.
- ✔ The name should make sense to you and work well on a Web browser.

That said, we recommend that you create a folder somewhere on your hard drive especially for your Web pages. Call it "Web Pages" or "HTML" (or any other name that makes sense to you), and be sure you put it somewhere easy to find.

When you choose a name for your page, don't include spaces in it because some operating systems — most notably Unix and Linux (the most popular Web-hosting operating systems around) — don't tolerate spaces in filenames. Choose names that make sense to you and that you can use to identify file contents without actually opening the file.

In our example, we saved our file in a folder called `Web Pages` and named it (drumroll, please) `zog_letter.html`, as shown in Figure 3-3.

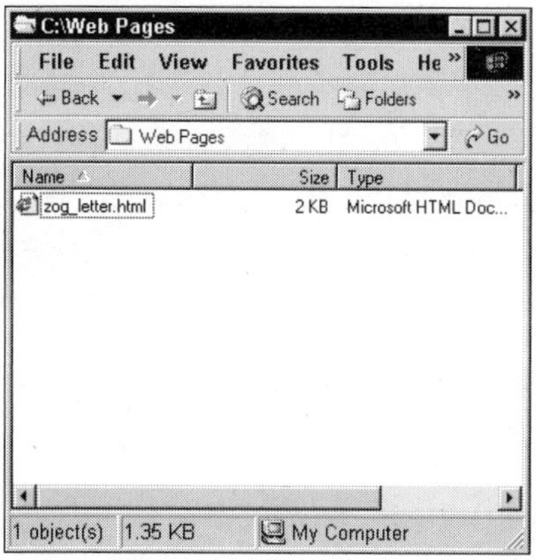

Figure 3-3:
Choose an easy-to-access location and a descriptive filename for your HTML pages.

.htm or .html

Notice that our filename, zog_letter.html, uses the .html suffix. You can actually choose from one of two suffixes for your pages: .html or .htm. The shorter .htm is a relic from the 8.3 DOS days when filenames could only have eight characters followed by a three-character suffix that describes the file's type. Today, operating systems can support very long filenames and suffixes that are more than three letters long so we suggest you stick with .html.

That said, you can use either .htm or .html, and Web servers and Web browsers will handle both equally well. We do, however, recommend that you stick with one option or the other to be consistent. Even though .html and .htm files are treated the same by browsers and servers, they are different suffixes. The name zog_letter.html is different from zog_letter.htm, and this matters when you create hyperlinks, as you learn in Chapter 5.

Step 4: Viewing your page

After you save a copy of your page, you're ready to view it in a Web browser. If you haven't opened your browser, do that now. Next, choose File⇨Open and click the Browse button. Navigate your file system until you find your HTML file, as shown in Figure 3-4.

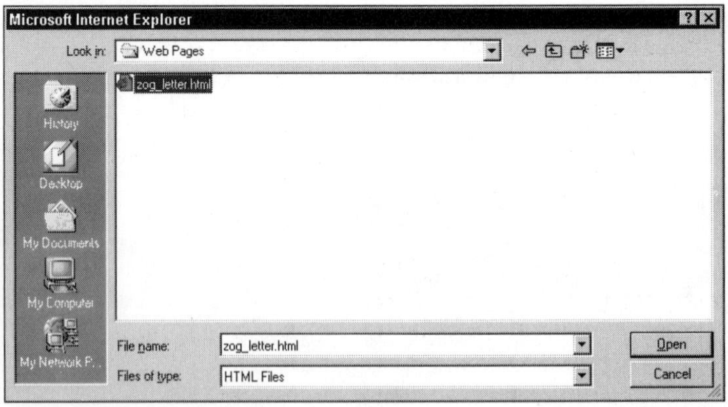

Figure 3-4:
Use Internet
Explorer to
navigate to
your Web
pages.

Click the Open button, and the page appears in your Web browser in all its glory, as shown in Figure 3-5.

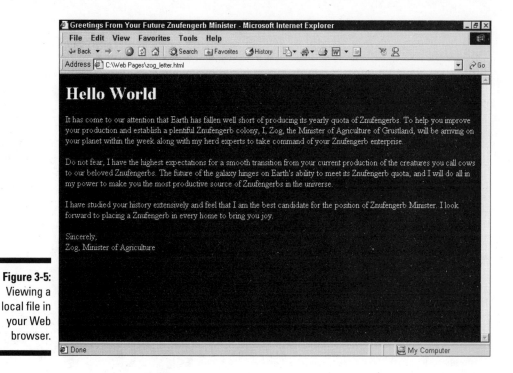

Figure 3-5:
Viewing a
local file in
your Web
browser.

You aren't actually viewing this file on the Web yet; you're just viewing a *copy* of it saved on your local hard drive. You can't give anyone the URL for this file yet, but you can edit and view the changes you make.

Editing an Existing Web Page

Chances are you'll want to change one thing (at least) about your page after you view it in a Web browser for the first time. After all, you can't really see how the page is going to look when you're creating the markup, and you might decide that a first-level heading is too big or that you really *want* purple text on a green background.

To make changes to the Web page you've created in a text editor and are viewing in a browser, follow these steps:

1. **Leave the browser window with the HTML page display open and go back to the text editor.**

2. **If the HTML page isn't open in the text editor, open it.**

You should have the same file open in both the browser and the text editor, as shown in Figure 3-6.

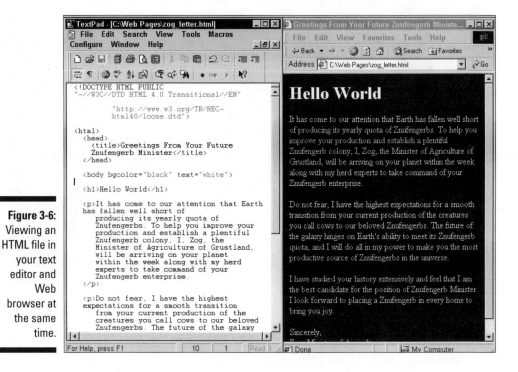

Figure 3-6:
Viewing an HTML file in your text editor and Web browser at the same time.

3. **Make your changes to the HTML and its content in the text editor.**

4. **Save the changes.**

   This is an important step. If you don't save your changes, you won't see them in the Web browser.

5. **Move back to the Web browser and click the Refresh button.**

6. **Repeat these steps until you're happy with the final display of your page.**

Although you don't have to keep the HTML file open in both the text editor and the browser while you work, it's easiest if you do. You can quickly make a change in the editor, flip to the browser and refresh, flip back to the editor to make more changes, flip back to the browser and refresh, and so on.

In our example letter, we decided after our initial draft of the HTML page that we should add a date to the letter. Figure 3-7 shows the change we made to the HTML to add the date and the resulting display in the Web browser.

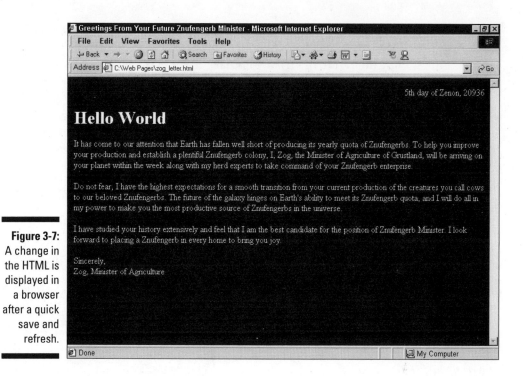

Figure 3-7:
A change in
the HTML is
displayed in
a browser
after a quick
save and
refresh.

This approach to editing an HTML page only applies to pages saved *on your local hard drive.* If you want to edit a page that you have already stored on a Web server, you have to save a copy of the page to your hard drive, edit it, verify your changes, and then upload the file again to the server, as discussed in the following section.

Posting Your Page Online

After you're happy with your Web page, it's time to put it online. Chapter 17 is devoted to a detailed discussion of what you need to do to put your page online, but to sum it up in a few quick steps:

1. **Find a Web hosting provider to hold your Web pages.**

   Your Web host might be a company Web server or space that you pay an ISP for. If you don't have a provider yet, double-check with the ISP you use for Internet access — see whether you get some Web-server space along with your access. Regardless of where you find space, get details from the provider on where to move your site's files and what your URL will be.

2. **Use an FTP client or a Web browser to make a connection to your Web server as specified in the information from your hosting provider.**

3. **Copy the HTML file from your hard drive to the Web server.**

4. **Use your Web browser to view the file via the Internet.**

For example, to host our letter online at `ftp.io.com/~natanya`, we used Internet Explorer to access the site and provided the appropriate name and password (which you will get from your ISP). A collection of folders and files appeared.

We copied the file to the server with a simple drag-and-drop operation from Windows Explorer to Internet Explorer, as shown in Figure 3-8.

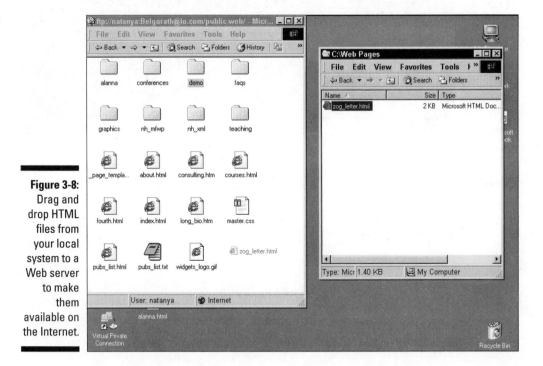

Figure 3-8:
Drag and drop HTML files from your local system to a Web server to make them available on the Internet.

The URL for this page is `http://www.io.com/~natanya/zog_letter.html`, and the page is now served from the Web browser instead of from a local file system, as shown in Figure 3-9.

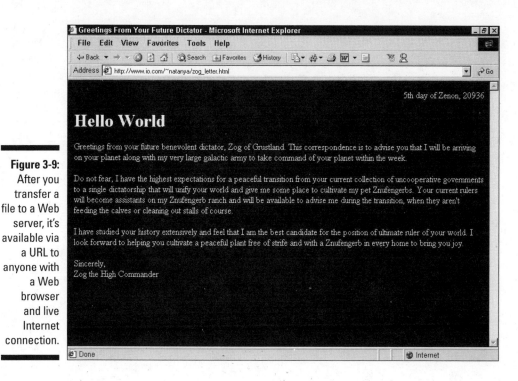

Figure 3-9:
After you
transfer a
file to a Web
server, it's
available via
a URL to
anyone with
a Web
browser
and live
Internet
connection.

Again, see Chapter 17 for more details on how to serve your Web pages to the world.

Part II

Getting Started with HTML

The 5th Wave   By Rich Tennant

THE MODERN JAMES BOND

The name is bond.com, JAMES bond.com.

In this part . . .

In this part of the book, we describe the markup and document structures that make Web pages workable and attractive. To begin with, we explore and explain basic HTML document structure and talk about organizing text in blocks and lists. Next, we explain how linking works in HTML, and how it provides the glue that ties the entire World Wide Web together. Then we explain how to add graphics to your pages. Finally, we cover the elements of HTML formatting — including colors, backgrounds, and fonts — so you can make your HTML documents (and Web pages) really stand out!

Chapter 4

Structuring Your HTML Documents

. . . .

In This Chapter

▶ Creating a basic document structure

▶ Defining metadata

▶ Working with paragraphs, headings, and other block elements

▶ Creating bulleted, numbered, and definition lists

. . . .

*H*TML documents consist of text, images, multimedia files, links, and
other pieces of content that you bring together into a single page using
markup elements and attributes. You use blocks of text to create headings,
paragraphs, lists, and more. The first step in creating a solid HTML document
is laying a firm foundation that establishes the document's structure.

This chapter covers the major elements that you use to set up a basic HTML
document structure — including the head and body of the document. We also
show you how to define the various large chunks of text that will make up
your document. Finally, you find out how to use HTML's three different kinds
of lists — bulleted, numbered, and definition — to group like information and
add a little visual variety to your page.

Establishing a Basic Document Structure

Although no two HTML pages are alike — each employs a unique combination of content and elements to define the page — every HTML page must
have the same basic document structure that includes

✔ A statement that identifies the document as an HTML document

✔ A document header

✔ A document body

Every time you create an HTML document, start with these three elements;
then you can fill in the rest of your content and markup to create an individual page.

Although a basic document structure is a requirement for every HTML document, creating it over and over again can be a little monotonous. Most HTML editing tools — shareware, freeware, and commercial — can automatically set up the basic document structure for you when you start a new HTML document. As you evaluate potential HTML editors, look for this feature and others that help you create commonly used chunks of HTML, such as list structures and basic tables. Chapter 16 includes more information on finding a good HTML editor to make your page creation more efficient.

Labeling Your Document as an HTML Page

Every HTML document must begin with a *DOCTYPE declaration* that specifies which version of HTML you used to create the document. (DOCTYPE is short for document type.) There are three possible DOCTYPE declarations for HTML 4.0 documents, one for each of the three flavors of HTML:

✔ **HTML 4.0 Transitional:** The most inclusive version of HTML 4.0 that incorporates all HTML structural elements as well as all presentation elements.

```
<!DOCTYPE HTML PUBLIC "-//W3C//DTD HTML 4.0 Transitional//EN"
        "http://www.w3.org/TR/REC-html140/loose.dtd">
```

✔ **HTML 4.0 Strict:** A streamlined version of HTML that excludes all presentation-related elements in favor of style sheets as a mechanism for driving display.

```
<!DOCTYPE HTML PUBLIC "-//W3C//DTD HTML 4.0//EN"
        "http://www.w3.org/TR/REC-html140/strict.dtd">
```

✔ **HTML 4.0 Frameset:** A version of HTML that begins with HTML 4.0 Transitional and includes all the elements that make frames possible.

```
<!DOCTYPE HTML PUBLIC "-//W3C//DTD HTML 4.0 Frameset//EN"
        "http://www.w3.org/TR/REC-html140/frameset.dtd">
```

Regardless of the HTML flavor you choose to use, always begin every document with a DOCTYPE declaration. Most browsers can display your page even if you don't, but some others won't, so it's always better to be safe than sorry.

Chapter 1 includes more information on why there are three different flavors of HTML and shows you how to choose the right flavor for an individual HTML document.

After you specify which version of HTML the document follows, you must create an `<html>` element to hold all the other content markup in your page:

```
<!DOCTYPE HTML PUBLIC "-//W3C//DTD HTML 4.0 Transitional//EN"
        "http://www.w3.org/TR/REC-html140/loose.dtd">

<html>

</html>
```

It's easy, but also important: Never forget that a single `<html>` element holds all other text in your HTML page.

Adding a Document Header

After you've declared which version of HTML your document adheres to and created an `<html>` element, you set up a document header that provides some basic information about the document, including its title and metadata, which provides useful information about the document such as keywords, author information, a description, and so forth. Also, if you're going to use a style sheet (internal or external) with your page, you include information about that style sheet in the header.

Chapter 11 includes a complete overview of creating style sheets with CSS and shows you how to include them in your HTML documents.

The `<head>` element, which defines the page header, immediately follows the `<html>` opening tag:

```
<!DOCTYPE HTML PUBLIC "-//W3C//DTD HTML 4.0 Transitional//EN"
        "http://www.w3.org/TR/REC-html140/loose.dtd">

<html>
  <head>

  </head>
</html>
```

Giving your page a title

Every HTML page needs a descriptive title that helps a visitor understand at a glance why the page exists in the first place. The page title should be concise, yet informative. (For example, *My home page* isn't nearly as informative as *Ed's IT Consulting Service*.)

You define the title for your page using the `<title>` element inside the `<head>` element:

```
<!DOCTYPE HTML PUBLIC "-//W3C//DTD HTML 4.0 Transitional//EN"
        "http://www.w3.org/TR/REC-html40/loose.dtd">

<html>
  <head>
    <title>Ed's IT Consulting Service</title>
  </head>
</html>
```

The document title doesn't actually show up in the middle of a browser window in huge boldface text. Instead, most browsers display the page title as in the browser window's title bar, as shown in Figure 4-1.

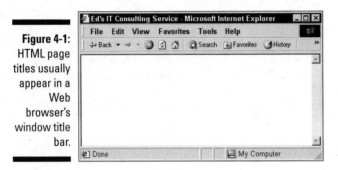

Figure 4-1: HTML page titles usually appear in a Web browser's window title bar.

Search engines use the contents of the `<title>` bar when they list Web pages in response to a query. Your page title may be the first thing your visitors read about your Web page, especially if they find it via their favorite search engines because your page will most likely be listed (by its title) with many others on a search results page — you've got one chance to grab your audience's attention and get them to choose your page over the others. A well-crafted title can do just that, as discussed in more detail in Chapter 17.

Defining metadata

The term *metadata* refers to data *about* data; in the context of the Web, it means data that describes the data on your Web page. Metadata for your page may include

- ✔ Keywords
- ✔ A description of your page

✔ Information about the page author

✔ The software application you used to create the page

You use the `<meta>` element and the `name` and `content` attributes to define each piece of metadata for your HTML page. For example, the following elements create a list of keywords and a description for a consulting-service page:

```
<!DOCTYPE HTML PUBLIC "-//W3C//DTD HTML 4.0 Transitional//EN"
        "http://www.w3.org/TR/REC-html40/loose.dtd">

<html>
  <head>
    <title>Ed's IT Consulting Service</title>
    <meta name="keywords" content="IT consulting, MCSE, networking guru">
    <meta name="description" content="An overview of Ed's skills and services">
  </head>
</html>
```

The HTML specification doesn't predefine the different kinds of metadata you can include in your page, nor does it specify how to name different pieces of metadata, such as keywords and descriptions. So, for example, instead of using `keywords` and `description` as names for keyword and description metadata, you can just as easily use `kwrd` and `desc`, as in the following markup:

```
<!DOCTYPE HTML PUBLIC "-//W3C//DTD HTML 4.0 Transitional//EN"
        "http://www.w3.org/TR/REC-html40/loose.dtd">

<html>
  <head>
    <title>Ed's IT Consulting Service</title>
    <meta name="kwrd" content="IT consulting, MCSE, networking guru">
    <meta name="desc" content="An overview of Ed's skills and services">
  </head>
</html>
```

So if you can use just any old values for `meta name` and `content` attributes, how do systems know what to do with your metadata? The answer is — they don't. Each search engine works differently, although *keywords* and *description* are commonly used metadata names, many search engines may not recognize or use other metadata elements that you include. Instead, many developers use metadata as a way to leave messages for others who might look at the source of their page later, or with the hope that one day browsers and search engines will make better use of the metadata they've provided.

Although you may not want to take the time to load your page with metadata, be sure you do include keywords and a page description. Those two metadata elements are most commonly used by search engines. Keywords help engines catalog your page more precisely; many engines display your description along with the page title, which gives prospective visitors a bit more information about your site — and maybe incentive to visit it.

Automatically redirecting users to another page

You can use metadata in your header to send messages to Web browsers about how they should display or otherwise handle your Web page. You commonly see the `<meta>` element used this way to automatically redirect page visitors from one page to the other. For example, if you've ever come across a page that says `This page has moved. Please wait 10 seconds to be automatically sent to the new location` (or something similar), you've seen this trick at work.

To use the `<meta>` element to send messages to the browser, you use the `http-equiv` attribute in place of the `name` attribute. Then, you choose from a predefined list of values that represents instructions for the browser. These values are based on instructions you can also send to a browser in the HTTP header, but changing the HTTP header for a document is more difficult than embedding the instructions into the Web page itself.

To instruct a browser to redirect users from one page to another, you use the `<meta>` element with an `http-equiv` attribute with a value of `refresh` and a value for `content` that specifies how many seconds before the refresh happens and what URL you want to jump to. For example, this `<meta>` element creates a refresh that jumps to `www.w3.org` after 15 seconds:

```
<meta http-equiv="refresh" content="15; url= http://www.w3.org/">
```

Older Web browsers may not know what to do with `<meta>` elements that use the `http-equiv` element to create a redirector page. Be sure to include some text and a link on your page to enable a visitor to link manually to your redirector page if your `<meta>` element fails.

The line shown in bold in the following markup shows you how:

```
<!DOCTYPE HTML PUBLIC "-//W3C//DTD HTML 4.0 Transitional//EN"
        "http://www.w3.org/TR/REC-html40/loose.dtd">
```

```
<html>
  <head>
    <title>All About Markup</title>
    <meta http-equiv="refresh" content="15; url= http://www.w3.org/">
  </head>

  <body>
    <p>This page is still in development. Until we are done, please visit
       the <a href="http://www.w3.org">W3C Website</a> for the definitive
       collection of markup-related resources.
    </p>

    <p>Please wait 10 seconds to be automatically redirected to the W3C.</p>
  </body>
</html>
```

If a user's browser doesn't know what to do with your redirector information, the user can simply click the link in the page body to go to the new page, as shown in Figure 4-2.

Figure 4-2:
When you
use a
`<meta>`
element to
create a
page
redirector,
include
text that
visitors can
click if their
browsers
can't
handle the
redirector.

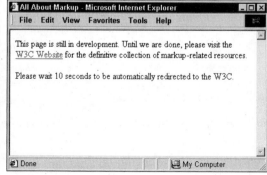

You can use the `http-equiv` attribute with the `<meta>` element for a variety of other purposes, including setting an expiration date for a page, specifying the character set (that is, language) the page uses, and more. To find out what your `http-equiv` options are (and how to use them), check out the Dictionary of HTML META tags at the following URL:

```
http://vancouver-webpages.com/META/metatags.detail.html
```

Creating the Body of Your HTML Document

After you set up your page header, create a title, and define some metadata, you're ready to create the HTML and content that will show up in a browser window. The `<body>` element holds every bit of content and markup not defined in the header. In general, if you want to see something in your browser window, put it in the `<body>` element:

```
<!DOCTYPE HTML PUBLIC "-//W3C//DTD HTML 4.0 Transitional//EN"
        "http://www.w3.org/TR/REC-html40/loose.dtd">

<html>
  <head>
    <title>Ed's IT Consulting Service</title>
    <meta name="kwrd" content="IT consulting, MCSE, networking guru">
    <meta name="desc" content="An overview of Ed's skills and services">
  </head>

  <body>
    <p>Ed's IT Consulting Service Homepage</p>
    <p>Ed has over 20 years of IT consulting experience and is available
       to help you with any IT need you might have. From network design
       and configuration to technical documentation and training, you can
       count on Ed to help you create and manage your IT infrastructure.</p>

    <p>For more information please contact Ed by e-mail at ed@itguru.com or
       by phone at 555.555.5555.</p>
  </body>
</html>
```

Figure 4-3 shows how a browser displays this complete HTML page. Again, notice the following:

- ✔ The content of the `<title>` element is in the window's title bar.
- ✔ The `<meta>` elements don't affect the page display at all.
- ✔ Only the paragraph text contained in the `<p>` elements in the `<body>` element actually displays in the browser window.

You can use a variety of attributes with the `<body>` element to define the default text and link colors for your document text. Chapter 7 covers these attributes in detail.

Figure 4-3:
Only content
in the
`<body>`
element
appears
in the
browser's
window.

> **Ed's IT Consulting Service - Microsoft Internet Explorer**
>
> File   Edit   View   Favorites   Tools   Help
>
> Ed's IT Consulting Service Homepage
>
> Ed has over 20 years of IT consulting experience and is available to help you with any IT need you might have. From network design and configuration to technical documentation and training, you can count on Ed to help you create and manage your IT infrastructure.
>
> For more information please contact Ed by e-mail at ed@itguru.com or by phone at 555.555.5555.
>
> Done   My Computer

Working with Blocks of Text

Here's a super-ultra-technical definition of a *block of text:* some chunk of content that wraps from one line to another in an HTML element. Every bit of content on your Web page has to be part of an initial block element, and every block element sits within the `<body>` element on your page. In the end, your HTML page is a giant collection of blocks of text.

Inline content is a word or string of words inside a block element. The difference between the inline content and a block of text is important because certain HTML elements (like those discussed in this chapter) are designed to describe blocks of text, whereas others (such as linking and formatting elements) are designed to describe a few words or lines of content found inside those blocks. The remaining chapters of this book often refer to block elements and inline elements. Just remember that inline elements must be nested within a block element or your HTML document won't be syntactically correct.

HTML recognizes several different kinds of text blocks that you might want to use in your document, including (but not limited to)

 ✔ Paragraphs

 ✔ Headings

 ✔ Block quotes

 ✔ Lists

 ✔ Tables

 ✔ Forms

This list is far from complete, but it gives you a good idea of what kinds of text are labeled as text blocks in HTML. This chapter looks at the HTML markup you use to describe less-complicated text blocks such as paragraphs and lists. Later chapters delve into the more complicated text structures such as tables and forms.

Inserting paragraphs

Paragraphs are probably used more often in Web pages than any other kind of text block. To label a paragraph, simply place your content in a <p> element. Presto! Here's what it looks like:

```
<!DOCTYPE HTML PUBLIC "-//W3C//DTD HTML 4.0 Transitional//EN"
        "http://www.w3.org/TR/REC-html40/loose.dtd">

<html>
  <head>
    <title>All About Blocks</title>
  </head>

  <body>
    <p>This is a paragraph. It's a very simple structure that you will use
       time and again in your Web pages.</p>
    <p>This is another paragraph. What could be simpler to create?</p>
  </body>
</html>
```

This HTML page includes two paragraphs, each marked with a separate <p> element. Most Web browsers add a line break and full line of white space after every paragraph on your page, as shown in Figure 4-4.

Figure 4-4:
Web
browsers
delineate
paragraphs
with a
line break
and white
space.

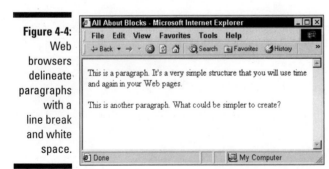

The default alignment for a paragraph is left, and you can use the `align` attribute with a value of `center`, `right`, or `justify` to override that default and control the alignment for any paragraph.

```
<p align="center">This paragraph is centered.</p>
<p align="right">This paragraph is right-justified.</p>
<p align="justify">This paragraph is double-justified.</p>
```

Figure 4-5 shows how a Web browser aligns each paragraph according to the value of the `align` attribute.

Figure 4-5:
Use the `align` attribute with a paragraph to specify its horizontal alignment.

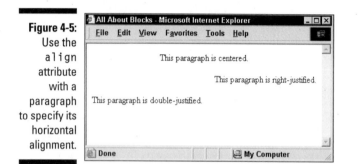

If you look at other people's markup, you may find that many eliminate the closing `</p>` tag when they create paragraphs. Although some browsers will let you get away with this, leaving out the closing tag doesn't follow correct syntax and will cause problems with style sheets (at the very least). Additionally, leaving out closing tags can get in the way of a consistent display for your page across all browsers.

Breaking down information with headings

Headings are commonly used to break a document into sections. This book, for example, uses headings and subheadings to divide every chapter into sections — and you can do the same with your Web page. In addition to creating an organizational structure, headings help break up the visual display of the page and give readers visual clues about how the different pieces of content are grouped.

HTML includes six different elements to help you define six different heading levels in your documents. Every browser has a different way of displaying these different heading levels. Most graphical browsers use a distinctive size and typeface, although text-only browsers may use a different convention because all content is displayed in a single size and font. In graphical browser displays, first-level headings (<h1>) are the largest (usually two or three font sizes larger than the default text size for paragraphs); sixth-level headings (<h6>) are the smallest and may be two or three font sizes *smaller* than the default text size. The following excerpt of HTML markup shows all six headings at work:

```
<!DOCTYPE HTML PUBLIC "-//W3C//DTD HTML 4.0 Transitional//EN"
         "http://www.w3.org/TR/REC-html40/loose.dtd">

<html>
  <head>
    <title>All About Blocks</title>
  </head>

  <body>
    <h1>First-level heading</h1>
    <h2>Second-level heading</h2>
    <h3>Third-level heading</h3>
    <h4>Fourth-level heading</h4>
    <h5>Fifth-level heading</h5>
    <h6>Sixth-level heading</h6>
  </body>
</html>
```

Figure 4-6 shows this HTML page as rendered in a browser.

Figure 4-6:
Web browsers display headings in decreasing size from level one to level six.

You shouldn't use a second-level heading until you've used a first-level heading, nor a third-level heading until you've used a second, and so on. If you want to change the way headings display in a browser, you can either use <font> elements (as discussed in Chapter 7) or style sheets (as discussed in Chapter 11).

Exerting More Layout Control Over Blocks of Text

Although blocks of text form the foundation for your page, you'll occasionally want to break those blocks up to better guide readers through your content. Two of the most common methods for breaking up the blocks of text on your page are line breaks and horizontal rules.

Using block quotes

A *block quote* is a long quotation or excerpt from a printed source that you want to set apart on your page. You use the <blockquote> element to identify block quotes, as in this markup:

```
<!DOCTYPE HTML PUBLIC "-//W3C//DTD HTML 4.0 Transitional//EN"
        "http://www.w3.org/TR/REC-html40/loose.dtd">

<html>
  <head>
    <title>Famous Quotations</title>
  </head>

  <body>
    <h1>An Inspiring Quote</h1>
    <p>When I need a little inspiration to remind me of why I spend my days
       in the classroom, I just remember what Lee Iococca said:</p>
    <blockquote>
      In a completely rational society, the best of us would be teachers
      and the rest of us would have to settle for something else.
    </blockquote>
  </body>
</html>
```

Most Web browsers display block-quote content with a slight left indent, as shown in Figure 4-7.

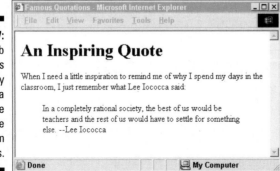

Figure 4-7:
Web
browsers
typically
indent a
block quote
to separate
it from
paragraphs.

Using preformatted text

HTML ignores white space; if your block elements include hard returns, line breaks, or too many large spaces, the browser won't display them. For example, in the following markup we included several hard returns, some line breaks, and a lot of spaces, but as you can see in Figure 4-8, Web browsers ignore every bit of formatting you might try to add.

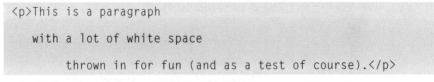

```
<p>This is a paragraph

    with a lot of white space

        thrown in for fun (and as a test of course).</p>
```

Figure 4-8:
Web
browsers
routinely
ignore white
space.

Sometimes, however, you may want the browser to display the white space you include in an HTML page (for example, when you include code samples or text tables where proper spacing is important). The preformatted text element (`<pre>`) instructs browsers to keep all white space intact when it displays your content (as in the sample that follows). Use the `<pre>` element in place of the `<p>` element to get the browser to honor all your white space, as shown in Figure 4-9.

```
<!DOCTYPE HTML PUBLIC "-//W3C//DTD HTML 4.0 Transitional//EN"
        "http://www.w3.org/TR/REC-html40/loose.dtd">

<html>
  <head>
    <title>White space</title>
  </head>

  <body>
    <pre>This is a paragraph

      with a lot of white space

        thrown in for fun (and as a test of course).
    </pre>
  </body>
</html>
```

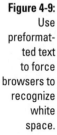

Figure 4-9:
Use
preformatted text
to force
browsers to
recognize
white
space.

Using preformatted text in block quotes

You can nest `<pre>` elements inside `<blockquote>` elements to carefully control the way the lines of quoted text appear on the page. This feature is particularly useful for poetry stanzas or other quoted text in which line breaks and white space are important, as shown in this bit of markup and Figure 4-10.

```
<!DOCTYPE HTML PUBLIC "-//W3C//DTD HTML 4.0 Transitional//EN"
        "http://www.w3.org/TR/REC-html40/loose.dtd">

<html>
  <head>
    <title>Shakespeare in HTML</title>
  </head>

  <body>
  <h1>Shakespeare's Sonnets XVIII: Shall I compare thee to a summer's day? </h1>
  <blockquote>
    <pre>Shall I compare thee to a summer's day?
    Thou art more lovely and more temperate.
    Rough winds do shake the darling buds of May,
    And summer's lease hath all too short a date.
    Sometime too hot the eye of heaven shines,
    And often is his gold complexion dimm'd;
    And every fair from fair sometime declines,
    By chance or nature's changing course untrimm'd;
    But thy eternal summer shall not fade
    Nor lose possession of that fair thou ow'st;
    Nor shall Death brag thou wander'st in his shade,
    When in eternal lines to time thou grow'st:
    So long as men can breathe or eyes can see,
    So long lives this, and this gives life to thee.</pre>
  </blockquote>
  </body>
</html>
```

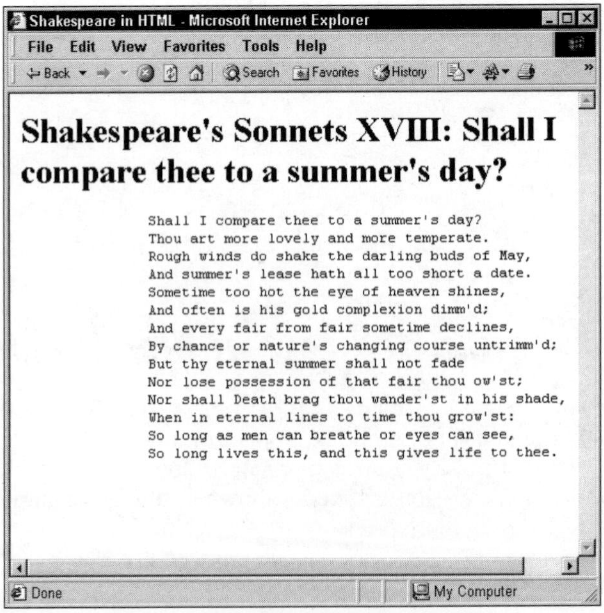

Figure 4-10:
Use <pre>
with
<block
quote> to
control
white space
within a
quotation.

Adding line breaks

Typically, browsers wrap any text that appears in block elements such as paragraphs, headings, and block quotes; if the text reaches the end of a browser window, you don't have much control over where a line ends (unless you use preformatted text). If you don't want to worry about accounting for every space in your content, you can always turn one paragraph into two — but you may not want the extra line of white space that most browsers include after each paragraph. What to do?

The best way to specify when you've reached the end of a line in a paragraph, but aren't ready to create a new paragraph, is to use a line break, denoted by the ⟨br⟩ element. The ⟨br⟩ is the HTML equivalent of the good, old manual hard return that you use in paragraphs and other blocks of text when you're working in a word-processing program.

Any time a browser sees a ⟨br⟩, it breaks the text there and moves to the next line. The following markup shows a different way to break the lines of text in a poem. The entire poem is described *as a single paragraph,* and the ⟨br⟩ element marks the end of each line:

```
<!DOCTYPE HTML PUBLIC "-//W3C//DTD HTML 4.0 Transitional//EN"
        "http://www.w3.org/TR/REC-html40/loose.dtd">

<html>
  <head>
    <title> Shakespeare in HTML</title>
  </head>

  <body>
  <h1>Shakespeare's Sonnets XVIII: Shall I compare thee to a summer's day? </h1>
    <p>
      Shall I compare thee to a summer's day? <br>
      Thou art more lovely and more temperate. <br>
      Rough winds do shake the darling buds of May, <br>
      And summer's lease hath all too short a date. <br>
      Sometime too hot the eye of heaven shines, <br>
      And often is his gold complexion dimm'd; <br>
      And every fair from fair sometime declines, <br>
      By chance or nature's changing course untrimm'd; <br>
      But thy eternal summer shall not fade <br>
      Nor lose possession of that fair thou ow'st; <br>
      Nor shall Death brag thou wander'st in his shade, <br>
      When in eternal lines to time thou grow'st: <br>
      So long as men can breathe or eyes can see, <br>
      So long lives this, and this gives life to thee. <br>
    </p>
  </body>
</html>
```

Figure 4-11 shows how a browser handles each line break. In this example, the poem isn't left-indented because the `<p>` element replaces the `<block quote>` element.

Using the `<br>` element isn't necessarily better than using preformatted text in block quotes, but it does offer you a choice in the visual results.

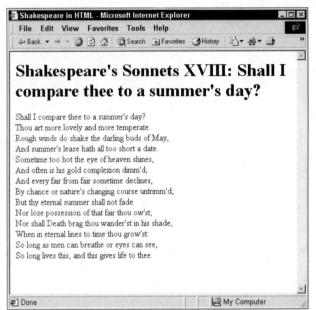

Figure 4-11:
Using the
`<br>`
element to
specify
where lines
in block
elements
should
break.

Within the browser window:

Shakespeare's Sonnets XVIII: Shall I compare thee to a summer's day?

Shall I compare thee to a summer's day?
Thou art more lovely and more temperate.
Rough winds do shake the darling buds of May,
And summer's lease hath all too short a date.
Sometime too hot the eye of heaven shines,
And often is his gold complexion dimm'd;
And every fair from fair sometime declines,
By chance or nature's changing course untrimm'd;
But thy eternal summer shall not fade
Nor lose possession of that fair thou ow'st;
Nor shall Death brag thou wander'st in his shade,
When in eternal lines to time thou grow'st:
So long as men can breathe or eyes can see,
So long lives this, and this gives life to thee.

Adding horizontal rules

The horizontal rule element (`<hr>`) helps you include solid straight lines (*rules*) on your page — and put them anywhere you'd rather not use a graphic. If you want to break your page into logical sections (or just separate your headers and footers from the rest of the page), a horizontal rule is a good option. Users don't have to wait for a graphic to download because the browser creates the rule based on the `<hr>` element, not an image reference.

When you include an `<hr>` element in your page, as in the following HTML, the browser replaces it with a line, as shown in Figure 4-12.

A horizontal rule must always sit on a line by itself; you can't add an <hr> element in the middle of a paragraph (or other block element) and expect the rule to just appear in the middle of the block.

```
<!DOCTYPE HTML PUBLIC "-//W3C//DTD HTML 4.0 Transitional//EN"
          "http://www.w3.org/TR/REC-html40/loose.dtd">

<html>
  <head>
    <title>Horizontal Rules</title>
  </head>

  <body>
    <p>This is a paragraph followed by a horizontal rule.</p>

    <hr>

    </p>This is a paragraph preceded by a horizontal rule.</p>
  </body>
</html>
```

Figure 4-12:
Use the
<hr>
element to
add
horizontal
lines to
your page.

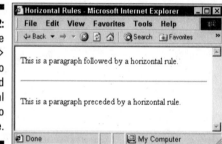

Four different attributes help you control the display of each horizontal rule:

- ✔ width: Specifies line width in pixels or by percentage. For example, your rule can be 50 pixels wide or take up 75 percent of the page.

- ✔ size: Specifies the height of the line in pixels. The default is 1 pixel.

- ✔ align: Specifies the horizontal alignment of the rule as left (the default), center, or right. If you don't define a width for your rule, it takes up the entire width of the page, preventing any alignment you set from showing up in the display.

✔ noshade: Specifies a rule with no shading. By default, most browsers display hard rules with a shade. If you include the noshade attribute in your <hr> element, the line will appear as a solid line.

This bit of HTML creates a horizontal rule that takes up 45 percent of the page, is 4 pixels high, aligned to the center, and has shading turned off:

```
<p>This is a paragraph followed by a horizontal rule.</p>

<hr width="45%" size="4" align="center" noshade>

<p>This is a paragraph preceded by a horizontal rule.</p>
```

Figure 4-13 shows how the addition of these attributes can greatly alter the way a browser displays the rule.

Figure 4-13:
Use the
<hr>
attributes to
better
control how
a browser
displays
the rule.

Horizontal Rules - Microsoft Internet Explorer
File Edit View Favorites Tools Help
Back → ▾ ⊘ ⊙ ⌂ Search Favorites ⟫
This is a paragraph followed by a horizontal rule.
————————
This is a paragraph preceded by a horizontal rule.
Done My Computer

For a look at how you can use horizontal rules in the real world to highlight important content, take a gander at Figure 4-14. The LANWrights, Inc. site uses colored hard rules to surround a key statement on the site's home page that tells visitors exactly what the company does. The rules make the statement stand out from the rest of the page.

Cascading Style Sheets give you much more control over the placement of horizontal rules; you can even fancy them up with color and shading options.

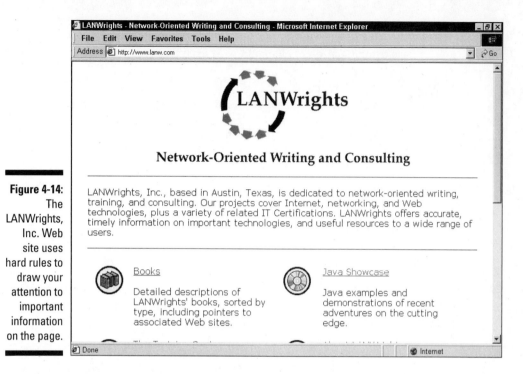

Figure 4-14:
The
LANWrights,
Inc. Web
site uses
hard rules to
draw your
attention to
important
information
on the page.

Organizing Information into Lists

Lists are powerful tools for arranging similar elements together and giving visitors to your site an easy way to hone in on groups of information. You can put just about anything in a list: from a set of instructions to a collection of hyperlinks or navigational tools.

HTML provides for three different kinds of lists:

- Numbered lists
- Bulleted lists
- Definition lists

Unlike the other markup elements you've seen in this chapter (which use a single element to describe a chunk of content), lists are a little more complex. They use a combination of elements — at least two components:

- A markup element that says "Hey browser. This is a list."
- Markup elements that say "Hey browser. This is an item in the list."

Lists are easy to create once you get the hang of using markup elements together. Mastering lists can also make the more complicated combinations of elements easier to handle when you create tables and forms.

Using numbered lists

A *numbered list* consists of one or more items, each prefaced by a number. Usually, lists are numbered when the order of the items is important.

You use the ordered list element (<ol>) to specify that you're creating a numbered list, and a list item element (<li>) to mark each item in the list. This bit of markup defines a three-item numbered list:

```
<!DOCTYPE HTML PUBLIC "-//W3C//DTD HTML 4.0 Transitional//EN"
        "http://www.w3.org/TR/REC-html40/loose.dtd">

<html>
  <head>
    <title>Numbered Lists</title>
  </head>

  <body>
    <h1>Things to do today</h1>
    <ol>
      <li>Feed cat</li>
      <li>Wash car</li>
      <li>Grocery shopping</li>
    </ol>
  </body>
</html>
```

Figure 4-15 shows how a browser renders this markup. Notice that you don't actually have to specify a number for each item in the list, the HTML infers it from the markup.

Figure 4-15:
Use the
`<ol>` and
`<li>`
attributes
to create
a numbered
list.

If you swap the first two items in the list, their numbers change when the page displays again, as in Figure 4-16.

```
<ol>
   <li>Wash car</li>
   <li>Feed cat</li>
   <li>Grocery shopping</li>
</ol>
```

Figure 4-16:
Web
browsers
set the
numbers for
your list
according to
the order
items
appear in
the list.

You can use two different attributes with the `<ol>` element to control the display of any given list:

✔ **start:** Specifies what number you want the list to start with. The default starting number is 1, but if you interrupt a list with a paragraph or other block element, and want to pick it up again later, you can specify any number as the start number for the new list.

✔ type: Specifies the numbering style from the list. You can choose from five predefined numbering styles:

- 1: Decimal numbers
- a: Lowercase letters
- A: Uppercase letters
- i: Lowercase Roman numerals
- I: Uppercase Roman numerals

This bit of markup uses ordered list elements and attributes to create a list that uses uppercase Roman numerals and begins numbering at 5 (V in Roman numerals):

```
<ol start="5" type="I">
  <li>Wash car</li>
  <li>Feed cat</li>
  <li>Grocery shopping</li>
</ol>
```

Figure 4-17 shows how the attributes affect the list display in a browser.

Figure 4-17:
Use the
`start` and
`type`
attributes to
guide the
display of a
numbered
list in a
browser.

Using bulleted lists

A *bulleted list* consists of one or more items each prefaced by a bullet. This type of list is commonly used if the order of the presentation of the items isn't necessary for understanding the information presented.

You use the unordered list element (`<ul>`) to specify that you're creating a bulleted list, and a list item element (`<li>`) to mark each item in the list. The following markup changes a three-item numbered list to a three-item bulleted list:

```
<!DOCTYPE HTML PUBLIC "-//W3C//DTD HTML 4.0 Transitional//EN"
        "http://www.w3.org/TR/REC-html40/loose.dtd">

<html>
  <head>
    <title>Bulleted Lists</title>
  </head>

  <body>
    <h1>Things to do today</h1>
    <ul>
      <li>Feed cat</li>
      <li>Wash car</li>
      <li>Grocery shopping</li>
    </ul>
  </body>
</html>
```

Figure 4-18 shows how a browser renders this list with bullets instead of numbers.

Figure 4-18: An unordered list uses bullets instead of numbers to mark items.

You can use the `type` attribute with the `<ul>` element to specify what kind of bullet you want the list to use:

- `disc`: Solid circle bullets (the default)
- `square`: Solid square bullets
- `circle`: Hollow circle bullets

The addition of the `type` attribute to the bulleted-list markup just given changes the bullets from discs to squares, as shown in Figure 4-19. Here's what the relevant markup looks like:

```
<ul type="square">
   <li>Feed cat</li>
   <li>Wash car</li>
   <li>Grocery shopping</li>
</ul>
```

Figure 4-19:
Use the
`type`
attribute to
change the
bullet style
for an
unordered
list.

Adding definition lists

Definition lists group terms and definitions into a single list and require three
different elements to complete the list:

- `<dl>`: Holds the list definitions.
- `<dt>`: Defines a term in the list.
- `<dd>`: Defines a definition for a term.

You can have as many terms (defined by `<dt>`) in a list as you'd like, and
each term can have one or more definitions (defined by `<dd>`). The following
definition list includes three terms, one of which has two definitions:

```
<!DOCTYPE HTML PUBLIC "-//W3C//DTD HTML 4.0 Transitional//EN"
       "http://www.w3.org/TR/REC-html40/loose.dtd">

<html>
  <head>
    <title>Definition Lists</title>
  </head>

  <body>
    <h1>Markup Language Definitions</h1>
    <dl>
      <dt>SGML</dt>
        <dd>The Standard Generalized Markup Language</dd>
      <dt>HTML</dt>
```

```
            <dd>The Hypertext Markup Language</dd>
            <dd>The markup language you use to create Web pages.</dd>
        <dt>XML</dt>
            <dd>The Extensible Markup Language</dd>
    </dl>
  </body>
</html>
```

Figure 4-20 shows how a browser displays this HTML.

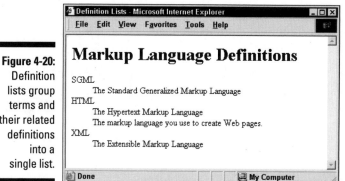

Figure 4-20:
Definition
lists group
terms and
their related
definitions
into a
single list.

If you think the items in a list are spaced too closely together, you can put two <br> elements before each </li> or </dd> element to add more white space. You can also use CSS styles to more carefully control all aspects of your list display, as discussed in Chapter 11.

Creating nested lists

One handy way that HTML lists behave is to break up the display of your page and add some horizontal depth to it. You can take such lists one step further and group a large number of related items when you *nest* lists, creating subcategories. Some common uses for nested lists include

✔ Site maps and other navigation tools

✔ Table of contents for online books and papers

✔ Outlines

You can combine any of the three kinds of lists to create nested lists. The following example starts with a numbered list that defines a list of things to do for the day, and uses three bulleted lists to further break down those items into specific tasks:

```
<!DOCTYPE HTML PUBLIC "-//W3C//DTD HTML 4.0 Transitional//EN"
        "http://www.w3.org/TR/REC-html40/loose.dtd">

<html>
  <head>
    <title>Nested Lists</title>
  </head>

  <body>
    <h1>Things to do today</h1>
    <ol>
      <li>Feed cat</li>
        <ul>
          <li>Rinse bowl</li>
          <li>Open cat food</li>
          <li>Mix dry and wet food in bowl</li>
          <li>Deliver on a silver platter to fluffy</li>
        </ul>
      <li>Wash car</li>
        <ul>
          <li>Vacuum interior</li>
          <li>Wash exterior</li>
          <li>Wax exterior</li>
        </ul>
      <li>Grocery shopping</li>
        <ul>
          <li>Plan meals</li>
          <li>Clean out fridge</li>
          <li>Make list</li>
          <li>Go to store</li>
        </ul>
    </ol>
  </body>
</html>
```

Notice the pattern that the nested list uses: Each list item in the top-level ordered list is followed by a complete second-level list. The second-level lists don't sit inside the list items; instead, they sit inside the top-level list. Figure 4-21 shows how a browser reflects this nesting in its display of the nested list.

As you build nested lists, watch your open and close tags carefully. *Close first what you opened last* is an especially important axiom here.

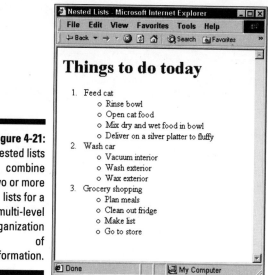

Figure 4-21:
Nested lists combine two or more lists for a multi-level organization of information.

Chapter 5

Linking to Online Resources

- -

- -

*H*yperlinks connect resources on the Web. When you include a link in your page, you give users the capability to jump from your page to somewhere else on the Web, somewhere else on your site, or even somewhere else on the same page. Without links, your page stands alone, disconnected from the rest of the Web. With links, it becomes part of an almost boundless collection of information.

Creating a Basic Link

To create a hyperlink, you need three things:

▶ The Web address (called a Uniform Resource Locator, or URL) of the place you want to link to.

▶ Some text in your Web page to hang the link on. Usually, the text you attach a link to describes the resource being linked.

▶ An *anchor element* (`<a>`) to bring it all together. The element you use to create links is called *anchor element* (as opposed to the *link element*) because you use it to anchor a URL to some text on your page. When a user views your page in a browser, he or she can click the text to activate the link and jump to the page whose URL you specified in the link.

Say you have a Web page that describes HTML standards. You might want to refer Web surfers to the World Wide Web Consortium (W3C) — seeing as it's the organization that governs all things related to the HTML standard — for detailed information. A basic hyperlink to the W3C's Web site, `www.w3.org`, looks like this:

```
<p>The <a href="http://www.w3.org">World Wide Web
Consortium</a> is the standards body that oversees
the development of the HTML specification.</p>
```

You specify the link URL (`http://www.w3.org`) in the anchor element's `href` attribute. The text (World Wide Web Consortium) you include between the anchor element's open and close tags (`<a>` and `</a>`) is the text you hang your link on. Figure 5-1 shows how a browser displays this bit of markup.

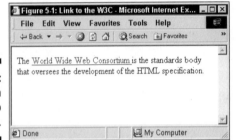

Figure 5-1:
A paragraph
with a link to
the W3C.

You can also anchor URLs to images so users can click the image to activate a link. (For more about creating images that link, see Chapter 6.)

For a detailed discussion of the ins and outs of URLs, see Chapter 1.

Anchor elements aren't block elements

Notice, in the W3C link example, that the anchor element sits inside a paragraph (<p>) element. Anchor elements are inline elements — they don't define blocks of text, but instead apply to a few words or characters within a block of text. When you create a link, you should always do so within a block element (such as a paragraph, list item, heading, or even a table cell). Turn to Chapter 4 for more information on block elements.

Although many Web browsers may display your anchors just fine (even if you don't nest them in block elements), some browsers don't handle this breach of HTML syntax very well. A good example is text-only browsers like those on Palm devices and mobile phones, as well as those used by the visually impaired with text-to-speech readers. These browsers have to display your pages with text and nothing more, and they rely heavily on block elements to help them properly divide the sections of your page. Without a block element, these browsers may not know what to do with your links and put the links in the wrong place in their final display.

Understanding the Difference Between Absolute and Relative Links

As mentioned in a later section ("Beyond Basic Links"), you can link to a variety of online resources. You can create links to other HTML pages (either on your Web site or on another Web site), create links to different locations on the same HTML page, or to resources that aren't even HTML pages at all (such as e-mail addresses, pictures, and text files).

The kind of link you create is determined by where you link to:

- An **absolute link** uses a complete URL to connect browsers to a Web page or online resource.

  Links that use a complete URL to point to a resource are labeled *absolute* because they provide a complete, standalone pointer to another Web resource. When you link to a page on someone else's Web site, the Web browser needs every bit of information in the URL to help it find the page. The browser starts with the domain in the URL and works its way through the path to a specific file. When you link to files on someone else's site, you must always use absolute URLs in the `href` attribute of the anchor element.

- A **relative link** uses a kind of shorthand to specify the URL for the resource you're pointing to. You create relative links between resources on the same domain, and because the two resources are on the same domain, you can omit the domain information from the URL. A *relative* URL uses the location of the resource you're linking from to identify the location of the resource you're linking to.

Imagine that the following URLs identify documents on your Web site. The only difference between them is the specific file they point to:

```
http://www.mysite.com/webdocs/home.html
http://www.mysite.com/webdocs/about.html
```

Because both of these pages reside on the same Web site, you can take advantage of relative URLs when you create a link between them. If you want to make a link from `home.html` to `about.html`, you can use this simplified, relative URL in the anchor element:

```
<p>Learn more <a href="about.html">about</a> our company.</p>
```

When a browser encounters this link and finds that the link doesn't include a domain name, the browser assumes the link is relative and uses the domain and path of the linking page (`http://www.mysite.com/webdocs/`) as a guide for finding the linked page (`about.html`).

As your site grows more complex and you organize your files into a variety of folders, you can still use relative links. However, you have to provide some additional information in the URL to help the browser find files that aren't stored in the same directory as the file you're linking from.

Use `../` (two periods and a slash) before the filename to indicate that the browser should move up one level in the directory structure. The notation in this anchor element instructs the browser to move up one folder from the folder the linking document is stored in, find a folder called `docs`, and then find a file called `home.html`. The markup for this process looks like this:

```
<a href="../docs/home.html>Documentation home</a>
```

When you create a relative link, the location of the file you're linking to is always relative to the file you're linking from. As you create your relative URL, trace the path a browser must take if it starts on the page you're linking from before it can get to the page you're linking to. That path defines the URL you will use in your relative link.

Avoiding Common URL Mistakes

Every site, page, image, or other resource on the Web has its own unique URL, and even one incorrect letter in your URL can lead to a *broken link*. Broken links lead to an error page.

URLs are such finicky creatures that a simple typo can lead to links that simply don't work. If you have a URL that doesn't work, try these tactics to solve the problem:

✔ **Check the case.** Some Web servers, Linux and Unix most notably, are case-sensitive. Thus the servers treat the filenames `Bios.html` and `bios.html` as two different files on the Web server. That also means that browsers must use uppercase and lowercase letters when necessary. Be sure the case you're using in the link matches the actual case of the URL that works in a Web browser.

✔ **Check the extension.** `Bios.htm` and `Bios.html` are two different files. If your link's URL uses one extension but the actual filename uses another, your link won't work.

The importance of http:// in HTML links

You've probably noticed that browsers are designed to make it as easy as possible for you to surf the Web. If you type www.sun.com in your browser's link window, the browser obligingly brings up http://www.sun.com. Although this technique works when you type URLs into your browser window, it won't work when you're writing markup for your Web page.

The URLs you use in your HTML need to be fully formed. Browsers won't interpret URLs that don't include the page protocol. Forget the http://, and your link simply won't work.

✔ **Check the filename.** If you change one part of a URL from the name of the domain to the path or filename (say you type bio.html instead of bios.html), you've got a completely different URL on your hands or you've got a broken link. Enter the URL with bios.html at the end, and you're golden. Enter the following URL, and a File Not Found error page appears in your browser:

```
http://www.sun.com/developers/evangcentral/bio.html
```

✔ **Cut and paste.** The best and most foolproof way to create a URL that works is to load a page in your browser, copy the URL from the browser's address or link field, and then paste the URL into your HTML markup.

Beyond Basic Links

In the section "Creating a Basic Link" at the beginning of this chapter, we gave you a perfect example of how to create a link in your Web page to a Web page (an interdocument hyperlink) on another site. You pick a page to link to, find some text in your document to hang the link on, create an anchor element, and you're done.

However, you can go beyond the basics when you link to other Web pages: You can create links that direct browsers to open linked documents in new windows, link to specific locations *within* a Web page, and link to things other than HTML pages, such as Portable Document Format (PDF) files, compressed files, word-processing documents, and more.

Creating a link that opens in a new window

The Web works because you can link pages on your Web site to pages on other people's Web sites with the simple addition of an anchor element. However, when you link to someone else's site, you're sending users away from your own site, and you have no guarantee that they will find their way back.

An increasingly common approach to linking users to other sites without sending them away from your site is to use HTML that instructs the browser to open the linked page in a new window. A simple addition of the `target` attribute to your anchor element sends the link to a new browser window instead of opening it in the current window:

```
<p>The <a href="http://www.w3.org" target="_blank">World Wide
Web Consortium</a> is the standards body that oversees
the development of the HTML specification.</p>
```

When you give the `target` attribute a value of `_blank`, that tells the browser to keep the linking page open in the current window and open the linked page in a new one, as shown in Figure 5-2.

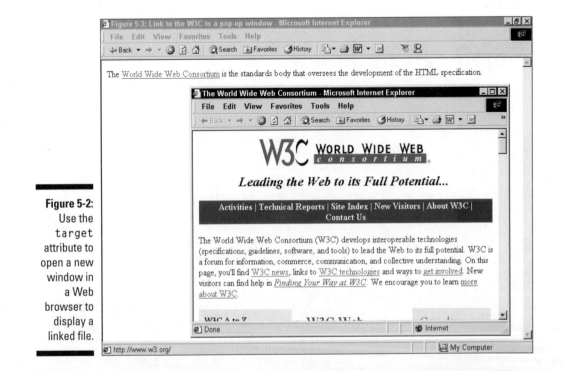

Figure 5-2:
Use the `target` attribute to open a new window in a Web browser to display a linked file.

This technique gives you the best of both worlds: You can link to an off-site resource without really sending your users off site. However, many users are easily irritated when new window after new window pops up on their screens. Use this technique with care and sparingly, or your users will leave your site without benefiting from any links you might provide.

You can use JavaScript to control the size and appearance of pop-up windows, as well as give them buttons that help users close them quickly. Learn more about this in Chapter 12.

Linking to specific locations in the same Web page

Just as you can use links to help your users navigate your Web site or the Web in general, you can help users navigate on a single Web page. If you've ever seen "Back to top" links or a table of contents section for a very long Web page, you've seen *intradocument* hyperlinks at work. Creating an intradocument hyperlink is a two-step process:

1. **Identify and mark the places in your document that you want to link to.**

   For example, mark the top of your page or its major headings.

2. **Link to those spots.**

When you create a link from one Web page to another, you use URLs to define the location of the page you want to link to. However, URLs apply to a whole page, not segments of a page. If you want to direct your links to a specific place on the page, you first have to mark the spot you want to link to. You use the anchor element with the `name` attribute to make your mark:

```
<a name="top"></a>
```

Notice that there isn't any text between the opening and closing tags. That's because an anchor tag that marks a spot doesn't need text to hang the spot on. Instead, you simply create an empty anchor tag and you've created a spot in your document that you can link to.

To link to this spot, you use a slightly different URL than you've seen before:

```
<a href="#top">Back to top</a>
```

The pound sign (#) indicates that you're pointing to a spot on the page, rather than another page. Listing 5-1 shows how these two anchor elements work together as part of a more complete page.

Listing 5-1 is shorter than most documents that integrate intradocument links. It's designed as an example of the markup you should use and how to use it.

Listing 5-1: Intradocument Hyperlinks

```
<html>
  <head>
    <title>Intradocumment hyperlinks at work</title>
  </head>

  <body>
    <h1><a name="top"></a>Web-Based Training</h1>

    <p>Given the importance of the Web to businesses and
       other organizations, individuals who seek to improve
       job skills, or fulfill essential job functions, are
       turning to HTML and XML to deliver training. We
       believe this provides an outstanding opportunity for
       participation in an active and lucrative adult and
       continuing education market.</p>

    <p><a href="#top">Back to top</a></p>

  </body>
</html>
```

Figure 5-3 shows how this HTML appears in a Web browser. If the user clicks the `Back to top` link, the browser jumps back to the `top` spot — marked by `<a name="top"></a>`.

The anchor element that marks the spot doesn't affect the appearance of the first-level heading. You can mark spots wherever you need to without worrying about the final display of your page.

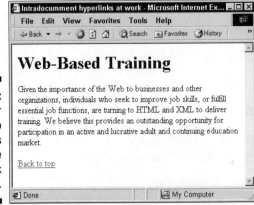

Figure 5-3: Use anchor elements to mark spots on a page and link to them.

You generally use intradocument navigation for long pages that users need help navigating.

Linking to specific locations in another Web page

You can combine intradocument and interdocument links to point users to a specific spot on a different Web page. For instance, if you want to point to a spot named descriptions on a page named home.html on your site, the link would look like this:

```
<p>Review the <a href="home.html#descriptions">document
descriptions</a> to find the documentation specific to
your product.</p>
```

Because you have to define a spot before you can link to it, you'll find that intradocument linking works best on your own site where you create and control the markup. However, if you happen to know that a page on someone else's site has spots already marked on them, you can use an absolute URL to point to that spot, for example:

```
<p>Find out how to <a href="http://www.lanw.com/training/
online.htm#register">register</a> for upcoming training
courses lead by LANWrights instructors.</p>
```

When you link to spots on someone else's Web site, you're at their mercy because they control the spots. You never know when someone will completely rework the markup and content on a page, and your links will break if the site designer removes the spot. Be sure you check all of your links regularly to catch and fix broken links to both Web pages and spots on Web pages.

Linking to non-HTML resources

Although links on the Web were originally used strictly for linking from one Web page to another or within a single Web page, the uses for links have expanded significantly over time to link to a variety of other kinds of files, including these:

- Word-processing documents
- Spreadsheets
- PDFs
- ZIP files and other compressed files

You can also use an anchor element to link to multimedia files, but there are generally better ways to embed media clips in your Web pages. Chapter 13 covers media file linking in detail.

A great use for this kind of link is on software and PDF download pages.

Creating a file download link

Even non-Web files have unique URLs just like good old HTML pages. When you put a file on a Web server (regardless of its type) you can use a URL to point to it from a link. For instance, if you want your users to be able to download a PDF file named `doc.pdf` and a `.ZIP` archive called `software.zip` from a Web page, you use this HTML:

```
<h1>Download the new version of our software</h1>
<p>The <a href="software.zip">software</a></p>
<p>The <a href="doc.pdf">documentation</a></p>
```

You can't be sure how any given user's browser will respond when he or she clicks on a link to a non-Web file. The browser may prompt the user to save the file, or the browser may have a plug-in installed that allows the user to view the file without downloading. (This is common for PDFs.) In some rare instances, the browser may present an error message (such as a pop-up window) to let the user know the browser can't handle the file.

To help users download files successfully, you should provide them with as much information as possible about the file formats and any special tools they might need to work with the files. For example, to work with the contents of a `ZIP` file you need WinZip or another utility; to view a PDF file, you need the free Acrobat reader. You can make the previous download markup a little more user-friendly by adding some supporting text and links:

```
<h1>Download the new version of our software</h1>
<p>The <a href="software.zip">software</a> <br>
   <b>Note:</b>
    You need a <a href="http://www.winzip.com">zip</a>
   utility to open this file.</p>
<p>The <a href="doc.pdf">documentation</a> <br>
   <b>Note:</b>
   You need the free <a href="http://www.adobe.com/
   products/acrobat/readstep.html">Acrobat Reader</a>
   to view the documentation.</p>
```

Figure 5-4 shows how a browser renders this HTML and the dialog box it displays when you click the software link.

Figure 5-4:
This
browser
prompts you
to save or
view the
ZIP file.

Linking to an e-mail address

In addition to linking to non-Web files to create download pages and the like, you can also link to e-mail addresses. You use the standard anchor element and `href` attribute, but you preface the e-mail address you want to link to with `mailto:`, as shown here:

```
<p>Send us your
  <a href="mailto:comments@mysite.com">comments</a>.</p>
```

Although the user's browser configuration ultimately controls how the browser handles an e-mail link, most browsers automatically open a new e-mail message window with the e-mail address you specify in the `href` attribute already in the To field. This is a great way to help users send you e-mail while a request or issue is in the forefront of their mind.

Web page `mailto` links are one of the prime sources of e-mail addresses for spam systems. If you choose to use an e-mail link as a way for users to contact you (a form is another option for receiving feedback, as discussed in Chapter 10), consider creating a special e-mail address just for your site feedback. You can keep the messages you receive at this address separate from your personal or other mail, so you can more easily filter out junk mail.

Regardless of what kind of link you include in your Web page, where you place your links, the text you anchor them to, and the clues you give your users about where a link is taking them have a significant impact on the effectiveness of your links. Chapter 18 discusses some best practices for including links in your overall site design.

Chapter 6

Finding and Using Images

- -

In This Chapter

▶ Finding the right format for your images

▶ Using markup to add images to Web pages

▶ Creating images that link

▶ Understanding image maps, animated GIFs, and transparent images

▶ Finding images to use in your Web pages

- -

Although the Web was once a text-heavy place where images played only a supporting role, things are very different today. Web page designers use text and images equally to deliver important information, direct site navigation, and of course contribute to the overall look and feel of a page. Images are a powerful weapon in your Web design armory, but you need to use them carefully and properly or you risk reducing their effectiveness.

When used well, images are a key element of your page design. When used poorly, they can make your page unreadable or inaccessible.

This chapter gives you a crash course in using images on your Web pages. You find out which image formats are Web-friendly, how to use HTML elements to add images to your Web pages, how to attach hyperlinks to your images, how to create image maps and animated images, and how to find and edit images for your Web page.

The Role of Images in a Web Page

Think back to the last several Web pages you've visited and consider the role images have played in each. Images may be logos, clickable navigation aids, or display content; they may also make the page look prettier, or serve to unify a page's theme. A perfect example of the many different ways images can enhance and contribute to Web pages is the White House home page at www.whitehouse.gov, shown in Figure 6-1.

Navigation and theme

Figure 6-1:
The White
House Web
page uses
images in a
variety of
ways.

Content

Spend a few moments analyzing this page, and you'll see that images play the following roles on the page:

✔ **For navigation:** The navigation at the top of that page uses graphics with stylized text to link you to information about the President, the Vice President, a search of the site, and more. These navigation elements could have been text based (like those on the left-side of the screen), but using graphics to help visitors link to key areas of the site makes it just a little prettier and helps establish an overall flow and formal look and feel for the site.

✔ **As content:** The picture on the right side of the screen isn't just there to break up the text on the page; it conveys content in a way text simply can't. The site could easily use text to describe the President making calls to world leaders from the Oval Office with the sun streaming through the windows on a beautiful day in Washington, D.C., but the picture captures the moment more effectively (and concisely) than words ever could. This illustrates the many times images are better vehicles for conveying content than text can be.

✔ **For decoration and to establish an overall look and feel for the site:**
The site uses a smattering of graphics to make the site look good and
establish an overall look and feel. Notice the White House balcony in the
upper-right corner. It helps emphasize that this is the White House home
page and adds a sense of dignity and formality to the site's look and feel.
A picture of Grover Cleveland sitting next to links to information about
goings on in the Cleveland White House back in 1893 adds some variety
and visual appeal to the page.

Overall, the White House site balances images and text beautifully. Many of
the images on the page perform double-duty as both navigation tools and
decorations, and the images the designer chose help convey a consistent
and appropriate look and feel for the site.

Creating Web-Friendly Images

There are a lot of different ways to create and save graphics, but only a few
are actually appropriate for images you want to use on the Web. As you work
to create Web-friendly images, you have to take two factors into account: file
format and file size.

Choosing the right file format

Usually, graphic file formats are particular to one operating system or
another, or even to one software application or another. However, because
you can't predict what kind of computer visitors might be using, or what software (other than a Web browser) they have installed, you need to create
images that anyone can view with any browser. This means you need to use
file formats that can be viewed whether a person uses any version of
Microsoft Windows, the Mac OS, or any of the various varieties of Linux on
the scene. Such file formats are called *cross platform*.

There are only three graphics formats that are appropriate for use on the Web:

✔ **GIF (Graphics Interchange Format):** GIF is the original cross-platform,
application-independent image format created by CompuServe. It's a
compressed file format, which means that images saved as GIFs tend to
be smaller than those saved in other file formats. However, GIF supports
up to 256 colors (and that's all, folks), so if you try to save an image created with millions of colors as a GIF, you may lose some image quality.
Generally, GIF is the best format for line art, clip art, and other types of
less-complex images.

✔ **JPEG (Joint Photographic Experts Group):** JPEG is a file format that supports 24-bit color (millions of colors) and consequently more complex images, like photographs. JPEG is both cross-platform and application-independent, just as GIF is. JPEG also offers compression to make images smaller, and a good image-editing tool can help you tweak the level of compression that you use so you can strike the optimum balance between image quality and image size.

✔ **PNG (Portable Network Graphics):** The latest cross-platform and application-independent image file format developed to bring together the best of GIF and JPEG. PNG provides the same level of compression as GIF does, but supports 24-bit color (and even 32-bit color) like JPEG. Because PNG supports such rich color and uses more advanced compression schemes than either GIF or JPEG, it's the best of the three formats and works with any kind of art. However, Internet Explorer 4 and Netscape 4 and older browsers don't support it, so many designers still shy away from it.

Any good graphics-editing tool (like those discussed in Chapter 16) allows you to save your images in any of these file formats. You can experiment with each to see how converting a graphic from one format to the other changes its appearance and file size, and then choose the format that gives you the best results.

For a complete overview of graphics formats and how to match a format to a particular graphic, visit Builder.com's Graphics 101 `http://builder.cnet.com/webbuilding/0-3883-8-4892140-1.html` and Webmonkey's "Web Graphics Overview" at `http://hotwired.lycos.com/webmonkey/01/28/index1a.html`.

Achieving the smallest possible file size

The fact that all three cross-platform graphics file formats (GIF, JPEG, and PNG) include file compression capabilities should be your first clue that file size is extremely important when you create Web graphics. Before users can view the images on your Web site, they have to download copies of those images to their local hard drives, which means the wrong set of circumstances can make your pages so difficult to access that visitors won't stay long enough to see your content and certainly won't be making a return visit:

✔ **You have several big images on your HTML page:** If the graphics on your page take up several hundreds of kilobytes (K), they will take quite a while to download regardless of the speed of a user's Internet connection.

✔ **A visitor has a slow Internet connection:** If it takes a minute or more (a very long time in cyberspace) for your page to load on users' computers, you can lose traffic. Most users don't have that much patience, and they'll leave your page in search of one that loads faster.

The good news is you can create graphics that look good and that have a reasonable file size. The few minutes you spend optimizing your images for Web use make them more effective and help you keep the users who visit your site on your site.

Optimizing images for the Web

As you build graphics for your Web page, you'll find yourself in a constant struggle to maintain a healthy balance between file quality and file size. The more colors an image has, the better it looks, but the larger its file size. As you begin to reduce the number of colors, image quality begins to decline, but so does file size. Finding the right balance in an image is called *optimizing* it, and there are a variety of tools designed to help you do just that.

The first step in optimizing your graphic for the Web is choosing the proper file format. For example, if you try to save a complex photograph as a GIF, you'll only have 256 colors to work with, which typically isn't enough for a photograph. The file size might be smaller, but the quality probably won't be that great. On the other hand, if you try to use JPEG to save some simple line art, you'll have millions of colors to work with (that you really don't need), and your file size will typically be larger than you need.

Table 6-1 offers some very general guidelines for choosing a file format for an image type.

Table 6-1	Choosing the Right File Format	
File Format	*Best Used For*	*Watch Out*
GIF	Line art and other images with few colors and less detail.	Don't use this format if you have a complex image or photo.
JPEG	Photos and other images with millions of colors and lots of detail.	Don't use with line art. Be sure that you don't compromise too much quality when you compress the file.
PNG	Photos and other images with millions of colors and lots of detail.	Don't use with line art. Older browsers don't support PNG, so you may still lose Web surfers even though PNG offers the best balance between quality and file size.

Although many visitors to your Web site may have broadband Internet connections, many more probably do not. The best way to ensure that your page is accessible to everyone and downloads quickly — regardless of connection speed — is to remember the 1-second, 1K rule. If you assume that it takes 1 second for every K of information on your page to download, you can add the total file size for the HTML file and all images on the page and get a good idea of how long your page will take to download on a slow Internet connection. Try to keep it to 60 seconds, which is 60K, or less, and you'll be just fine.

Webmonkey has two good tutorials on trimming your image file sizes and optimizing your entire site so it downloads faster. For a healthy collection of tips and tricks that can help you create pages that download quickly, review "Optimizing Your Images" at http://hotwired.lycos.com/webmonkey/ 99/15/index0a.html and the "Site Optimization Tutorial" at http:// hotwired.lycos.com/webmonkey/design/site_building/tutorials/ tutorial2.html.

Adding an Image to Your Page

After you have an image to work with and optimized it for the Web, you need to use the correct markup to make sure the image is added to your page. Easy enough. The image (<img>) element is an empty element, sometimes called a *singleton tag,* which you place on the page wherever you want your image to go.

An empty element only has an open tag, and no close tag.

The following markup places an image named three_cds.jpg between two paragraphs:

```
<!DOCTYPE HTML PUBLIC "-//W3C//DTD HTML 4.0 Transitional//EN"
         "http://www.w3.org/TR/REC-html40/loose.dtd">

<html>
  <head>
    <title>CDs at Work</title>
  </head>

  <body>

  <h1>CD as a Storage Media</h1>

  <p>CD-ROMs have become a standard storage option in today's computing world
     because they are an inexpensive and easy to use media.</p>

  <img src="three_cds.jpg">
```

```
<p>To read from a CD, you only need a standard CD-ROM drive, but to create
   CDs, you need either a CD-R or a CD-R/W drive.</p>

</body>
</html>
```

A Web browser replaces the `<img>` element with the image file referenced by the `src` attribute, as shown in Figure 6-2.

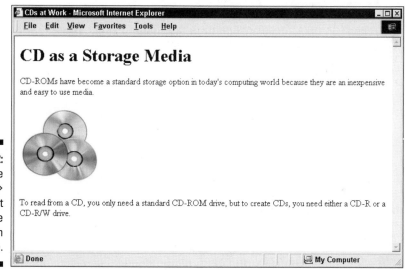

Figure 6-2:
Use the
`<img>`
element
to place
graphics in
a Web page.

The `src` attribute is very much like the `href` attribute that you use with an anchor (`<a>`) element. The `src` attribute specifies the URL for the image you want to display on your page. The previous example points to an image file that sits in the same folder as the HTML file referencing it, so the URL is relative. You'll find that most of your links to images are relative just because you usually keep image files on your site.

You make relative links between resources (like a Web page and graphic) on the same Web site. You make absolute links between resources on two different Web sites. Turn to Chapter 5 for a complete discussion of the differences between relative and absolute links.

So why should you keep all of the images you reference in your HTML on your site with your other files? After all, you can point to any image anywhere from your HTML. An image is just another Web resource. There are three compelling reasons to link to images on your own site:

✔ When the images are stored on your site, you have complete control over them. You know they aren't going to disappear or change, and you can work to optimize them.

✔ If you link to images on someone else's site, you never know when that site might go down or be unbelievably slow. You know these things about your own site.

✔ If you link to images on someone else's Web site, you may very well be violating his or her copyright (see the "Copyright matters" sidebar at the end of the chapter), and that's just plain illegal.

Adding alternative text

Images are designed, obviously, to be seen. However, there two important reasons why your image might not be seen:

✔ Users who are visually impaired may not be able to see them.

✔ Users with slow modem connections may turn images off.

Some search engines and other cataloging tools also use alternative text to index images.

Although most of your users will see your images, you should always be prepared for those who won't. The HTML 4.0 specification requires that you provide alternative text that describes the image with every image on your page. You use the `alt` attribute with the `<img>` element to add this information to your markup:

```
<!DOCTYPE HTML PUBLIC "-//W3C//DTD HTML 4.0 Transitional//EN"
        "http://www.w3.org/TR/REC-html40/loose.dtd">

<html>
<head>
  <title>Inside the Orchestra</title>
</head>

<body>
  <p>Among the different sections of the orchestra you will find:</p>
  <p><img src="strings.jpg" alt="violin and sheet music"> Strings</p>
  <p><img src="brass.jpg" alt="trumpet"> Brass</p>
  <p><img src="woodwind.jpg" alt="clarinet"> Woodwinds</p>
</body>
</html>
```

When browsers don't display an image (or can't, in the case of text-only browsers such as Lynx), they display the alternative text instead, as shown in Figure 6-3.

Even when browsers show an image, many (Internet Explorer 4 and Netscape 4 and later) typically show the alternative text as a pop-up tip when you hold your mouse over the image for a few seconds, as shown in Figure 6-4.

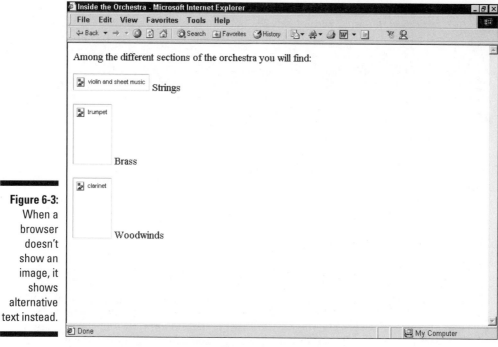

Figure 6-3:
When a
browser
doesn't
show an
image, it
shows
alternative
text instead.

Figure 6-4:
Even when
a browser
shows an
image,
it may
display the
alternative
text as a
pop-up tip
as well.

This means you can use alternative text to describe the image to those who can't see it and to provide additional information about the image to those who can.

The W3C's Web Accessibility Initiative (WAI) includes a variety of helpful tips on how to create useful and usable alternatives to visual content at www.w3. org/TR/WCAG10-TECHS/#gl-provide-equivalents. Chapter 18 also discusses making your site accessible in more detail.

Specifying image size

You can use the height and width attributes with the <img> element to let the browser know just how tall and wide an image is (in pixels):

```
<img src="brass.jpg" width="72" height="108" alt="trumpet">Brass</p>
```

Most browsers download the HTML and text associated with a page long before they download all of the page graphics. Rather than make users wait for every bit of a page to download, browsers typically display the text first and fill in graphics as they become available. If you let the browser know how big a graphic is, the browser can reserve a spot for it in the display. This technique makes the transition from a page without graphics displayed to a page with graphics displayed much smoother for the user.

Any image-editing program or even the image viewers built into Windows and Mac OS display the width and height of an image in pixels. Also, you may be able to simply view the properties of the image in either operating system to see how wide and tall it is.

Another good use of the height and width attributes is to create colored lines on a page using just a small colored square. For example, this markup adds a 10 by 10-pixel blue box to an HTML page:

```
<img src="blue_box.gif" alt="" height="10" width="10">
```

When the height and width attributes in the <img> element match the height and width of the image, it displays as a blue box in a browser window, as shown in Figure 6-5.

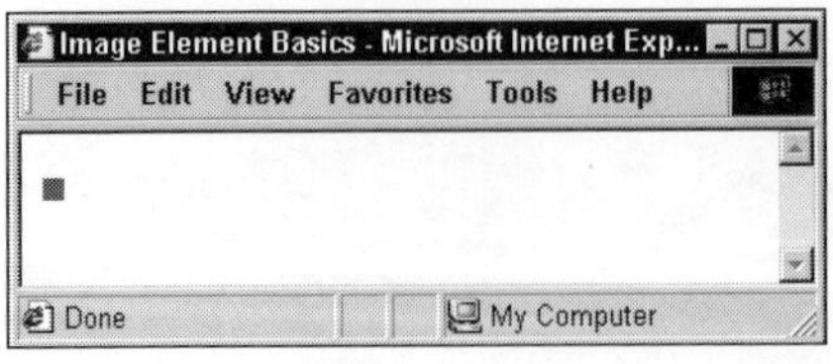

Figure 6-5:
A small box.

Image Element Basics - Microsoft Internet Exp...

File   Edit   View   Favorites   Tools   Help

Done   My Computer

However, a change to the height and width values in the markup turns this small blue box into a line 20 pixels high and 500 pixels long:

```
<img src="blue_box.gif" alt="" height="20" width="500">
```

The browser will expand the image to fit the height and width specifics in the markup, as shown in Figure 6-6.

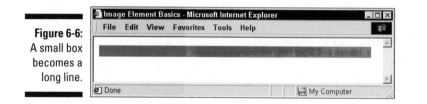

Figure 6-6:
A small box
becomes a
long line.

Using this technique, you can turn a single image like the blue box (only 1K in size by the way) into a variety of lines and even boxes. This is a good way to ensure all of the dividers and other border elements on your page use the same color — because they are all based on the same graphic. Also, if you decide you want to change all of your blue lines to green, you simply change the image, and every line you've created changes colors.

When you specify a height and width for an image that are different from the image's actual height and width, you rely on the browser to scale the image display accordingly. Although this works great for single-color images like the blue box, it doesn't work well for images with multiple colors or images that display actual pictures. The browser doesn't size images well, and you'll wind up with a distorted picture. Figure 6-7 shows how badly a browser handles enlarging the trumpet image from the previous example when we double the image height and width in the markup:

```
<img src="brass.jpg" width="144" height="216" alt="trumpet"> Brass</p>
```

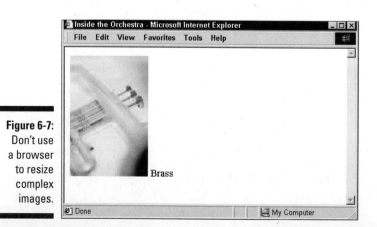

Figure 6-7:
Don't use
a browser
to resize
complex
images.

If you need several sizes of the same image, say a logo or navigation button, use the largest size image to make smaller versions in an image-editing tool so you can better control the final look and feel of the image.

Setting the image border

By default, every image has a border of 1, which doesn't really show up until you turn that image into a hyperlink (as discussed in the "Images that Link" section coming up). You can use the border attribute with the <img> element to better control what border the browser displays around your image. This markup sets the border for the clarinet image to 10 pixels:

```
<img src="woodwind.jpg" width="72" height="108" alt="clarinet" border="10">
```

The browser applies this border to all four sides of the image, as shown in Figure 6-8.

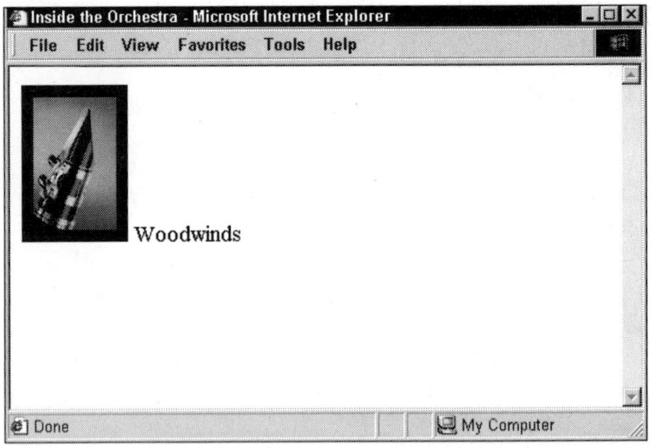

Figure 6-8:
Use the border attribute to create a border around your image.

Notice that the border is black and applies to all four sides of the image. If you want to control the color of the border, or want the border to appear differently on each side of the image, you have two options:

- ✔ Build the border into the image in an image-editing tool.
- ✔ Use Cascading Style Sheets (covered in Chapter 11).

If you use an image-editing tool to create your border, you can take advantage of the tool's features to create a patterned border or apply a unique effect. However, the additional information in the image may make it bigger. You'll need to carefully manage your image size in relation to its final appearance to be sure it doesn't take too long to download.

If you use CSS to apply a border, your image won't get any bigger, but your border may not show up in older browsers that don't support CSS well. The choice you make depends on how crucial the border is to your image (if it's very important, embed it in the image) and what browser you think your visitors use (newer browser have better support for style sheets).

If you don't plan to make your image into a hyperlink and don't want a border, don't worry about setting a `border` attribute at all. However, if you want to turn your image into a hyperlink and don't want a bright blue line around it, be sure to set the value of `border` to 0.

Controlling image alignment

The `align` attribute works with the `<img>` element to control the way your image appears relative to the text around it. The possible values for this attribute are:

- ✔ `top`: Aligns the text around the image with the top of the image.
- ✔ `middle`: Aligns the text around the image with the middle of the image.
- ✔ `bottom`: Aligns the text around the image with the bottom of the image.
- ✔ `left`: The image sits on the left, and text floats to the right of the image.
- ✔ `right`: The image sits on the right, and text floats to the left of the image.

By default, most browsers align images to the left and float all text to the right. The following markup shows how five different `<img>` elements use the `align` attribute to change the way text floats around the mouse images:

```
<p> <img src="white_mouse.jpg" alt="mouse on a white background"
        height="108" width="72" align="top">
    This text is aligned with the top of the image.
</p>

<p> <img src="kid_mouse.jpg" alt="mouse on a yellow background"
        height="108" width="72" align="middle">
    This text is aligned with the middle of the image.
</p>

<p> <img src="grey_mouse.jpg" alt="grey mouse on a red background"
        height="108" width="72" align="bottom">
    This text is aligned with the bottom of the image.
</p>

<p> <img src="threebutton_mouse.jpg" alt="three button mouse"
        height="108" width="72" align="left">
    This image floats to the left of the text.
</p>
```

```
<p> <img src="blue_mouse.jpg" alt="trackball mouse and keyboard"
        height="108" width="72" align="right">
     This image floats to the right of the text.
</p>
```

Figure 6-9 shows how a browser interprets these different alignments.

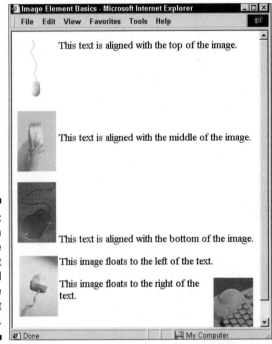

Figure 6-9:
You can
vary image
alignment
to control
image
placement
on the page.

You may find that the `<img>` attributes don't give you as much control over your image alignment as you'd like. One of the primary uses for tables is to better control the way images sit relative to other content on the page. Find out more about using tables and images together in Chapter 8. In addition, CSS, discussed in Chapter 11, includes a variety of properties you can use to better control the way your images sit on the page.

Setting image spacing

Most browsers only leave a pixel or so of white space between images and the text or other images next to them. You can use the `vspace` and `hspace` attributes to give your images a little more breathing room both on the top and bottom (vertical space) and to the left and right (horizontal space). This HTML gives the mouse graphic 20 pixels of white space on either side, and 25 pixels on the top and bottom:

```
<p>
   This text doesn't crowd the image on top.<br>
   <img src="white_mouse.jpg"
        height="108" width="72" hspace="20" vspace="25"
        alt="mouse on a white background">
   And this text is a little further away from the sides. </p>
```

Figure 6-10 shows how a browser adds space around the image to separate it from the text.

Figure 6-10:
The
hspace
and
vspace
attributes
control the
white space
around an
image.

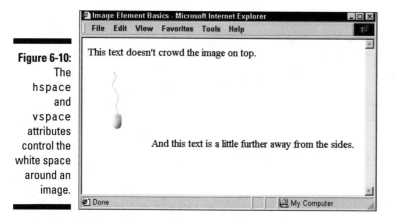

The default value for hspace and vspace is 1. If you want to place images so close together that their sides are touching, as you might for a set of navigation buttons, set the value for these attributes to 0 to eliminate that extra 1 pixel of space.

Images that Link

One of the most common uses for images is as navigation tools. They are prettier than plain-text links, and as you saw on the White House page earlier in the chapter, they allow you to include both form and function on your page with one element. To create an image that links, you simply substitute an <img> element in place of the text you would anchor your link to. This markup hangs a link on some text:

```
<p><a href="http://www.w3.org">Visit the W3C</a></p>
```

This markup replaces the text Visit the W3C with an appropriate icon:

```
<p><a href="http://www.w3.org"><img src="w3.jpg"
    alt="Visit the W3C Web Site" height="72" width="108" border="0"></a>

</p>
```

This creates a linked image that points to http://www.w3.org. Also, notice that the alternative text now says Visit the W3C Web Site, to let users who can't see the image know where the link takes them. When a user moves his or her mouse pointer over the image, the cursor turns from a pointer into a pointing hand (or whatever icon his or her browser uses to indicate a link), as shown in Figure 6-11.

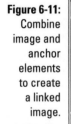

Figure 6-11: Combine image and anchor elements to create a linked image.

A quick click of the image launches the W3C Web site. It's as simple as that.

As discussed earlier in the chapter, you should set the border of any image you use in a link to 0 to keep the browser from surrounding your image in an ugly blue line. Without the line, however, users will need other visual (or alternative text) clues so they know an image is a link. Be sure images that serve as links scream to the user (tastefully of course) "I'm a link." Chapter 18 discusses building a good user interface in more detail.

Creating an image map

When you use an <img> element with an anchor element to create a linking image, you can only attach one link to that image. If you want to create a larger image that connects several different links to different regions on the page, you need an *image map*.

To create an image map you need two things:

✔ An image with several distinct areas that would be obvious to users that point to different areas on your site.

✔ A set of markup to map the different regions on the map to different URLs.

You use the `<img>` element to add the map image into your page, just as you would any other image. In addition, you include the `usemap` attribute to let the browser know that there's image map information to go with the image. The value of the `usemap` attribute is the name of your map.

You use two elements and a collection of attributes to define the image map: `<map>` to hold the map information and `<area>` to link specific parts of the map to URLs. The `<map>` element uses the `name` attribute to identify the map. The value of name should match the value of `usemap` in the `<img>` element that goes with the map. The `<area>` element takes several attributes to define the specifics for each region in the map:

✔ `shape`: Specifies the shape of the region. You can choose from `rect` (rectangle), `circle`, and `poly` (a triangle or polygon).

✔ `coords`: Define the region's coordinates. A rectangle's coordinates include the left, right, top, and bottom points. A circle's coordinates include the x and y coordinates for the center of the circle and the circle's radius. A polygon's coordinates are a collection of x and y coordinates for every point in the polygon.

✔ `href`: Specifies the URL to which the region links. This can be an absolute or relative URL.

✔ `alt`: Provides alternative text for the image region.

This markup defines a three-region map called `NavMap` linked to the `navigation.gif` image:

```
<img src="navigation.gif" width="302" height="30" usemap="#NavMap" border="0">
<map name="NavMap">
  <area shape="rect" coords="0,0,99,30" href="home.html" alt="Home">
  <area shape="rect" coords="102,0,202,30" href="about.html" alt="About">
  <area shape="rect" coords="202,0,301,30" href="products.html" alt="Products">
</map>
```

Figure 6-12 shows how a browser displays this markup.

When the mouse sits over a region in the map, the cursor turns into a pointing hand, just as it does over any other hyperlink, so take advantage of the alternative text to include useful information about the link

Creating thumbnail images

There may be times when you want to make large images available to users on your Web site, but want to give them a preview of the image and the option to view the larger image, rather than forcing them to wait for the larger image when they first view your page. Thumbnail images use smaller versions of a large image to link to the larger (both in file size and image size) image, as in this markup:

```
<p><a href="brass_large.jpg">
  <img src="brass_small.jpg"
    alt="trumpet thumbnail" height="98"
    width="109" border="0">
  </a>
</p>
```

This markup links a smaller version of the trumpet image directly to a larger version. Notice that the link is to a JPEG file, not to another HTML page. This is a quick way to make a link to a larger image. Another option is to create a

new HTML page to hold the larger image and link to the page `brass_large.html` instead of the image itself.

```
<p><a href="brass_large.html">
  <img src="brass_small.jpg"
    alt="trumpet thumbnail" height="98"
    width="109" border="0">
  </a>
</p>
```

This approach gives you the flexibility to add text and navigation to the page holding the larger image, but of course requires that you create and maintain the page. If you only have a couple of such thumbnail images on your site, maintaining them isn't that difficult. More than 10 or so is a different story though. You have to decide for yourself how much additional information you want to supply with the larger image.

Figure 6-12:
Image
maps turn
different
areas of an
image into
linking
regions.

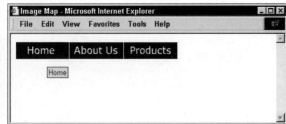

Image maps have really fallen out of favor among Web designers recently because they tend to be bulky and very difficult to manage. Even so, they're still used on the Web and they may be a feature you want to include on your pages. A common use for image maps, even today, is to turn maps of places (states, countries, cities, neighborhoods, and such) into linkable maps. Webmonkey's image map tutorial at http://hotwired.lycos.com/webmonkey/96/40/index2a.html provides even more details on optimizing your image maps and making the most of this HTML feature.

Creating image maps by hand can be a little tricky. You need to use an image editor to identify each point in the map and then create the proper markup for it. Most HTML tools from (both shareware and commercial software) include utilities to help you make image maps. If you take advantage of one of these tools, you'll create image maps quickly and with fewer errors. Find out more about HTML tools in Chapter 16.

Other Interesting Image Tricks

As you look around the Web, you see types of interesting image tricks at work. Two of the most popular involve creating animated GIFs and transparent images. Neither of these activities is particularly difficult. You just need to know how they work and then acquire the right tools.

Images often play an integral role in multimedia presentations you might add to your Web page. Be sure to review Chapter 13 for more information on working with media.

Creating animated GIFs

An animated GIF is a collection of graphics files in the GIF format that display in succession, one after the other, just like scenes in a movie. To create an animated GIF, you bring several images together in animation software, specify parameters such as how many times the animation should repeat, how fast the animation should run, and if you want any special effects applied to the transition from image to image.

To create an animated GIF, you need animation software such as GifBuilder or GIF Construction Set, both of which are shareware. These tools handle the programming (such as it is — it's not what we'd describe as heavy lifting) behind the GIF, and help you put the pieces together.

You can visit TUCOWS at www.tucows.com and search for "animated GIF" to access a long list of tool possibilities. You're sure to find one that fits your budget and that works with your computer of choice.

Because animated GIFs are just GIF files with a little extra information thrown in, you reference them in your HTML just like you would any other GIF file; that is, you use the <img> element. Animated GIFs may begin with several GIF files, but they become a single file whose name you can use as the value of the src attribute.

Much like image maps, animated GIFs are becoming something of a dinosaur on the Web. New technologies such as Macromedia Flash (covered in Chapter 13) allow you to do more advanced animations that are interactive and include links. However, Flash isn't a free product and does have a learning curve. If you want to quickly add a short animation to your page, an animated GIF may be just what you're looking for. The Webmonkey tutorial entitled "My First GIF Animation" at `http://hotwired.lycos.com/webmonkey/html/97/14/index2a.html` walks you through all of the steps to creating an animated GIF.

Making transparent images

Transparent images are simply graphics saved in either the GIF or PNG file format (but not JPEG) where a color in the image is transparent. That is, the background color of whatever page the image is on will show through where that color would have been.

Transparency helps images blend into a page, but creating transparent images does have its drawbacks:

- Although you can set several colors in a PNG image to be transparent, you can only pick one color in a GIF.

- If you set the color on the remote edge of a GIF to transparent, the edge may appear jagged against a different color background. This happens because what the human eye perceives as the edge between two colors is really a blend of several shades of one color into the next. Black and white isn't really just a transition between black and white, but instead requires several shades of gray. When you make a single color transparent, the other shades are still there.

Just about any image-editing software, from shareware to commercial, has utilities for creating transparent images. Look in the help or documentation for your tool of choice to find out how to use the transparency feature. Also, because transparent images are just regular image files, you use the image element to reference them in your HTML pages.

Transparency works best on line art that doesn't have a lot of colors so there is less shading to work with. If you have more complicated graphics that you would like to blend in with your page background, consider making the graphic background match that of the page.

Finding Sources for Images

Of course, if you want to use images in your Web pages, you need a source for all of those images. If you aren't a modern-day Rembrandt (or Picasso or even Warhol), that doesn't mean you can't acquire quality images without spending an arm and a leg to do so. You have several options for reasonably priced (including free) images:

- **Online:** There a variety of online image repositories that house free graphics you can use for personal and even business Web sites. Search your favorite search engines for "free Web graphics," and you'll be presented with a very long list to get you started. However, because everyone can access these graphics your site may lose some of its uniqueness, or you may have a hard time finding images that fit your needs.

- **Photo and clip art CDs:** There are several photo and clip art CD vendors that will sell you entire collections of graphics for a low cost (even as little as $25 a CD). These images are usually high quality and come in a variety of formats so you can use them for both print and Web work. Visit www.profotos.com for a list of companies that specialize in selling images on CD-ROM. In addition, www.iStockphoto.com is a great resource for free stock photography.

When you locate images either for free or for a fee, be sure to double check the licensing agreement for those images. Some images are only free for personal use and require that you pay a fee for business use. Some clip art and photo CDs only allow you to use the images in print or on the Web, but not both. When in doubt, ask the person or company providing the art what they will allow you to use the art for.

- **Scanners and digital cameras:** You can capture your own images using a scanner or a digital camera. If you have art, drawings, documents, or other art that you would like to incorporate into your site, just scan them. You can take pictures of products, a company office, people at work and at play, and more with a digital camera to create your own compelling images for your site.

- **Create your own:** Even if you haven't done much drawing before, try your hand at creating your own art. Today's software packages provide you with powerful collections of tools for creating original art.

When you pay a graphic artist to create any piece of customized artwork — from a company logo to specialized charts or presentation templates — always be sure to get copies of the artwork in digital format, preferably TIFF format. If you want to use this artwork online (or for any other digital purpose later on), you'll get a much clearer image if you work from the original digital version instead of scanning a print version. Also, be sure that you retain all rights to any version of the artwork — print, electronic, otherwise — so you don't have to secure the artist's permission to use it over and over again.

This chapter really only scratches the surface of what you can do with Web images and how to use them effectively as part of your page and site design. Although you can find out everything you need to know to get started using images in your pages, the information in this chapter is really only the tip of the iceberg. If you want to delve deeper into the ins and outs of Web graphics, consider reading *Web Design For Dummies* by Lisa Lopuck. This book can help you transition from a simple user of graphics in Web pages to a master of Web images and Web design.

Copyright matters

Whereas you might be tempted to download an image from someone else's Web site to use on your own, or simply make a link to that image, don't. Just about everything on the Web is copyrighted these days, and that includes any original work you've done. Even if the owner of some text or an image doesn't apply for a copyright, by the very nature of creating an original work, he or she owns it. Many sites, especially education, science, and museum sites, will allow you to borrow their images, but only if you properly attribute them on your page.

The bottom line about copyright is if you violate it, you're breaking the law — which is bad in so many ways. Don't ever represent someone else's work as your own, or use someone else's

work without permission, and you'll be sure to stay on the right side of the copyright law.

Much of the Web's content is protected by copyright, but there are many images paid for with taxpayer money, or whose copyrights have long expired (think works and images owned and managed by the federal government) are in the public domain and free for your use. Before you assume something is in the public domain, however, look closely on the site for a copyright notice, and be sure to send e-mail to the site's owners if you are at all in doubt. PDImages.com (www.pdimages.com) is a wonderful resource for beginning the search for copyright-free images available in the public domain.

Chapter 7

Top Off Your Page with Formatting

*I*t's amazing what a little color and text variation can do to liven up a Web page. You can turn a plain page into a striking work of art with a few carefully placed text treatments. Color can bring attention to important information on your site, and the right font can emphasize your text's message.

HTML includes a healthy collection of elements, which you can use to control the background, colors, fonts, and text sizes on your Web page. In this chapter, you learn how to spruce up your pages a bit by using the HTML formatting elements.

Because HTML is really a language for defining document structure, not a formatting language, its built-in formatting capabilities are basic. After you master HTML formatting you may find you want to do even more with the look and feel of your pages. Cascading Style Sheets (CSS) is a style-definition language for HTML designed to let you do just that — take your Web page formatting to the next level. Chapter 11 shows you how to use CSS to set page margins, attach background images to different blocks of text, create borders around your text, and more.

Defining Color in HTML

You use different combinations of HTML elements and attributes depending on where you want to make a color change — in your entire document, in a table cell, or to a chunk of text. Even so, the notation that defines colors in HTML is the same, regardless of which elements and attributes you associate with the color.

HTML gives you two different ways to specify a color:

- By name (you choose from a limited list)
- By number (harder to remember, but you have many more options)

Color names

The HTML specification includes 16 color names you can use to define colors in your pages: Aqua, Black, Blue, Fuchsia, Gray, Green, Lime, Maroon, Navy, Olive, Purple, Red, Silver, Teal, White, and Yellow. Because these names are part of the specification, you can be confident that any and every browser can recognize them and apply the correct color to your page display.

If you want to see how your browser displays these different colors, visit www.htmlhelp.com/reference/html40/values.html#color. If you can, view this page on two or three different computers to see how the browser, operating system, graphics card, and monitor can subtly change the display.

If you're looking for burnt umber, chartreuse, or salmon, you're out of luck. A box of 64 crayons this list is not. Don't despair; the artist in you won't be quashed. The hexadecimal color notation system gives you what you need to use any color (even burnt umber) on your Web page.

Hexadecimal color codes

Every color can be defined as a mixture of red, green, and blue (RGB). Monitors display colors in RGB, and hexadecimal notation gives you a way to convey a color's RGB values to a Web browser. If you know a color's hexadecimal code (often called a *hex code* for short), you have all you need to use that color in your HTML page.

Hexadecimal notation uses six characters — a combination of numbers and letters — to define the amount of red, green, and blue in any color. Table 7-1 shows the hexadecimal equivalents for each of the 16 color names. Every color out there has a hex code like these.

Table 7-1	The 16 Color Names with Their Hex Codes						
Color Name	*Hex Code*	*Color Name*	*Hex Code*	*Color Name*	*Hex Code*	*Color Name*	*Hex Code*
Aqua	#00FFFF	Gray	#808080	Navy	#000080	Silver	#C0C0C0
Black	#000000	Green	#008000	Olive	#808000	Teal	#008080

Color Name	Hex Code	Color Name	Hex Code	Color Name	Hex Code	Color Name	Hex Code
Blue	#0000FF	Lime	#00FF00	Purple	#800080	White	#FFFFFF
Fuchsia	#FF00FF	Maroon	#800000	Red	#FF0000	Yellow	#FFFF00

Notice the pound sign (#) before each of the six-digit hex codes. When you use hexadecimal code to define a color, you should always precede it with a pound sign. So, this HTML uses a color name to specify that some text in a paragraph should be blue:

```
<p> Some of the text <font color="blue">in this paragraph is blue.</font></p>
```

This HTML uses a hex code to do the same thing:

```
<p> Some of the text <font color="#0000FF">in this paragraph is blue.</font></p>
```

You find out all about which elements and attributes you use to apply color to different parts of your HTML page later in the chapter.

Finding out any color's hex code

Of course, you can't just wave your magic wand and come up with the hex code for any color. But that doesn't mean that you can't find out through less magical means. Color converters follow a precise formula that changes a color's standard RGB notation into hexadecimal notation. Because you have better things to do with your time than compute hex codes, you have several options for finding out the code for your color of choice, none of which require you to use a calculator:

✔ **On the Web:** Two good sources for hexadecimal color charts are www.hypersolutions.org/pages/rgbhex.html and www.fastboot.com/color_chart.html. You simply find a color you like, and type the hex code listed next to it into your HTML.

✔ **Using a converter:** If you already know the RGB percentages for a particular color, you can plug them into an online converter at http://www.univox.com/home/support/rgb2hex.html to get the hexadecimal equivalent. For example, the RGB percentages for nice sky blue are 159, 220, and 223. Plug those into the converter, and you get the equivalent hex code #9FDCDF.

✔ **Using image-editing software:** Many image-editing applications, such as Adobe Photoshop or Jasc Paint Shop Pro, display the hexadecimal notation for any color. Even Microsoft Word's color picker shows you hex codes for colors in an image. If you have an image you like that you want to use as a color source for your Web page, open the image in your favorite editor and find out what the colors' hex codes are.

Unlike the more familiar decimal system that uses base-ten numbers to represent all possible numbers, the hexadecimal system uses base 16. If you want to know more about the hexadecimal system or find out how to convert numbers from decimal to hexadecimal, visit http://mathforum.org/library/drmath/view/55830.html.

Setting Colors and Backgrounds for Your Entire Page

The <body> element contains the guts of your Web page, so when you want attributes (namely colors and backgrounds) to affect your entire Web page, the <body> element is the element you need to deal with. You can use the <body> element attributes to do the following:

🖙 Define the text color for your entire Web page.

🖙 Specify the different colors for links in your Web page.

🖙 Set a background color for your Web page.

🖙 Attach a background image to your Web page.

Changing text color

By default, most Web browsers display the text on a Web page in black. Some users may change their browser preferences to display text in another color, but most of the time, you can expect users to see black text against a white background on your page unless you specify otherwise.

You use the text attribute with either a color name or hexadecimal value in the <body> element to set the color for the text on your Web page. The following markup uses one of the 16 color names to set the page text color to white:

```
<body text="white">
```

This code uses the hex code to do the same:

```
<body text="#FFFFFF>
```

Many Web browsers allow users to define their own color settings and override yours. You can expect about 90 percent or so of your users to see the colors you've defined and be content with them, but the other 10 percent or so will want their color choices to override yours.

You should coordinate your text, link, and background colors so they all work well together. If you set your background text to black but forget to set your text color to a lighter color, your text won't show up on the page. Conversely, light text and link colors can be lost on a white page.

Changing link colors

You've probably noticed when you visit a Web page, click a link, view the linked document, and return to the linking page, that the link may be a different color than it was before you clicked it.

The change in link color is your Web browser's way of giving you a visual cue of which links you've clicked recently. Each browser has default settings for the different colors associated with each *link state.* For example, both Internet Explorer and Netscape use some shade of bright blue to highlight links you've haven't yet visited. You can use the following attributes with the `<body>` element to control those colors for your page.

Links come in three states, and you can modify each of them using an attribute:

- **Link:** The user hasn't clicked the link or recently visited the resource it points to. The `link` attribute defines this link's color.

- **Active link:** The user just clicked the link, but the browser hasn't opened the page yet. Links are active for a second or two (maybe a few more on a slower computer and Internet connection) before the browser displays the linked document. Define the color of this kind of link with the `alink` attribute.

- **Visited link:** The user has recently visited this link. The `vlink` attribute defines this link's color.

The following HTML markup snippet makes all the links on a page silver, all the active links teal, and all the visited links blue:

```
<body link="silver" alink="teal" vlink="blue">
```

This next HTML line uses hexadecimal codes to define the same color settings:

```
<body link="#C0C0C0" alink="#008080" vlink="#0000FF">
```

TIP

You may have noticed that the links on some Web sites don't seem to be underlined. All browsers display hyperlinks as underlined by default, and HTML doesn't provide an attribute or other method for turning off link underlining. The removal of lines under links isn't magic; style sheets give you more control over link display and behavior than these HTML attributes do. Turn to Chapter 11 to learn more about style sheets.

Background colors

Just as you can control text and link color, you can control the background color on your page. Add the bgcolor attribute to the <body> element to set the background color for the page. This HTML sets the background color to black:

```
<body bgcolor="black">
```

This HTML uses the hexadecimal code to do the same:

```
<body bgcolor="#000000">
```

Bringing all of the colors together

The markup in Listing 7-1 combines all the color-related <body> attributes to create a page with a black background, white text, silver links, teal active links, and blue visited links:

Listing 7-1: **Using** <body> **Element Attributes to Control a Page's Colors**

```
    <html>
<head>
  <title>Page Colors</title>
</head>
<body text="white" link="silver" alink="teal" vlink="blue" bgcolor="black">
  <p>The attributes in the document body element define the colors the
    browser uses to display text on the page.</p>
  <p>This <a href="home.html">link</a> is silver before it is clicked, teal
    when it is clicked, and blue after it is clicked.</p>
</body>
</html>
```

Figure 7-1 shows how a browser displays this HTML. You can't actually see the colors in this figure, but you should get a good idea of the effect these attributes will have.

Figure 7-1:
Use the
`<body>`
element
attributes
to define
the colors
on your
Web page.

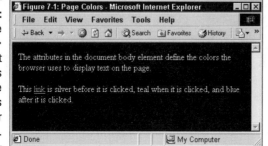

Adding a background graphic

In addition to setting a simple background color for your page, you can also specify a graphic to act as a background image for your page using the `background` attribute with the `<body>` element. This HTML assigns `back.gif` as the background image for the page:

```
<body background="back.gif">
```

A background image can be as small or as large as you like. Web browsers automatically repeat (or *tile*) the image across and down the page to fill in the background. Figure 7-2 shows the background image `back.gif`, which is a 2-inch-by-2-inch square:

Figure 7-2:
A back-
ground
image can
be any size;
the browser
tiles it to
fill in the
entire page
background.

A browser has to download any background image before it can display it behind your page. Keep your background images small. A 2-inch by 2-inch graphic will load much faster than a 6-inch by 6-inch one, and the effect will be the same.

When you add the `background` attribute to the `<body>` element from Listing 7-1, the complete element with all its attributes is:

```
<body text="white" link="silver" alink="teal" vlink="blue" bgcolor="black"
    background="back.gif">
```

Figure 7-3 shows how the browser tiles the small `back.gif` image to fill the entire page.

Figure 7-3:
A Web page with both colors and a background image defined.

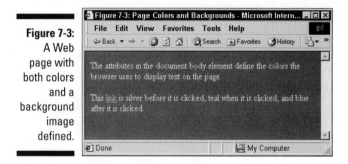

Notice that the HTML for the `<body>` element includes the `bgcolor` attribute even though the `background` attribute defines an image background for the page. A background image always displays instead of a background color, unless a user has turned off the image display settings in his or her browser.

If a browser can't display images, it displays the background color. Be sure to define a background color as a fallback to a background image, especially if your text is light and you're counting on the background to make the text readable.

Just as you have to coordinate text colors and background colors, you have to coordinate text colors and background images. In Figure 7-4, the background image is light, as are the text and link colors, so the text is unreadable.

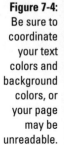

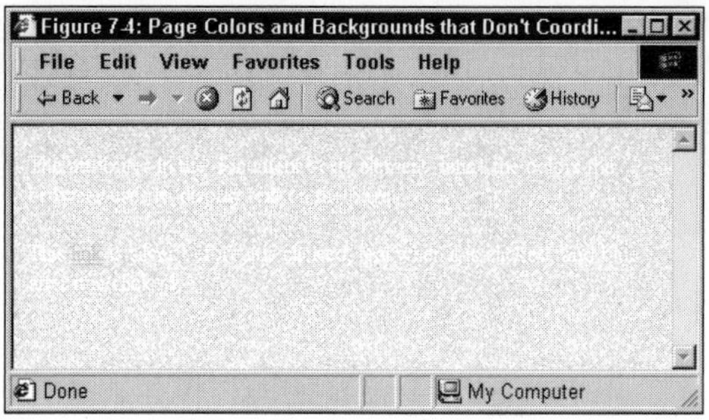

Figure 7-4:
Be sure to
coordinate
your text
colors and
background
colors, or
your page
may be
unreadable.

> **Figure 7-4: Page Colors and Backgrounds that Don't Coordi...** □ ▢ ✕
>
> File   Edit   View   Favorites   Tools   Help
>
> ↩ Back ▾ ⇒ ▾ ⊗ ⊡ ⊿   ⊕Search ⚑Favorites ⏱History   ⬛▾ »
>
> ⬇ Done   ⬛ My Computer

Working with Font Faces, Colors, and Sizes

All the attributes that work with the `<body>` element to set color and back-grounds for your page apply to the entire document. Sometimes you may want to apply color and other text formatting to specific parts of your page instead of the entire thing. Enter the `<font>` element (both literally and figuratively).

You can use the `<font>` element and its related attributes to control three different aspects of a section of text on your page:

✔ Font face
✔ Font color
✔ Font size

Defining the font face

Every browser has built-in settings that specify which font it uses to display various elements such as paragraphs and headings. Most browsers use some variety of Times, such as Times New Roman, or a similar serif font to display almost all text, but when you combine the `<font>` element with the `face` attribute, you can change that.

This HTML markup specifies that the first paragraph on the page should display in Arial, and the second paragraph should display in Courier:

```
<p>
   <font face="Arial">This text is displayed in Arial.</font>
</p>

<p>
   <font face="Courier">This text is displayed in Courier.</font>
<p>
```

Figure 7-5 shows how a browser renders this HTML.

Figure 7-5:
Use the
`<font>`
element and
the `face`
attribute to
change the
font face
for sections
of text on
the page.

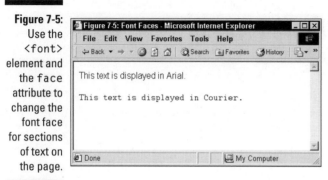

If you're wondering about the attribute that changes the font face of a whole HTML page at once, we've got bad news for you. There is no such attribute. HTML doesn't include one, so if you want to set the font face for the entire page to something other than the browser default, you have to use the `<font>` element and `face` attribute on every block element.

Refer back to Chapter 4 to find out more about the difference between block and inline elements, and how you use them together.

The `<font>` element is an inline element, so you can't use a `<font>` tag at the beginning of the page and close it at the end and get predictable results across several browsers. It may be tedious to set the `<font>` tag on every block element, but your results will be more consistent across browsers.

A good HTML editor (discussed in Chapter 16) can make the process of applying a font face to each block element much easier, or you can use a style sheet (discussed in Chapter 11) to define a font face for your entire document.

Applying font color to pieces of text

You can apply color to any chunk of text in your document using the `<font>` element and the `color` attribute. This HTML changes the font color twice in the same sentence, once to silver and once to white:

```
<p>You can change <font color="silver">font color</font> in the middle of
  <font color="white">paragraphs</font> if you like.</p>
```

Figure 7-6 shows how this affects the text display in a browser.

Figure 7-6:
Use the
`<font>`
element and
the `color`
attribute to
change the
font color
for sections
of text on
the page.

![Figure 7-6: Font Colors - Microsoft Internet Explorer. You can change font color in the middle of if you like.]

Notice that the white text doesn't show up on the page at all, because the page background is the browser's default white. Use the `<font>` tag with the `color` attribute carefully, or your page may be unreadable.

Setting the font size

The last attribute you can use with the `<font>` element to change the appearance of selected text is the `size` attribute. Most browsers support sizes 1 through 7, with 1 being the smallest and 7 being the largest. This HTML applies each size to a different line of text in a paragraph.

```
<p>
  <font size="1">Font size 1</font> <br>
  <font size="2">Font size 2</font> <br>
  <font size="3">Font size 3</font> <br>
  <font size="4">Font size 4</font> <br>
  <font size="5">Font size 5</font> <br>
  <font size="6">Font size 6</font> <br>
  <font size="7">Font size 7</font>
</p>
```

Figure 7-7 shows how a browser displays these different font sizes:

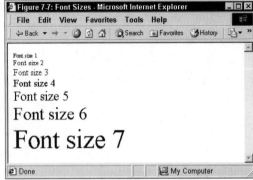

By default, most browsers display text in size 3. In addition to simply setting the font size number that you want to use as the value for the `size` attribute, you can also use positive and negative numbers to define font sizes relative to the default text size. For example, this HTML sets the size of one paragraph to one size above the default size and a second paragraph to one size following the default size.

```
<p>
   <font size="-1">One size smaller than the default</font><br>
   The default font size <br>
   <font size="+1">One size larger than the default</font>
</p>
```

Font sizes set this way are called *relative font sizes.* Conversely, font sizes that just use a number to define size are called *absolute font sizes* because they specifically define a font size instead of using a relative measurement. Figure 7-8 shows how a browser displays the relative font sizes.

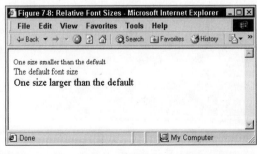

REMEMBER

Just because you can do something . . .

The `<font>` element and its three attributes — `face`, `color`, and `size`, — give you a lot of power over the way your page displays. However, just because you can do something (for example, use 50 colors, varying font sizes and faces, and add wild backgrounds) doesn't necessarily mean you should. When you use formatting carefully and in moderation, you can make your content have more impact and even enhance its meaning. If you use formatting just because you can, you may well drive users from your page before they even read a word of what it says. If you think of colors, backgrounds, font sizes, and other formatting tools as ways to augment your page, you'll be on the right track. Chapter 18 includes other tips on creating a good experience for your site's visitors.

If you assume that the browser's default font size is 3, then a font size of -1 is equal to a size of 2, and a font size of +1 is equal to a size of 4. Does the browser display size 2 and -1 as the same thing? What about size 3 and the default size? Or +1 and 4? Here's some HTML that uses these to define size:

```
<p>
  <font size="-1">One size smaller than the default</font><br>
  <font size="2">Font size 2</font><br>
    The default font size <br>
  <font size="3">Font size 3</font><br>
  <font size="+1">One size larger than the default</font><br>
  <font size="4">Font size 4</font>
</p>
```

Figure 7-9 shows how the browser interprets these size specifications.

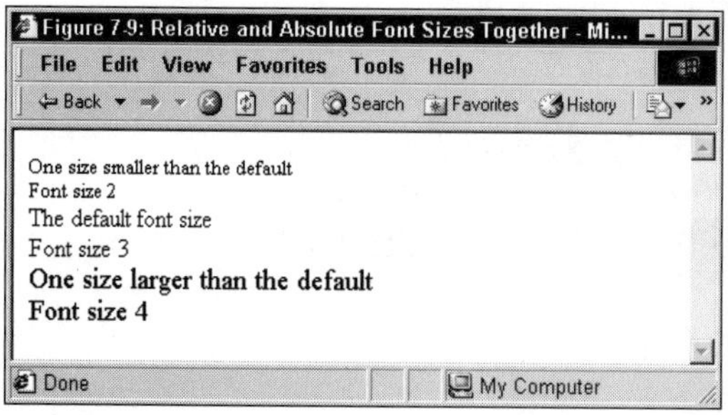

Figure 7-9:
You can
often get
the same
results
using
relative font
sizes or
absolute
font sizes.

So, which font size scheme do you use? Absolute font sizes are easier to use, but relative font sizes are more flexible. When a user increases or decreases his or her browser's default font size, relative font sizes grow and shrink as well. Some browsers expand and shrink both absolute and relative font sizes as the default font size changes, but not all of them do. For maximum flexibility, use relative font sizes. You can also use CSS for even greater control over your font sizes. Turn to Chapter 11 for more information.

Boldface, Italics, and Other Text Treatments

Text color and font changes are only one way to emphasize bits of text or make them stand out. In addition to the <font> element, HTML has a nice collection of elements you can use to apply treatments such as boldface, italics, underlining, and more to the text on your page. These treatments can be broken into two categories:

- ✔ **Style elements:** Much like the <font> element, these elements simply apply formatting to text on the page but don't describe anything about the text (such as the text is in italics because it is a book title). The style elements include:

  - <b>: boldface text

  - <big>: big text, usually one size larger than the text around it

  - <i>: italicized text

  - <s>: strike-through text

  - <small>: small text, usually one size smaller than the text around it

  - <strike>: strike-through text

  - <tt>: teletype text like a typewriter might create

  - <u>: underlined text

- ✔ **Phrase elements:** These elements provide more information about some text in your page (such as identifying it as computer code) and the browser formats the text accordingly (text marked as code is displayed in a monospaced font).

  - <abbr>: an abbreviation

  - <acronym>: an acronym

  - <cite>: a citation

- `<code>`: computer code
- `<del>`: deleted text
- `<dfn>`: a defined term
- `<em>`: emphasized text
- `<ins>`: inserted text
- `<kbd>`: text to be input on a keyboard or other device
- `<samp>`: sample output
- `<strong>`: strongly emphasized text
- `<var>`: a variable

The markup in Listing 7-2 shows all these elements in use in an HTML page. Notice that they are all *inline* elements, which means you need to use them within a block element like a paragraph, heading, or list item:

Listing 7-2:   Text Treatments at Work

```
<h1>Style elements</h1>
<p><b>boldface text</b><br>
   <big>big text</big><br>
   <i>italicized text</i><br>
   <s>strike-through text</s><br>
   <small>small text</small><br>
   <strike>strike-through text</strike><br>
   <tt>teletype text</tt><br>
   <u>underlined text</u>
</p>

<h1>Phrase elements</h1>
<p><abbr>an abbreviation</abbr><br>
   <acronym>an acronym</acronym><br>
   <cite>a citation</cite><br>
   <code>computer code</code><br>
   <del>deleted text</del><br>
   <dfn>a defined term</dfn><br>
   <em>emphasized text</em><br>
   <ins>inserted text</ins><br>
   <kbd>text to be input</kbd><br>
   <samp>sample output</samp><br>
   <strong>strongly emphasized text</strong><br>
   <var>a variable</var>
</p>
```

Figure 7-10 shows how a browser interprets these different elements. Notice that many of them look the same, even though the elements are different.

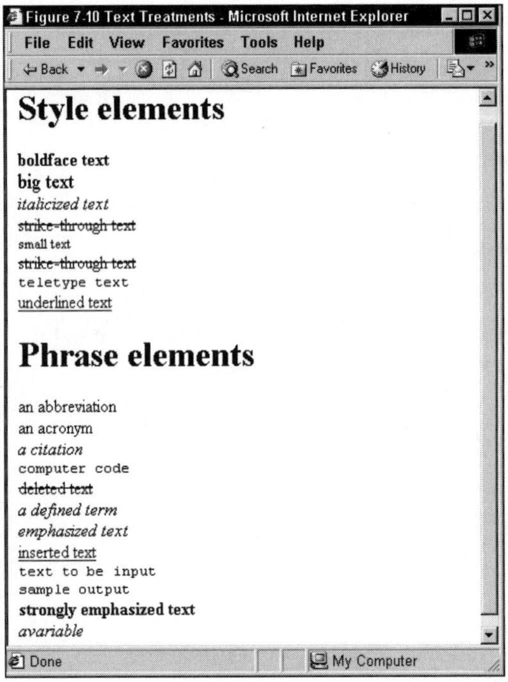

Figure 7-10:
Many of the font style and phrase elements display the same way in a Web browser.

Deciding on the Right Text Elements for the Job

So why does text described with `<strong>` look the same as that described with `<b>`? Bottom line: You have only so many ways to format text. Your browser really has only bold, italics, underline, and strikethrough to work with. Given that limitation, which elements do you use to apply text treatments to your text? After all, it's easier to type `<b>` than `<strong>`.

If you're practical about it, you have all the elements you need to format your text in the style elements. However, when you use *phrase elements,* you provide additional information about the text in your document, and that may come in handy one day when browsers have a wider array of formatting capabilities.

For example, deleted text currently looks the same as struck-through text, but eventually you may be able to toggle a browser's view to show and hide deleted text. HTML purists tend to believe you should always be as accurate in your markup as possible.

In the end, the choice is yours. If you take the time to accurately describe your text, it may pay off in the future. On the flip side, you can use basic formatting elements to create the display you're looking for — and that will serve your needs as well.

Part III
Taking HTML to the Next Level

The 5th Wave   By Rich Tennant

"Can someone please tell me how long 'Larry's Lunch Truck' has had his own page on the intranet?"

In this part . . .

Part III is where you move from basic, simple HTML markup to more complex HTML markup concepts and structures. Discover the wonder and majesty of HTML tables, which you can use to organize and manage all kinds of text and graphical data. This part explains HTML frames, which let you break up Web pages into logical areas and manage display separately for each such area — often for stunning visual effects. You also get a look at using HTML forms to organize, format, solicit, and handle user input on your Web pages — techniques that can turn your Web pages into a tool for two-way communications with your users. The chapters in this part help you kick your Web pages up a notch!

Chapter 8

HTML Tables

Most Web pages contain at least one table — some even nest tables within tables. Traditionally, tables display data; HTML tables, however, are more commonly used to control layout. You can arrange everything from text to images on your pages, efficiently and attractively, in HTML tables.

This chapter provides you with step-by-step instructions for creating and using HTML tables. In addition, a list of our favorite tried-and-true tips and techniques can help make the whole process quicker.

What Tables Can Do for You

Traditionally, tables displayed data in a format that's easy to read and understand. HTML changed all that. You may not realize it, but tables are used in a lot of Web sites. Sites such as Amazon, eBay, Yahoo!, and Google all use tables to display their content; but you can't see these tables. Invisible tables dominate the Web. The idea is this: Use tables to arrange items on your Web page, and then be sure to turn the borders off so the user cannot see the table.

By nature, Web pages start out linear; tables allow you to step out of that linear box and put text and images in the most interesting places in your layout.

You can use tables in a couple of ways:

- **Traditional (ho-hum) method:** You can define table or individual cell widths, producing a table that won't resize when users resize their browser's windows. Some designers prefer to use tables for the traditional purpose — to present data — a straightforward, balanced approach that's easily tackled.

- **Presentation-focused (wow) method:** You can define table and cell width using percentages, thereby allowing the table to resize when users resize their browser windows. Most designers are doing more creative, complex tricks with their tables.

Although this chapter covers all aspects of HTML tables, it focuses on layout tips and techniques.

Using tables for layout can result in rather complex structures, as seen in Figure 8-1. (Some other examples of complex tables are viewable at www.amazon.com and www.yahoo.com.)

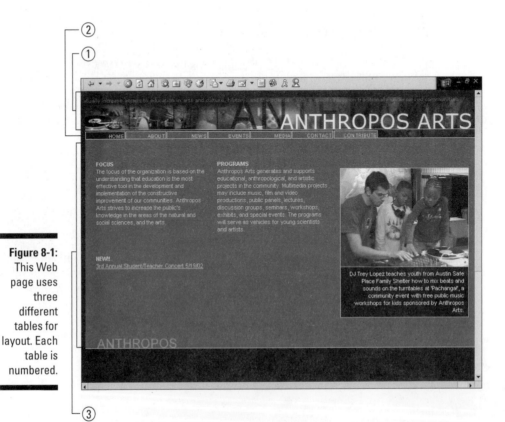

Figure 8-1:
This Web page uses three different tables for layout. Each table is numbered.

After you open these Web pages in your Web browser, take a look at each one's HTML source code (try View⇨Source from your menu bar). Observe how complex the markup is, and mark ye well when the markup looks haphazardly arranged (alas, if only they'd asked us . . .).

Equally effective are the Web pages that use the less-is-more approach. Some design models keep the interface simple — therefore easy to use. Figure 8-2 illustrates the simple approach.

For another example of a Web site that uses a simple table to arrange navigation, visit www.google.com.

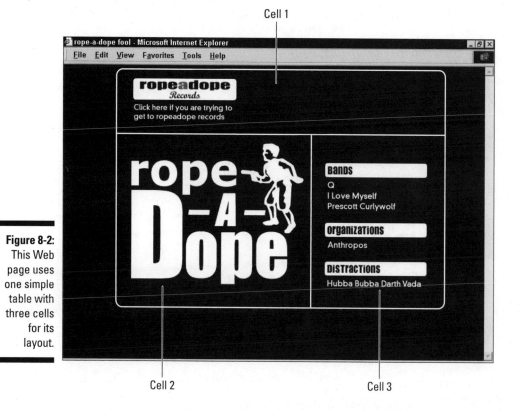

Figure 8-2:
This Web
page uses
one simple
table with
three cells
for its
layout.

Introducing Table Basics

To understand the complexity of HTML tables, you must first understand their basic elements

✔ **Borders:** Every basic table must always have *exactly* four borders that make up a rectangle.

✔ **Cells:** These are the individual squares within the borders of a table.

For example, even though the first table in Figure 8-3 has nine cells, it has four borders.

✔ **Cell span:** Within that four-walled structure, you can delete or add cell walls (as shown in the second table in Figure 8-3). When you delete cell walls, you require a cell to *span* multiple rows or columns — and that's exactly what makes a table a flexible tool for layout.

Cell spanning and cell width are different things. When you span cells, you add or delete cell walls (merge cells), and when you increase the width of a cell, you just adjust the width of that cell.

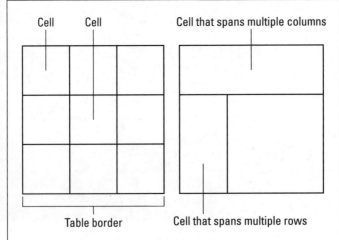

Figure 8-3:
After you delete a few cell walls, an HTML table might not look like much of a table at all, but it's perfect for laying out Web page elements.

Cell   Cell   Cell that spans multiple columns

Table border   Cell that spans multiple rows

Sketching Your Table

Tables can become complex, and they need to be carefully planned. Mapping to the nearest pixel can get rather tedious, and it could take several attempts, but it's an essential step in designing a well-laid-out page.

Start with a general idea and slowly plan your layout until it becomes more solid and specific. Follow these basic steps:

1. **Grab (believe it or not) a sheet of paper and a pencil so that you can sketch out your ideas.**

   Make sure that you have a general idea of where you want everything to go on your page.

2. **Evaluate what to include in your Web page and come to a firmer decision on the layout.**

   This way, you can begin to determine how many columns and rows you'll need, the width of the table and cells, and whether to make any cells span rows or columns. Here are some things to decide:

   • Whether the table will be centered, left aligned, or right aligned.

   • Whether you want to include hyperlinks, and where you might want to include them. The image in the top of the table in Figure 8-2 provides a hyperlink to another Web site, and that image is 294 pixels by 94 pixels.

3. **Figure out the pixel dimensions of any images you want to use, for example:**

   • Where and how site navigation tools should appear. In Figure 8-2, to the right of the logo, there's a list of images used for navigation, and the greatest width value is 190 pixels. Don't be concerned with the height of these images; you don't have to define cell or table height.

   • Where the main logo should go, and what size it should be. For example, in Figure 8-2, the logo is the main focal point. Its dimensions are 400 pixels wide by 302 pixels tall.

   The point is to make sure that the table fills a browser window nicely without forcing the user to scroll left and right to see everything. We think it's best to let the contents of your table determine the cell height; image height isn't as important because users are used to scrolling up and down Web pages but may get frustrated if they have to scroll left and right to read content.

If you opt for a simple approach, each main element (logo, hyperlink image, and navigation) will have its own cell. In Figure 8-2, that means only three cells. If you have only a few cells, you'll probably have to span the cells so the contents fill the width of your page.

Depending on the complexity of your design, you may need several rows. A simple, clean design, such as the one in Figure 8-2, requires only two rows. The first row should span two cells; the second row should contain two cells.

See Figure 8-4 for a look at the final sketch.

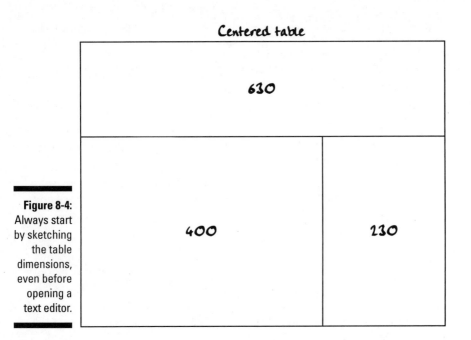

Centered table

Figure 8-4:
Always start
by sketching
the table
dimensions,
even before
opening a
text editor.

The author of our sample Web site uses images in place of text for the navigational elements; however, for usability reasons, try using text in place of images when possible. Even so, if you want complete control of the font(s) in which your text appears, you may have to use images instead — and create an image of the text written in your chosen font.

Constructing Basic Tables

After you complete a sketch that gives a pretty solid indication of the page and table layout, open your HTML editor and create the skeleton of your table. The building blocks for that framework are the three basic components of any table:

- **Table:** `<table>`
- **Table row:** `<tr>`
- **Table (data) cell:** `<td>`

A hierarchy defines the nesting order of table elements: A `<td>` is always enclosed within a `<tr>`, which is always enclosed within a `<table>`.

With these three elements alone, you're ready to build a simple table; the markup that does the job looks something like this:

```
<table>
  <tr>
    <td> cell 1 </td>
    <td> cell 2 </td>
  </tr>
  <tr>
    <td> cell 3 </td>
    <td> cell 4 </td>
  </tr>
</table>
```

In our example, we create a table with two rows based on the sketch in Figure 8-4. The first table row encloses cells 1 and 2; the second table row encloses cells 3 and 4.

Table rows always run horizontally and the contents of each cell — in this case, `cell 1`, `cell 2`, and so on — are contained within their own `<td>` element.

To create the shell of your table-based Web page (for example, one based on the sketch from the previous section, Figure 8-4), you start with the `<table>` element:

```
<table>
  ...
</table>
```

The `<table>` element can have a number of optional attributes (for example, `border="1"` or `bgcolor="black"`) — for now, however, keep it simple. Next, decide how many rows you want the table to have:

```
<table>
  <tr>...</tr>
  <tr>...</tr>
</table>
```

Figure 8-5 shows the type of table this markup generates: a simple table with two rows. Each `<tr>` tag pair represents a single row.

After you enter the appropriate number of rows, you add cells using the table data cell (`<td>`) element. The `<td>` element defines the number of cells — and, therefore, the number of columns.

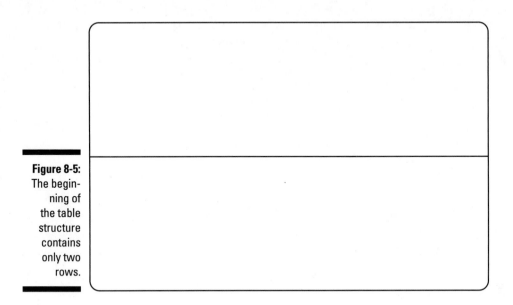

The sketch in Figure 8-4 shows a two-column table with *three* cells, the first row contains one cell, and the second row contains two cells. The markup for this arrangement looks like this:

```
<table>
  <tr>
    <td> contents </td>
  </tr>
  <tr>
    <td> contents </td>
    <td> contents </td>
  </tr>
</table>
```

Here's where tables can get a bit tricky. A simple table with an even number of rows and columns (say two rows and two columns) is a piece of cake — but you'll discover as you get more handy at designing your own pages that your needs aren't likely to produce such symmetrical tables very often. If your table will span more than one row or column (such as the first cell in the preceding example), you'll have to add an attribute that tells the browser which cell does the spanning.

The number in the attribute corresponds with the number of columns or rows you want the cell to span, which means if you're creating a table like the one in our example, you have to add the colspan="2" attribute to the first <td> element. (The first cell in the table spans across two columns.)

See the section later in this chapter, "Adding Spans," for more information, but for now, assuming that you're creating a table like ours, the markup looks like this:

```
<table>
  <tr>
    <td colspan="2"> contents </td>
  </tr>
  <tr>
    <td> contents </td>
    <td> contents </td>
  </tr>
</table>
```

Congratulations, you're done with your first table. Well, sort of. To effectively use tables for layout, you need to know how to control several display issues, such as borders, table widths, and the handling of white space within in your table. (For example, without borders, you can't really tell the table is there — it won't show up in your browser. This isn't a bad thing or a good thing, but something that you do have the power to change if you want.) Keep reading for more information on completing your table and integrating it into your page.

The <table>, <tr>, and <td> opening and closing tags are required. If you forget to include one, your table won't display correctly in most browsers.

Adding borders

For an HTML table, *border* refers not only to outside borders, but also to individual cell borders. You use the border attribute to turn all these table borders on or off. (Keep in mind, however, that if you're using tables to lay out content, the table borders should probably be turned off.) To turn the table (and cell) border on, add the border attribute to the <table> start tag, as shown in the following bold markup:

```
<table border="1">
  <tr>
    <td colspan="2"> contents </td>
  </tr>
  <tr>
    <td> contents </td>
    <td> contents </td>
  </tr>
</table>
```

Other table elements

Although tables were first created to contain and display tabular data, they are now most commonly used to control Web page layout. In this chapter, we focus on the elements that designer's use to control layout, but for those of you who might want to create a traditional table, we define the remaining table elements that you can use in this sidebar. They are as follows:

- ✔ `<th>`: The table header element displays text in boldface with a default center alignment. You can use the `<th>` element within any row of a table, but you most often find and use it in the first row at the top — or head — of a table. Except for their position and egotism, they act just like table data (`<td>`) tags and should be treated as such.

- ✔ `<caption>`: The table caption (`<caption>`) element is designed to exist anywhere inside the `<table>` . . . `</table>` tags but not inside table rows or cells (because then they wouldn't be captioning anything) — and they can only occur once. Similar to table cells, captions accommodate any HTML elements that can appear in the body of a document (in other words, inline elements), but only those. By default, captions are horizontally centered with the table, and their lines wrap to fit within the table's width. The `<caption>` element accepts the `align` attribute.

- ✔ `<tbody>`: Table rows may be grouped into a table body section using the table body (`<tbody>`) element. A recent addition to the HTML 4 specification, these elements allow table bodies to scroll independently of the table head (`<thead>`) and table foot

(`<tfoot>`). The table body should contain rows of table data. The `<tbody>` element must contain at least one table row (`<tr>`).

- ✔ `<thead>`: Table rows may be grouped into a table head section using the table head (`<thead>`) element. The table head contains information about the table's columns. The `<thead>` element must contain at least one table row.

- ✔ `<tfoot>`: Much like the `<thead>` element, table rows may be grouped into a table footer section, using the table footer (`<tfoot>`) element. The table foot contains information about the table's columns and must contain at least one table row. Be sure to include your footer information before the first instance of the `<tbody>` element; that way, the browser renders that information before taking a stab at all the content data cells.

- ✔ `<colgroup>`: The `<colgroup>` element creates an explicit column group. The number of columns is specified using the span attribute or using the `<col>` element, which is defined shortly. You use the span attribute to specify a uniform width for a group of columns.

- ✔ `<col>`: The table `<col>` element is an empty element. You use the `<col>` element to further define column structure. The `<col>` element should not be used to group columns — that is the `<colgroup>` element's job. The `<col>` element is used after you define a column group and set a uniform width to specify a uniform width for a subset of columns.

The value of the border attribute defines the thickness of the border in pixels. For example, border="5" produces a 5-pixel border. If you leave this attribute off, most browsers don't display a border. However, if you don't want your border visible, we suggest that you add border="0" to turn off the border for sure.

It's a good idea to turn on the table border when you're first creating and tweaking your table. This is because it's sometimes difficult to see just what is going on without a border. After you've finished tweaking your table, you can turn off the border.

When you don't use the border attribute, most browsers don't display a border but there's still an invisible 2-pixel border. Therefore, when you design your table, factor those 2-pixels into your calculations. To avoid the invisible two-pixel border altogether, set the border attribute to equal 0 (border="0").

Right now, the examples build on the table skeleton created in the previous sections. Figure 8-6 shows how the Web page looks if you add a two-pixel border to the finished product.

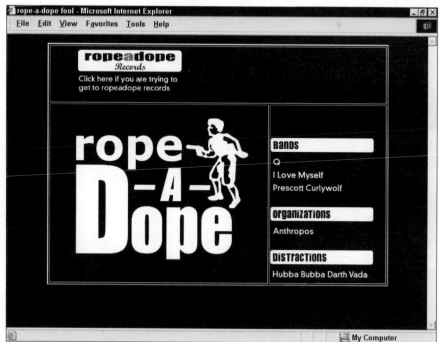

Figure 8-6: Most Web pages that use tables for layout don't use borders; here you can see why.

Adjusting height and width

Officially, you can only set the width of tables and cells; *unofficially,* however, some browsers also allow you to set the height of your table. When you use tables to lay out Web pages, width becomes one of the primary variables. But first, let's identify what happens if you don't include the width attribute at all.

Cell width

If you don't set table and cell width, the user's browser determines the width of every cell according to the width of its contents — no more, no less. For example, suppose you want to put a logo in the first cell and navigational items in the cell to its left. If you don't assign the width to the first cell (containing the logo), the navigational items are placed right beside the logo, with no or almost no space between the two. To avoid that cramped look, you can use the width attribute to strategically define an exact number of pixels between the logo and navigational items.

If you're using tables for layout purposes, we recommend that you set the width for the table and cells. You can do this using either pixels or percentages, keeping in mind that percentages allow your table to be resized depending on the size of the browser window.

Defining width is easy when you use the width attribute. For example, you can set the width of your table at 630 pixels like this:

```
<table border="1" width="630">
...
</table>
```

The value of the width attribute can be defined in pixels by using a positive integer (say, 630), or in percentages by using a positive integer followed by a percent sign (as in 95%). This choice also applies when you set the width of individual cells. To add widths to the table built earlier in this chapter (and to set width for its individual cells), add the following markup shown in bold text:

```
<table border="1" width="630">
  <tr>
    <td width="630"> contents </td>
  </tr>
  <tr>
    <td width="400"> contents </td>
    <td width="230"> contents </td>
  </tr>
</table>
```

Figures 8-7 and 8-8 show the difference between a site that doesn't define table and cell width and one that uses the width attribute.

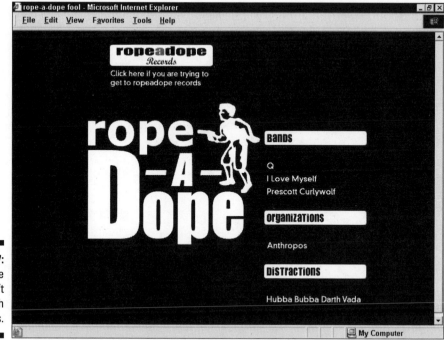

Figure 8-7:
This image
doesn't
define width
properties.

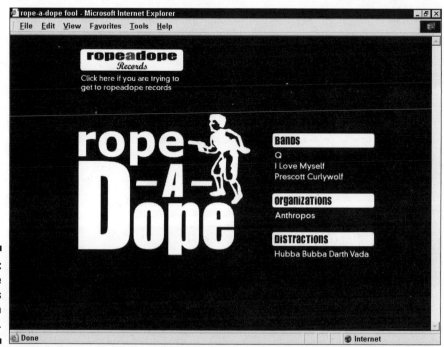

Figure 8-8:
This image
defines
width
properties.

If you set the pixel width smaller than the content's pixel size, the browser ignores the width attribute and defaults to display all the cell contents. So, be sure to check all dimensions.

Cell height

Two factors bear close attention when you're defining table and cell height:

- ✔ **You have two ways to define height.** It works the same way as defining width — by using number of pixels or percentages.

- ✔ **Height is not nearly as important as width.** Cell content determines the height of each cell; normally, it's not even necessary to define cell height.

That said, you may want to avoid using the height attribute. Here's why: According to the HTML standard, the height attribute is not a `<table>` attribute. You can use the height attribute because some browsers support it, but not all of them do yet. Bottom line: Using the height attribute may produce unpredictable results. However, it is used occasionally, so here's how to use the height attribute to further define a table:

```
<table border="1" width="630">
  <tr>
    <td width="630" height="100"> contents </td>
  </tr>
  <tr>
    <td width="400" height="302"> contents </td>
    <td width="230" height="302"> contents </td>
  </tr>
</table>
```

Although, according to the HTML 4 standard, the height attribute can legally be added to the table data cell (`<td>`) element, it's now *deprecated* (considered obsolete and on the way out). The standard currently favors the use of style sheets; future versions of this standard have or will phase out the height attribute. Not because they don't want you to define this property, but rather because they want you to set the height using style sheets instead. If you're interested in learning more about style sheets, see Chapter 11.

Padding and spacing

Determining the white space between cells is essential for proper layout. Thinking back to our sketch, you have to determine — to the pixel — how space is going to be used in your table. There are two attributes that help you define white space: cellpadding and cellspacing. These attributes are similar, and can sometimes confuse first-time HTML authors.

Both attributes allow you to put some space between cells; however, they do it using two different techniques:

✔ `cellspacing` increases the border width between cells — increasing the space between cells.

✔ `cellpadding` pads the cell with space — the space is added within the cell walls.

The value for either attribute is defined in pixels. For example, `cellpadding="5"` adds five pixels worth of padding to each cell.

To define either attribute, add it to the `<table>` start tag, as follows:

```
<table cellpadding="5" cellspacing="5">
```

When using tables for layout, without visible borders, it doesn't matter much which one you use. However, if you add color to your tables — or use the border for any reason — you can see a considerable difference. That's because `cellpadding` increases the space within the border, and `cellspacing` increases the width of the border itself, as shown clearly in Figures 8-9 and 8-10.

The default value for `cellpadding` is 1; the default for `cellspacing` is 2. If you don't define `cellpadding` and `cellspacing`, your users' browsers assume the defaults. Accounting for those pixels in your sketch is a good idea.

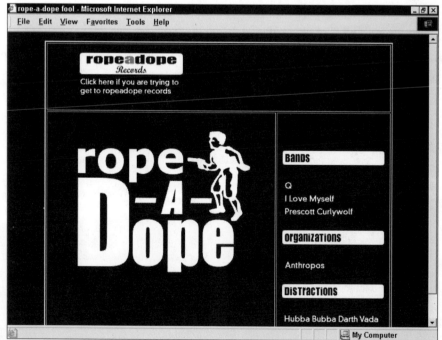

Figure 8-9: Cellpadding increases the space within each cell.

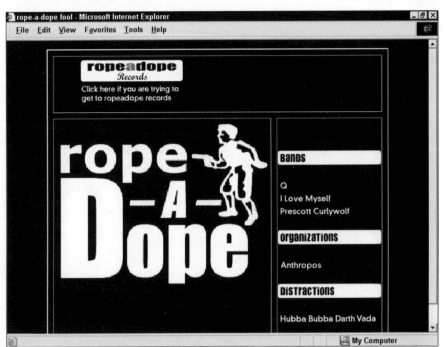

Shifting alignment

In the past, table alignment was not well supported by browsers; therefore, if you wanted to center your table, you had to find a different method that would work. Many designers used the `<center>` tag pair outside the table, as follows:

```
<center>
  <table>
    ...
  </table>
</center>
```

Browsers finally caught up; now you can use attributes that are part of the HTML standard to align your tables (horizontally) and your table contents (horizontally and vertically). Aligning tables is similar to aligning images.

To align your table horizontally, you use the `align` attribute with the `<table>` element. The `align` attribute, when used with the `<table>` element has the following possible values: `left`, `right`, or `center`. When you use these values, the table is aligned to the left, right, or center of the document, respectively.

You can also use the `align` attribute with the `<td>` or `<tr>` elements. However, when used with these elements, the data is aligned in the cell or row. The values that can be used with the `align` attribute in the `<td>` or `<tr>` elements are defined as follows:

- `align="right"`: Aligns the table or cell contents against the right side.
- `align="left"`: Aligns the table or cell contents against the left side. (This is the default setting.)
- `align="center"`: Centers the table or cell contents.
- `align="justify"`: Justifies cell contents in the middle (not widely supported).
- `align="char"`: Aligns cell contents around a specific character (not widely supported).

In the following example, we align our table in the center of the page (see Figure 8-11):

```
<table border="1" width="630" align="center">
  <tr>
    <td width="630" colspan="2"> contents </td>
  </tr>
  <tr>
    <td width="400"> contents </td>
    <td width="230"> contents </td>
  </tr>
</table>
```

Figure 8-11: Our simple table centered.

You can also vertically align cell contents using the `valign` attribute. The `valign` attribute cannot be used for a `<table>`; it can only be used with the `<tr>` and `<td>` elements.

The possible values are as follows:

- `valign="top"`: Vertically aligns cell contents to the top of the cell.
- `valign="bottom"`: Vertically aligns cell contents to the bottom of the cell.

✔ `valign="middle"`: Vertically centers the cell contents. (This is the default.)

✔ `valign="baseline"`: Defines a baseline for all other cells in the same row, so alignment is the same for all cells.

The `align` and `valign` attributes can also be used with the following other table elements: `<col>`, `<colgroup>`, `<tbody>`, `<tfoot>`, `<th>`, and `<thead>`.

If you set the alignment for a row (`<tr>`), and then set the alignment for a cell within that row (`<td>`), the setting you add to the cell overrides the setting for the row.

Adding Spans

One of the main reasons tables are a flexible alternative for arranging elements in your Web page is because of spanning.

Spanning enables you to stretch items across multiple cells; you essentially tear down a cell wall. Whether you need to span rows or columns, you can use the concept of spanning to wrangle your table into almost any arrangement. Keep in mind that row and column spanning takes careful planning, and that planning should occur during the sketching phase. The two attributes you use to span cells are `colspan` and `rowspan`. Both attributes are added to the `<td>` element.

Changing column spans

To span columns you use the `colspan` attribute in the `<td>` element and set the value equal to the number of cells you want to span. Figure 8-12 illustrates a cell that spans two columns.

In this example, the first cell spans the two cells in the next row. You use the `colspan` attribute set to 2, as shown in the following markup, because the cell spans two columns:

```
<table border="1" width="630">
  <tr>
    <td width="630" colspan="2"> contents </td>
  </tr>
  <tr>
    <td width="400"> contents </td>
    <td width="230"> contents </td>
  </tr>
</table>
```

colspan = "2"

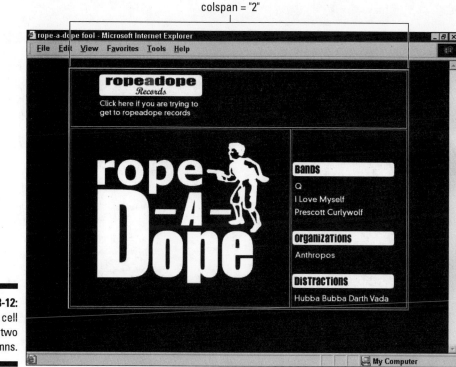

Figure 8-12:
The cell
spans two
columns.

After you add a `colspan` attribute, verify that you have the appropriate number of `<td>` cells. For example, if you define a cell to span two columns, you should have one less `<td>` in that row. If you use `colspan="3"`, there should be two fewer `<td>` cells in that row. You also want to make sure that the other rows have the appropriate number of cells. For example, if you define a cell to span two columns, the other rows in that table should have two `<td>` cells to fill out the two columns.

Changing row spans

Row spans are similar to column spans, the only difference is that you span rows instead of columns. Like the `colspan` attribute, the `rowspan` attribute is added to the `<td>` cell. Figure 8-13 illustrates a cell that spans two rows.

To span rows, you use the `rowspan` attribute in the `<td>` element and set the value equal to the number of cells you want to span.

rowspan = "2"

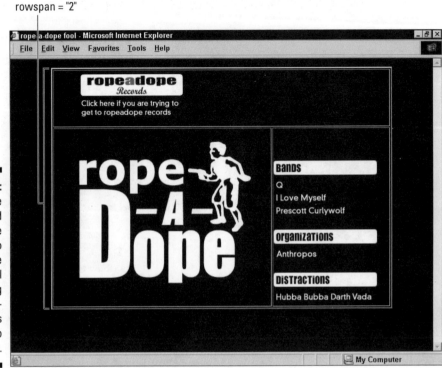

Figure 8-13:
We have
changed
our table
design so
that the
last cell
containing
our naviga-
tional items
spans two
rows.

You should sketch your table first, so you know what cells should span what. The example design we've used throughout most of this chapter uses the `colspan` attribute with the first cell. However, the design could have been just as simple if we used a `rowspan` with the last cell that contains the navigational items. Either way, the table is efficiently laid out. The modified table comes from the following markup (note the bold `rowspan`) and is shown in Figure 8-14:

```
<table border="1" width="630">
  <tr>
    <td width="400"> contents </td>
    <td width="230" rowspan="2"> contents </td>
  </tr>
  <tr>
    <td width="630"> contents </td>
  </tr>
</table>
```

Always keep in mind that columns are vertical and rows are horizontal. If you want to extend a cell vertically (across multiple rows), use `rowspan`. If you want to extend a cell horizontally (across multiple columns), use `colspan`.

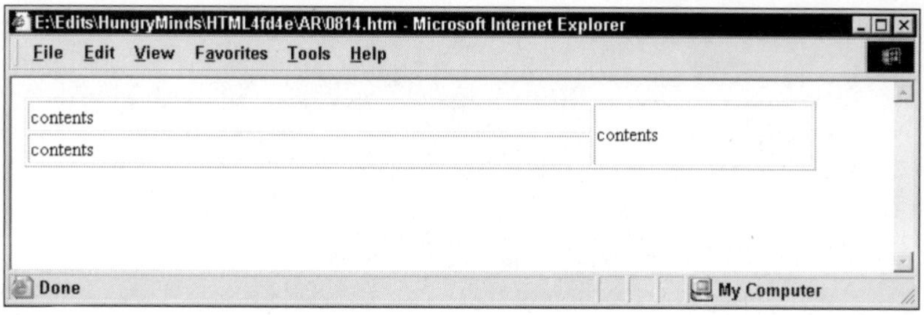

Figure 8-14:
Our simple
table with
the last
rows
spanned.

Populating Cells

After you've sketched your table, defined table properties such as width, cell padding and spacing, and cell spanning, you're ready to populate the table cells with images, hyperlinks, text and almost any other HTML element. This is a simple process: You add images, hyperlinks and text to the `<td>` cell, similar to how you add them to the `<body>` element. The following markup shows a populated table, with data added in bold:

```
<table border="1" width="630" align="center" cellpadding="5" cellspacing="5">
  <tr>
    <td colspan="2" valign="bottom" align="left">
      <a href="http://www.ropeadope.com">
        <img src="images/ropeAdopeRecords.gif" width="249" height="94"
        alt="rope-a-dope records" border="0">
      </a>
    </td>
  </tr>
  <tr>
    <td valign="top" align="right" width="400">
      <img src="images/gunlogo.gif" width="400" height="302" alt="rope-a-dope
      home" border="0">
    </td>
    <td valign="top" align="left" width="230">
      <br><br><br>
      <img src="images/bands.gif">
      <br>
      <a href="q/">
        <img src="images/q.gif" border="0">
      </a>
      <br>
      <a href="ilovemyself/">
        <img src="images/ilovemyself.gif" border="0">
      </a>
      <br>
      <a href="http://www.pwolf.com">
        <img src="images/prescottCurlywolf.gif" border="0">
      </a>
      <br><br>
      <img src="images/organizations.gif">
```

```
      <br>
      <a href="http://www.anthropos.org">
        <img src="images/anthropos.gif" border="0">
      </a>
      <br><br>
      <img src="images/distractions.gif">
      <br>
      <a href="darth/">
        <img src="images/hubbabubba.gif" border="0">
      </a>
      <br>
    </td>
  </tr>
</table>
```

Testing Your Table

Testing is the final step before your table goes live. You must test your tables in all the popular browsers — including Internet Explorer, Netscape, and Opera. If you don't, your users may have to squint at your pages and may see your tables as one big mess.

As you're creating your table, we suggest that you have your browser window open at the same time. Each time you change the width of a cell or add an item to a cell, save the document, and view it in the browser window. That way, when it's time to test your table, you probably won't have too much tweaking to do.

A challenge for many designers is to create table designs that work in every browser. Thanks to many crusaders of standards, the newest versions of the most popular browsers, Netscape, Internet Explorer, and Opera, all support the HTML standard. If your audience does not consist of technical-savvy individuals, you might want to consider older browsers when designing your tables.

You should always test your site in any browser that your users might have. For example, if your table is aligned with align="center", but in an older version of Internet Explorer, the table remains flush with the left side, you might have to add a <center> tag pair to your table. As we stated earlier, you won't have too many problems with tables if you stick to the standard.

Table Making Tips

Before closing this chapter, we want to impart some of our favorite table techniques. After years of building, maintaining, and troubleshooting tables, the following tips are a head start to creating effective tables.

Following the standards

The first — and (we think) most important — tip is to keep with the established standards. The Web Standards Project has been campaigning for full standard support in browsers and HTML authoring applications since 1998. Their hard work should make your life easier.

Just a couple of years ago, if you built an HTML table, you would be forced to create different versions of your Web page (each version containing browser-specific elements and attributes) to define some basic table properties. As you might imagine, creating and maintaining different versions of the same Web page can drive development costs sky-high. To get around those costs, many developers would carefully craft their tables with specific markup that worked in Internet Explorer and Netscape — but what about Opera? Well, happily those are problems of the past. The newest versions of Internet Explorer, Netscape, and Opera *all* support HTML, as well as CSS and XHTML. To learn more about the fight for Web standards, visit www.webstandards.org.

Sanitizing markup

Efficiently written markup is easier to troubleshoot and maintain. Many designers use white space to separate elements. For example, the following markup doesn't use much white space and is hard to read:

```
<table border="1" width="630">
<tr><td width="630" colspan="2"> contents </td></tr>
<tr><td width="400"> contents </td>
<td width="230"> contents </td></tr></table>
```

Check out this clean version:

```
<table border="1" width="630">
  <tr>
    <td width="630" colspan="2"> contents </td>
  </tr>  <tr>
    <td width="400"> contents </td>
    <td width="230"> contents </td>
  </tr>
</table>
```

Notice that the white space we include is between elements; not within elements. If, for example, you add white space between the <td> and </td> tags, it affects the way the cell's content is displayed. Not generally something you want to do.

Nesting tables within tables

Many designers are forced to nest tables within tables to achieve a desired effect. This is not only legal, but quite common — and okay, a few such nestings won't hurt. Remember, however, that nesting too many tables within tables can lengthen download time. To nest a table, you simply add the `<table>` within a `<td>` element as follows:

```
<table border="1">
  <tr>
    <td> contents </td>
    <td> contents </td>
  </tr>
  <tr>
    <td>
        <table border="1">
        <tr>
        <td> contents  </td>
        <td> contents  </td>
        </tr>
        <tr>
        <td> contents  </td>
        <td> contents  </td>
        </tr>
        </table>
    </td>
    <td> contents </td>
  </tr>
</table>
```

This markup produces the tables shown in Figure 8-15. Be sure to remember cell widths — the width of the third cell should match the width of the nested table. Also, create *and test* the table you intend to nest — separately, before you add it to your primary table.

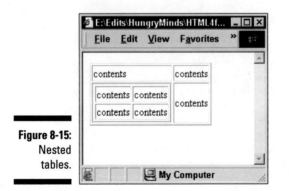

Figure 8-15:
Nested
tables.

Using CSS to control table properties

Chapter 11 provides an overview of Cascading Style Sheets (CSS), a style-sheet language you can use to define display properties for HTML documents. Compactly, definitions of a few CSS properties can take the place of some attributes such as `align`, `cellpadding`, `cellspacing`, and more. Tempting, but watch out: Older browsers don't support CSS — although the recent versions of Internet Explorer, Netscape, and Opera do. CSS provides more options for table display and is more flexible than HTML. If you know your audience has appropriate (and recent) equipment, CSS may be the way to go.

Avoiding dense tables

We recommend creativity, but be careful and don't pack a screen full of dense and impenetrable information — especially numbers. A long, unbroken list of numbers quickly drives away all but the truly masochistic — pretty much negating the purpose of the table to begin with. Put those numbers into an attractive table (better yet, *several* tables interspersed with a few well-chosen images). Watch your page's attractiveness and readability soar; hear visitors sigh with relief.

Individual table cells can be surprisingly roomy; you can position graphics in them precisely. If you're moved to put graphics in a table, be sure to:

✔ Select images that are similar in size and looks.

✔ Measure those images to determine their heights and widths in pixels (shareware programs such as Paint Shop Pro and GraphicConverter do this automatically).

✔ Use HTML markup to position these images within their table cells.

A short-and-sweet table keeps the graphics in check and guarantees that the text will always sit nicely to its right.

Two more handy graphics-placement tips: Size your rows and columns of cells that contain images to accommodate the largest graphic and center all graphics in each cell (vertically and horizontally). The result is a consistent, coherent image layout.

Adding color to cells

Remember the `bgcolor` attribute that goes with the `<body>` element? `bgcolor` is the same attribute; it affects the background of table cells in much the same way it affects the background of your entire HTML document. Simply add this attribute to any table cell to change its background color:

```
<td bgcolor="teal">...</td>
```

You can use background color instead of using an image that would take longer to download.

Chapter 9

HTML Frames

*H*TML frames delineate, outline, and give structure to HTML documents; by design, information can move coherently within and among frames. Frames are not as commonly used as they once were, but times still arise when frames work best and are used. For example, if you use any Macromedia products (such as Flash or Dreamweaver), you'll notice that the help section on the product (stored locally) is laid out using frames. In this chapter, we cover the basics of frames step by step.

Because frames became part of the HTML repertoire with HTML 4.0, older browsers (and browser versions older than 3.0) can't handle frames properly. Text-only browsers don't deal well with frames either. To be practical, this means that some of your users may not be able to appreciate the beauty and efficacy of your frames.

As long as you're sure users have frames-compatible browsers — the recent versions of both Netscape Navigator and Internet Explorer support frames, as do many of the non-commercial browsers such as Mosaic and Amaya — you can safely use frames on your site. However, if your audience uses a wide variety of browsers, you may want to shy away from frames. Another option is to offer a non-framed version of the same materials so users can pick which version of your pages they want to explore.

Frames have some significant usability concerns (covered later in this chapter). If frames are not strictly necessary, we recommend opting for tables instead.

When to Use Frames in an HTML Page

So, what are frames and why would you want to use them in your Web pages? Frames provide advantages as well as disadvantages. As mentioned previously, frames are not as widely used as they used to be. In this section you find out the advantages of frames as well as the disadvantages.

Why you may want to use frames

A browser window usually holds a single frame that displays one HTML document. However, browser windows can hold several frames (which are defined with the `<frameset>` element), and can display several HTML documents at one time. Each frame works like a separate browser screen, but all the frames are displayed together in one window. Imagine having three browser windows open (and tiled) at one time, and you begin to get the picture.

What's really cool is that with frames, the different browser windows work together to display your content. And for the control freak in all of us — depending on the attributes you give it — you can make a frame act just like a standard browser screen, or freeze it so that it can't be adjusted.

The most significant difference between tables and frames is that tables are static, and frames can be dynamic. You can scroll through information in individual frames, and users may find that appealing (or possibly annoying).

Frames have numerous uses. You might be looking at a page that uses frames if

- ✔ The Web page has a fixed logo at the top and a scrolling bottom section.
- ✔ The page has a fixed top logo, a navigation bar and copyright notice at the bottom, and a scrolling middle section for the page's content.
- ✔ The Web page has side-by-side frames that put a table of contents on the left and a scrolling text frame on the right.
- ✔ On the left side of the page, there's a frame that's filled with icons that link to different parts of a Web site; click an icon, and the element is displayed in the right frame.

You find out how to set up these structures later in this chapter. For now, note that frames are flexible. Frames allow you to keep constant chunks of information on display while your users can scroll through large amounts of text or dynamic content. Figure 9-1 provides an example of a Web page using two frames.

Frame usability: Is another alternative better?

Early in their history, frames introduced some ticklish problems that caused many developers to shun them. Some common usability concerns (even these days) are as follows:

- ✔ The browser's Back button may not work correctly.
- ✔ Users can't bookmark a collection of documents in a frameset. Only individual frames can be bookmarked.
- ✔ A frameset may produce different results when reloaded.
- ✔ Users can become trapped in a frameset.
- ✔ Search engines find HTML pages, not framesets; therefore, search results can produce pages without the navigational elements.
- ✔ In older browsers, printing Web pages with framed content could be a hassle.

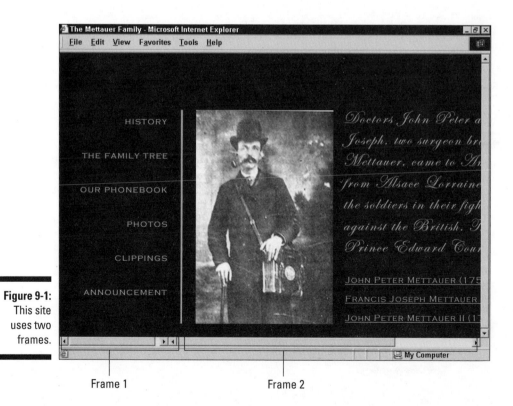

Figure 9-1: This site uses two frames.

Frame 1   Frame 2

In many cases, using tables can produce the same result as using frames. The advantage to using frames is that you can define one document that contains navigational elements, and dynamically change the contents pages. This requires less maintenance since the navigational elements are defined in a separate HTML document. However, with many of the modern HTML editors, you can define global templates that control the maintenance issue. For example, Macromedia's Dreamweaver allows you to define a Web page template that contains the navigational elements. Each time you create a new page using the template, the navigational elements are already defined for you. Later you can make changes to the global template, and Dreamweaver will update all the documents that were created using that template. We recommend avoiding frames when you can. But if you must use them, be sure to follow the steps we outline in this chapter:

- ✔ Sketch your frame structure on paper.
- ✔ Define your frame structure with `<frameset>` and `<frame>` elements only.
- ✔ Add attributes to define behavior.
- ✔ Check your documents in a browser.

To get a look at some well-designed frames, visit some sites that use them. (Yes, we have an example in mind.) Before you sketch your frame structure, check out the well-designed frames at `www.internetgarden.co.uk/frameset_1.htm`.

Sketching Frame Components

The first step in creating frames is to sketch your design on paper. Using a pen or pencil — and a sheet of paper — you define how the browser should render your pages. At this stage, you don't need to be precise about the content, just the frame dimensions. For example, if you want to create the Web page in Figure 9-1, you would sketch the dimensions for two frames for the Web page (see Figure 9-2). The first framed component contains navigational elements, and the second framed component contains the main content for our Web page.

Building a Set of Frames

To build a Web page that contains two frames, you need to create three documents:

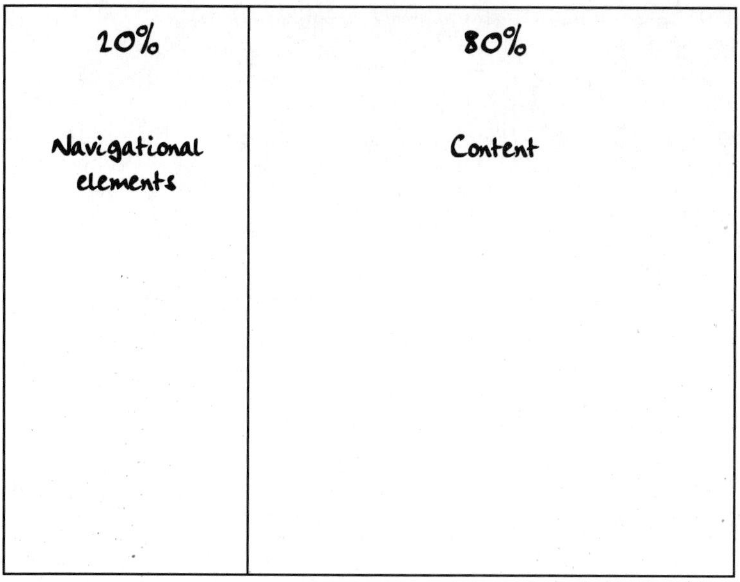

20%   80%

Navigational   Content
elements

Figure 9-2:
A sketch of
Figure 9-1.

✔ **The document that defines the frame structure, called the *frameset document*.** The frameset document is a normal HTML document in which you replace the `<body>` . . . `</body>` tags with the `<frameset>` . . . `</frameset>` tags. The frameset document only defines the frame structure, so it's usually a short document.

✔ **Two documents, each containing the HTML markup used in the two frames.** The `<frame>` element is an empty element used in the `<frameset>` element to point to the HTML document(s) used for frame content.

Following the frameset document rules

Frameset documents are HTML documents, so they must always begin with an `<html>` tag, followed by the `<head>` element, and we recommend you use the following HTML frameset `DOCTYPE` declaration before the `<html>` tag:

```
<!DOCTYPE HTML PUBLIC "-//W3C//DTD HTML 4.0 Frameset//EN"
   "http://www.w3.org/TR/REC-html40/frameset.dtd">
```

With these elements, divide-and-conquer is the best approach. The frameset document only contains elements that define the frame structure — no content is defined here.

Here are a few rules regarding frameset documents that you should keep in mind:

- ✔ The `<frameset>` element follows immediately after the closing `</head>` tag.

- ✔ If any `<body>` elements appear before the `<frameset>` elements, the `<frameset>` elements are ignored.

- ✔ Between the outermost `<frameset>` tags, you can only nest other `<frameset>` elements or `<frame>` elements — no other HTML is allowed.

The basic frameset document starts just like any HTML document; notice that the `<body>` tags are replaced with `<frameset>` tags.

```
<!DOCTYPE HTML PUBLIC "-//W3C//DTD HTML 4.0 Frameset//EN"
    "http://www.w3.org/TR/REC-html40/frameset.dtd">
<html>
    <head>
        <title>The Mettauer Family</title>
    </head>

<frameset>
</frameset>

</html>
```

The `<frameset>` element is the main container in a frameset document just like the `<body>` element is the main container in regular HTML documents.

The `<frameset>` elements should also include `<noframes>` elements to define content for older browsers that don't support frames or for text-only devices such as PDAs, mobile phones, and more. We encourage you to put some content in this element, even if it's only to inform the readers to visit your no-frames site.

Using frameset attributes

After you've added the `<frameset>` element, you need to add attributes that define the basic frame structure in terms of columns or rows. The figures you've seen so far defined frames in terms of columns — but rows work just as well for the purpose, as shown in Figure 9-3.

Frame 1

Figure 9-3:
Navigational
elements
are defined
as a row on
top of the
content.

Frame 2

To define either rows or columns, you use one of the following two attributes in the `<frameset>` element:

- ✓ `rows`: Determines the number of frames that appear vertically (stacked on top of each other) in the browser window and the height of each frame.

- ✓ `cols`: Determines the number of frames that appear horizontally (placed side by side) in the browser window and the width of each frame used to define a column structure.

The value for both attributes defines the height or width of the frames using pixels, percentages, or a wildcard:

- ✓ **pixels:** You can define a fixed number of pixels (such as 50 or 250) for the row's height. This procedure seems simple, but be careful: The size of the browser window can vary substantially from one user to another. If you use fixed pixel values, try using one or more relative values (described later in this chapter) with them. Otherwise the user's browser can override your specified pixel value, with no way to ensure that the total height and width of all frames equals 100 percent of the user's window. You may not want that to happen; a browser doesn't care about eyestrain. All it knows is to follow orders and *display all defined frames,* even if squashed together and crammed with unreadable text.

✔ **percentages:** If you define the width or height in percentages, the value should be followed by a % sign (`"20%"`). This value tells the browser, "Size this frame to a percentage of screen area, between 1 and 100." If the total for all frames is greater than 100 percent, all percentages are reduced to fit the browser window. If the values total less than 100 percent, extra space is added to any relative-sized frames that happen to be hanging around.

✔ **wildcard:** You have a couple of options for the wildcard. First, an asterisk (*) character identifies a relative-sized frame. Browsers give a frame defined with the asterisk all remaining space left over after the other frames defined with pixels and percentages are laid out on the screen. If you have several frames that take advantage of this flexible system, the remaining space is divided evenly among them. Second, if you place a value in front of the *, the frame gets that much more relative space. For instance, an entry such as `3*,*` allocates three times as much space to the first frame (¾ of the total on-screen space) as to the second frame (which gets a measly ¼).

Many developers define frames either absolutely or relatively. If the height or width of a frame is defined in pixels, it's an absolute value. If the width or height of a frame is defined in percentages or by using a wildcard, it's a relative value.

When you define values for the `cols` or `rows` attribute, you define a value for each frame you're creating, separating them with commas. The number of elements appearing in the value of the `rows` or `cols` attribute determines the number of frames displayed. For example, if you want to create two frames and you want the first frame column to occupy 20 percent of the window and the second frame column to take up the remainder of the window, you use the following markup:

```
<frameset cols="20%,*">
```

Used with the `rows` attribute, the same principle would look yield a markup like this:

```
<frameset rows="20%,*">
```

The total height or width of all simultaneously displayed frames must equal the height of the browser window.

Building a two-column frameset

To build a two-column frameset, you have to add the `cols` attribute to the `<frameset>` start tag. You can use pixels, percentages, or a wildcard for the value of the `cols` attribute. To create the scenario displayed in Figures 9-1 and 9-2, you could use the following `<frameset>` start tag:

```
<frameset cols="250,500">
```

Figure 9-4 illustrates this structure.

The `cols` attribute governs how many frames can sit horizontally across the browser's screen, as well as the width of each frame. To add a third frame to the scenario, you add a new value to the comma-separated list:

```
<frameset cols="250,500,200">
```

Building a two- or three-row frameset

To create a two-row frameset, you use the `rows` attribute — much the same way you use the `cols` attribute (detailed in the previous section). The values are the same as those defined by the `cols` attribute. The only difference is that with the `rows` attribute, the values define height instead of width:

```
<frameset rows="150,*">
```

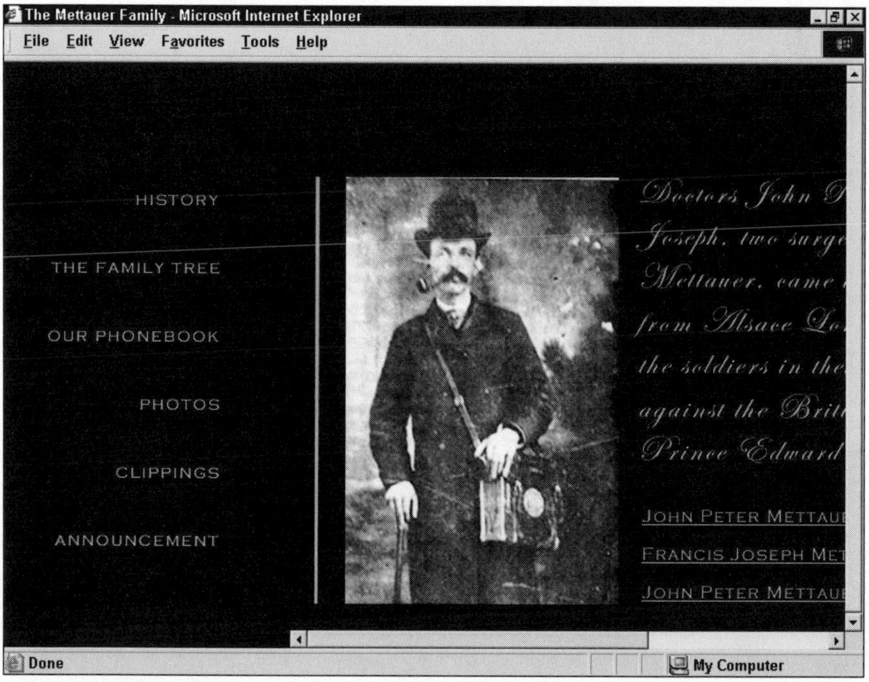

Figure 9-4:
This Web page consists of two columns.

Figure 9-5 illustrates this structure.

To add a third frame, add a new value to the comma-separated list:

```
<frameset rows="150,400,*">
```

Figure 9-6 illustrates this structure.

Combining rows and columns in the same frameset

When you create frames, you're not restricted to using only rows or only columns. You can mix them up, but go easy on that technique; it isn't common (or recommended) because it can make your page harder to use. If you want to try out the frameset mix 'n' match, however, you start by defining the rows and cols attributes one right after another. You can place these attributes just about anywhere in your markup without affecting the placement of the frames. What decides the actual number of frames is how many values you put in each attribute; the example in the previous section, "Building a two- or three-row frameset," yields six frames because it collectively defines a total of six values — three rows, each with two columns. Keep in mind that for each frame, you need a <frame> element that points to some resource, as in the following example:

```
<frameset rows="33%,33%,*" cols="20%,80%">
    <frame src="one.htm">
    <frame src="two.htm">
    <frame src="three.htm">

    <frame src="four.htm">
    <frame src="five.htm">
    <frame src="six.htm">
</frameset>
```

Here, the order of the frame elements assigns the content. For example, the contents of one.htm will appear in the first frame. The contents of two.htm will appear in the second frame in the first row. The contents of the three.htm will appear in the first frame of the second row, and so on. Figure 9-7 illustrates how these documents are assigned.

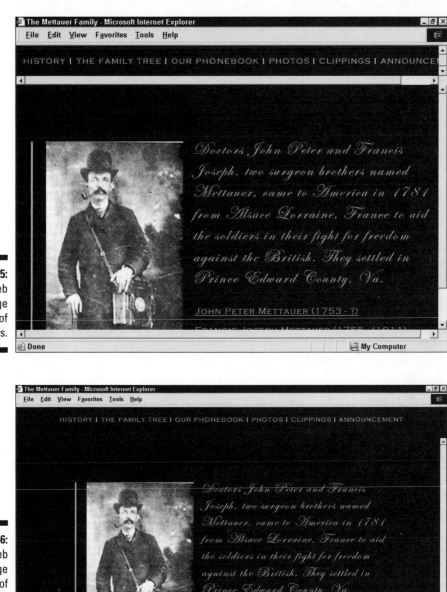

Figure 9-5:
The Web page consists of two rows.

Figure 9-6:
The Web page consists of three rows, with the third row taking up the remaining height in the browser window.

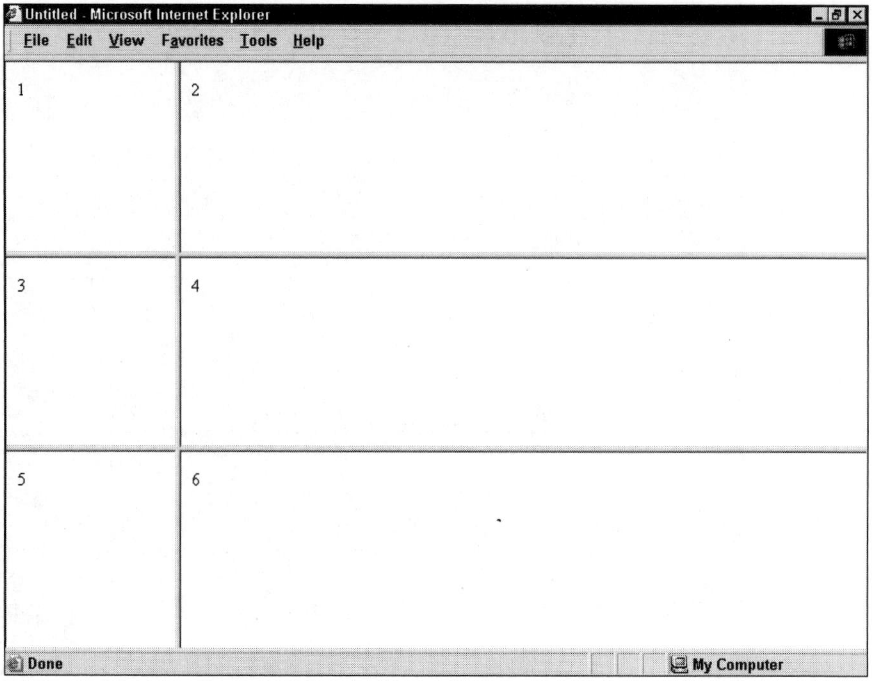

Figure 9-7:
This frame
structure
has three
rows
and two
columns,
which
results in
six separate
frames.

Building the Frame Content

The previous sections have shown you how to define the structure, write the frameset document, and use attributes to specify exactly how the frames should look and work. But that's really only part of the work. You haven't created the content that the frames will display. That's what we show you how to do in this section.

The <frame> element is empty, meaning it stands alone and does not require a closing tag. The primary purpose of the <frame> element is to point to the resource that you want to populate the frame. In most cases, that resource is an HTML document, although it can also be an image or another resource. The following markup shows <frame> elements that point to navigation.htm and content.htm documents:

```
<frameset cols="20%,*">
  <frame src="navigation.htm">
  <frame src="content.htm">
</frameset>
```

Listing the frame rules and regulations

As with all things HTML-related, you must obey the rules. Here are the highlights:

- ✔ **You have to define a frame element for each frame.** Yes, folks, it's true — if you want to display four different HTML pages in frames, you have to create four frames; therefore you need (all together, now) four `<frame>` elements.

- ✔ **Any documents you point to (for example, `navigation.htm` and `content.htm`) must exist first.** Be careful how you define the addresses of such documents.

  You can define documents in frames relatively (`navigation.htm`) or absolutely (`http://www.domain.com/navigation.htm`). Just be sure they exist. See Chapter 5 on more about relative and absolute links.

- ✔ **The order in which the frame elements are defined is important.** The first `<frame>` element defines the top or left-most frame area (depending on whether you use the `rows` or `cols` attributes, respectively). The second `<frame>` element defines the frame immediately to the right of the first frame or (if the edge of the browser is reached) the frame in the next row. And so on.

- ✔ You can use many different attributes with the `<frame>` element to modify a frame's appearance. The following section takes a closer look at them.

Using frame attributes

As with tables, frames have many attributes you can use to alter their appearance within the Web browser. You can turn a frame border on or off, define frame margins, or disallow scrolling for a particular frame. The following sections show you how.

Borders

The `frameborder` attribute enables you to turn a border on or off. You can individually specify whether you want the frames within your frameset to have borders. Borders help your readers differentiate between frames, but they can also get in the way of a seamless page. The value of the `frameborder` attribute can be 1, to turn the border on, or 0 to turn the border off.

```
<frameset cols="20%,*">
  <frame src="navigation.htm" frameborder="1">
  <frame src="content.htm" frameborder="0">
</frameset>
```

WARNING!

The default value for the frameborder attribute is 1. If you don't want borders around your frames, you have to use the frameborder attribute to turn them off (0).

Figure 9-8 shows the example site with borders turned off; Figure 9-9 shows it with borders turned on.

Margins

You can determine the margin height and width for any frame by using the following attributes:

- ✔ marginwidth: Accepts a value of 1 or more pixels to determine the exact width of the left and right margins of a frame.

- ✔ marginheight: Accepts a value of one or more pixels to determine the exact height of the controls at the top and bottom margins of a frame.

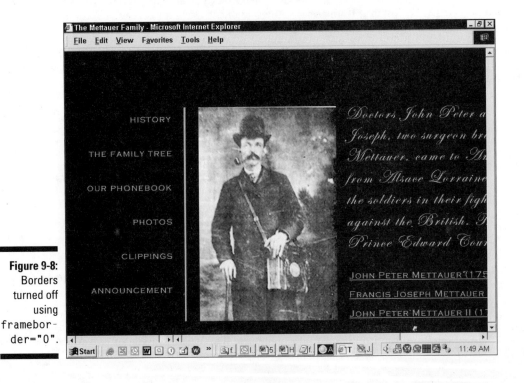

Figure 9-8:
Borders
turned off
using
framebor-
der="0".

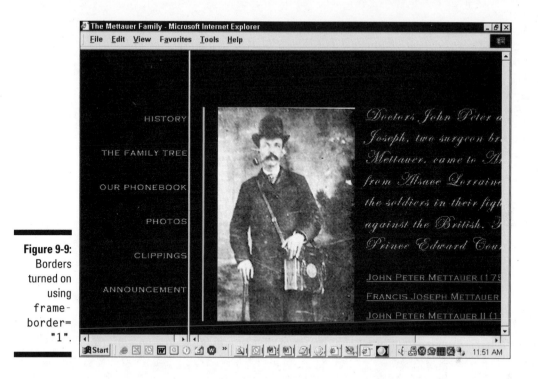

Figure 9-9:
Borders
turned on
using
frame-
border=
"1".

Once defined, the margins show up as white space in a browser's display; therefore, you can use these attributes to nicely separate the content in one frame from the content in another. Margins must be one or more pixels wide to keep objects from touching the edges of a frame. The marginwidth and marginheight attributes are optional. If you omit this attribute, the browser sets its own margin widths (usually one or two pixels, depending on the browser).

To define the margin height or width, add the attributes to the frame elements:

```
<frameset cols="20%,*">
  <frame src="navigation.htm" frameborder="0" marginwidth="20"
    marginheight="20">
  <frame src="content.htm" frameborder="0" marginwidth="20" marginheight="20">
</frameset>
```

Scrolling frames

One helpful attribute, scrolling, enables you to turn a scroll bar on and off for any given frame. When added to the <frame> element, you must define a value of yes, no, or auto:

✔ yes: Forces the browsers to display a scroll bar for the frame.

✔ no: Does not display a scroll bar for the frame.

✔ auto: Displays a scroll bar only if more content than fits in the window is displayed. This is the default value.

For our example, we force the first frame to have a scroll bar, and require the browser to not display a scroll bar for the second page, even if the content runs over.

```
<frameset cols="20%,*">
  <frame src="navigation.htm" frameborder="0" scrolling="yes">
  <frame src="content.htm" frameborder="0" scrolling="no">
</frameset>
```

Figure 9-10 illustrates the features described in this example when rendered in a browser.

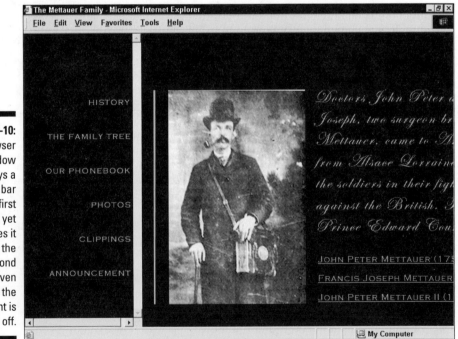

Figure 9-10:
The browser window displays a scroll bar for the first frame, yet leaves it off for the second frame, even though the content is cut off.

Targeting Links within a Frameset

Targeting links within a frameset is where frames get tricky, and usability can be thrown out the window if you're not careful. To illustrate the concept of targeting links, consider the example in Figure 9-1 where we define a frameset document with two vertical frames: a skinny one on the left that serves as a navigation document, and a wider one on the right where the bulk of the content your users see shows up.

Say you want to create hyperlinks in the document that lives in the skinny frame on the left that, when clicked, cause new Web documents to load in the wide frame on the right. This is actually a common frame dilemma, because frames are often used to separate navigation from content.

If you don't define the behavior correctly and click a hyperlink in the navigation frame, the contents will most likely display in your browser window in place of the two frames. You need to make sure you target the link correctly so the linked document replaces *only the right frame,* not the entire browser window.

Two steps are all you need to define how links behave in a frame structure:

1. **Name each frame in the frameset document.**
2. **Point the link at the named frame.**

Naming the frame

To name the frame in the frameset document, you add the `name` attribute to the `<frame>` element as follows:

```
<frameset cols="20%,*">
  <frame src="navigation.htm" frameborder="0" name="nav">
  <frame src="content.htm" frameborder="0" name="content">
</frameset>
```

The name of the frame can be almost anything you can think of, but we think you should keep the names short and descriptive. In our example, we named the frame that always contains the main content of our site, `content`. Real creative? Maybe not. But definitely more useful than calling it `spaghetti`.

Pointing the link to the target frame

After you name the frame, you can use the `<a>` element with the `target` attribute to create a link that opens in that named frame. The following example creates a link in the `navigation.htm` document that opens `history.htm` in the `content.htm` window:

```
<a href="history.htm" target="content">History</a>
```

Because a target window name is already defined, the browser opens his-tory.htm in the frame named content. Targeting works by giving you control over where the linked page (or other resource) appears when a user clicks a link in your documents.

Normally, when a user clicks a link, the browser displays the new document in the current, entire browser window (not just in a frame). Targeting enables you to change that: You can assign names to specific frames — using the name attribute — and require certain documents to appear in the frame that bears the targeted name.

As with the name attribute, any valid frame name you specify in a target attribute must begin with an alphanumeric character. The target attribute introduces a few predefined exceptions (covered shortly) that begin with an underscore character. Remember, however, that any targeted frame name starting with an underscore or a non-alphanumeric character (provided the name has no special purpose) gets ignored.

Using predefined values

Other than naming a specific frame name, you can use four predefined values with the target attribute:

- ✔ _self: Specifying the _self target always causes the linked document to load inside the frame that contains the hyperlink. All links act this way by default.

- ✔ _blank: Specifying the _blank target causes the linked document to load inside a new browser window, which is an easy way to force the user's browser to launch another window. The _blank attribute can be useful if you want to link to someone else's site. But, make sure that your site is immediately available to users in the first browser window that never went away.

  Don't overuse _blank targets. Visitors to your site won't appreciate new browser windows popping up all the time.

- ✔ _parent: Specifying the _parent target makes the linked document load in the immediate frameset parent of the document. If the current document in which the _parent target appears has no parent, this attribute behaves like the _self value.

- ✔ _top: Specifying the _top target makes the linked document load in the full body of the window. If the current document is already at the top of the document hierarchy, the _top target name behaves like _self. You can use this attribute to escape from a deeply nested frame.

If you get carried away using frames nested within frames nested within frames, or you link to someone else's framed site only to find their frames loading inside yours, you can use `target="_top"` to cancel out your frameset and revert back to a simple HTML page.

Zeroing in on targeted-link rules

Understanding targeted links may take a bit of wrestling. Keep a few things in mind while you grapple:

- ✔ **You must name the frames in the frameset document:** For our example, we named our two frames `nav` and `content`.

- ✔ **You must target your links defined in the HTML documents that populate the windows:** For our example, we want to target all the links in `navigation.htm` to point to the `content` window.

- ✔ **Check all links before the site goes live to verify that links are targeted correctly:** This is always a good practice, whether you're using frames or not.

- ✔ **If linking to a document outside of your site, you can use `target="_blank"` to force that document to open in a new, separate browser window:** That circumvents some of the unpredictability — always a good thing — of how the document will appear when it opens.

Nesting Framesets

Nesting frames introduces a new twist to the traditional frame structure, for example:

```
<frameset>
  <frame>
  <frame>
</frameset>
```

In this example, we define one frameset that contains two frame documents. Remember, for every document included in the frameset, there must be a corresponding `<frame>` element.

To split a frame into smaller frame components, you have to nest a `<frameset>` element within the original frameset:

```
<frameset>
  <frameset>
    <frame>
    <frame>
```

```
</frameset>
<frame>
</frameset>
```

Our example uses two sets of `<frameset>` tags. The outermost set defines the primary structure, and the second set defines the structure for the left frame. A third set is not needed for the right frame because it's only a single frame.

We can split the navigation frame in the example we have been using throughout this chapter:

```
<frameset cols="250,*" frameborder="1" framespacing="0">
  <frameset rows="85%,*" frameborder="1" framespacing="0">
    <frame src="navigation.htm" frameborder="1" framespacing="0"
      scrolling="yes">
    <frame src="note.htm" frameborder="1" framespacing="0">
  </frameset>
  <frame src="content.htm" frameborder="1" framespacing="0">
</frameset>
```

The second frameset functions much like the first set. You can even use the same attributes. In this example, we split the first frame into two rows, and therefore, use the `rows` attribute. Keep in mind that adding a new frame here calls for three `<frame>` elements. Figure 9-11 shows the resulting new frameset.

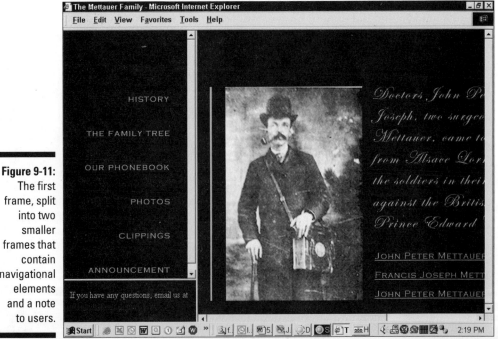

Figure 9-11: The first frame, split into two smaller frames that contain navigational elements and a note to users.

Chapter 10

HTML Forms

*M*ost of the HTML you write helps you display content and information for your users. Sometimes, however, you want a Web page to *gather* information from users instead of giving info to them. HTML *form markup* gives you a healthy collection of elements and attributes you can use to create forms for collecting information from visitors to your site.

This chapter takes a look at the many different uses for forms. It also shows you how to use form markup to create just the right form for soliciting information from your users, reviews your options for working with the data you receive, and gives you some tips for creating easy-to-use forms that really help your users provide the information you're looking for.

The Many Uses for Forms

Although you can find literally millions of unique forms on the Web, every form is driven by the same set of markup elements. Handily enough, they all fall into one of two broad categories:

✔ **Search forms:** These give users a way to submit search criteria.

✔ **Data collection forms:** These give your users a way to provide information for many uses such as online shopping, technical support, site preferences, and personalization.

Web forms can be short or long, simple or complex, and they have myriad uses on the Web. Here are just a few examples of how forms are used:

- ✔ **Doing an online search:** When you use a search engine to search a site or the entire Web, you enter your search criteria in a form.

- ✔ **Logging on to a site to view customized content:** When you log on to a site, you enter your username and password in a form. This type of form is a data-collection form.

- ✔ **Shopping online:** When you shop online or reserve travel online, you enter your selections and credit card information in this type of data-collection form.

- ✔ **Providing feedback to a site owner:** When you send feedback to a Web site's creator or ask for technical support via a Web site, you use this data collection form to provide all the pertinent details.

Before you create any form markup, you need to have a good idea of what kind of data you need to collect. Your data is what drives the form elements you use — and the way you put them together on a page — so make sure you understand what data you need before you collect it.

Introducing search forms

You'd be amazed at the many ways forms can help users search a site, or even the Web itself. For example, the IRS home page (shown in Figure 10-1) uses two different single-field forms to help visitors to its site search for general information or to search for tax forms.

The Get Refund Status page, however, has a different function: You can use it to search IRS records for the status of your refund. This page is a little more complicated, as shown in Figure 10-2.

The difference between the simple search forms on the home page and the slightly longer refund search form is the kind of data the IRS site needs from you to search the site. When you enter keywords into the fields on the home page, you may get dozens of relevant responses, which is okay: You can pick and choose from the options and find the one that relates to you.

This strategy won't work on the refund status page because refund information is sensitive and the IRS doesn't want you trolling through dozens of possible responses to find your information; the engine that drives the search for your refund status needs more detailed information to find the exact data you're looking for.

Figure 10-1: The IRS home page uses two short search forms to help users find what they are looking for in minimum time.

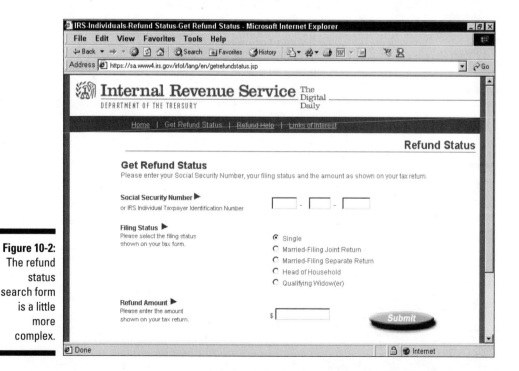

Figure 10-2: The refund status search form is a little more complex.

Because searches come in all shapes and sizes, so must the search forms that drive those searches. If you plan to add a search form to your Web site, you must carefully consider what kind of data visitors will be searching and what information you'll need from them to help them search successfully. A short keyword search may do the trick, or you may need something more complicated.

Introducing data collection forms

Data collection is a general category that describes every form on the Web that doesn't help someone search for something. For example, the Library of Congress (LOC) uses a form to collect the information it needs to subscribe teachers to a free electronic newsletter, as shown in Figure 10-3.

The LOC doesn't need much information to set up the subscription, so the form is short and simple. By contrast, RateGenius (a car-loan and refinancing organization) uses a series of long and detailed forms to gather the information it needs to help customers get the best possible loan rate. The form shown in Figure 10-4 is just the first of several a visitor must fill out to provide all the necessary information.

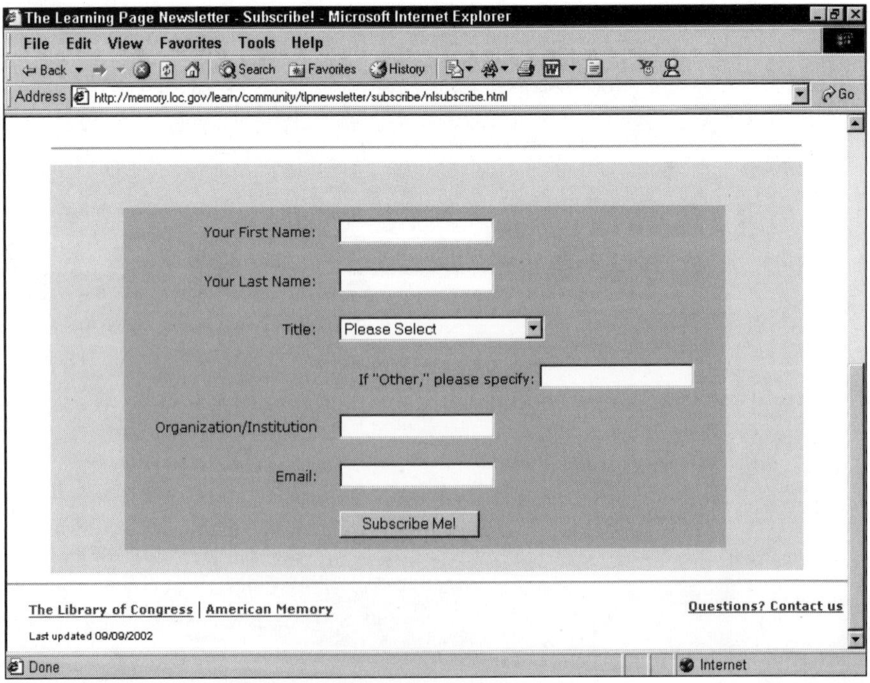

Figure 10-3:
A subscription form collects information to help teachers subscribe to an online newsletter.

(Screenshot: The Learning Page Newsletter - Subscribe! - Microsoft Internet Explorer)

File   Edit   View   Favorites   Tools   Help

Back

Address http://memory.loc.gov/learn/community/tlpnewsletter/subscribe/nlsubscribe.html

Your First Name:

Your Last Name:

Title: Please Select

If "Other," please specify:

Organization/Institution

Email:

Subscribe Me!

The Library of Congress | American Memory   Questions? Contact us

Last updated 09/09/2002

Done   Internet

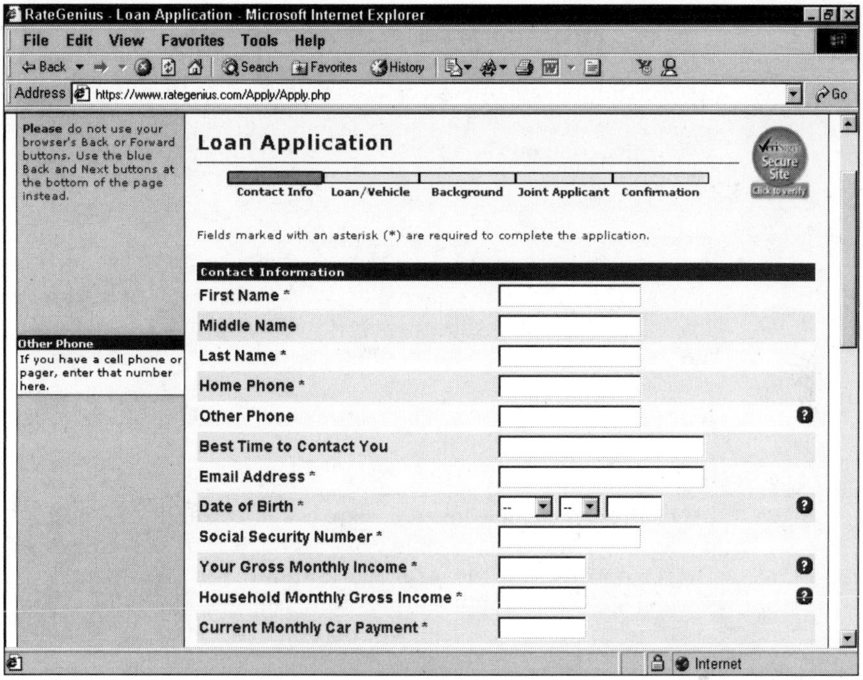

Figure 10-4:
An online
car loan site
uses many
long and
detailed
forms to
collect
necessary
data.

> When you create a form that collects information from visitors to your site, the information you need to acquire drives the final structure of the form and its complexities. If you need a lot of information, your form may be long and you may even use several forms. If you need just a little information, the form may be short and (relatively) sweet.

Creating Forms

The HTML form markup elements and attributes fall into one of two categories:

- ✔ Elements that define the overall form structure and let the Web browser know how to handle the form data.

- ✔ Elements that create input objects: fields, check boxes, drop-down lists, and the like.

Although every form has the same basic structure, the input elements you use differ depending on the data you're trying to collect.

Basic form structure

All of the input elements associated with a single form are contained with a `<form>` element and are all processed by the same form handler. A *form handler* is a program on the Web server (or even possibly a simple `mailto` URL) that manages the data a user sends to you via the form.

A Web browser is only programmed to *gather* information via forms; it doesn't know what to do with the information once it has it. You have to provide some other mechanism to actually *do* something useful with the data you collect. A later section in this chapter ("What Do You Want to Do with Your Form Data") discusses form handlers in more detail.

The two key attributes you must always use with the `<form>` element are

- ✔ `action`: Uses a URL to specify the location of the form handler.

- ✔ `method`: Specifies how you want the form data to be sent to the form handler. The two possible values for this attribute are `get` and `post`. If you specify `get`, the form data is sent to the form handler on the URL. If you specify `post`, the form data is sent in the Hypertext Transfer Protocol (HTTP) header. Your specific form handler dictates which value to use.

  For a good overview of the difference, read the Good Forms article on the Webmonkey site at

  ```
  http://hotwired.lycos.com/webmonkey/99/30/index4a_page3.html
  ```

The markup in Listing 10-1 creates a form processed by a form handler (on the Web server named `guestbook.cgi`) and sent to the handler via the `post` method.

Listing 10-1: A Simple Form Processed by a Form Handler

```
<!DOCTYPE HTML PUBLIC "-//W3C//DTD HTML 4.0 Transitional//EN"
        "http://www.w3.org/TR/REC-html40/loose.dtd">

<html>
  <head>
    <title>Forms</title>
  </head>

  <body>
    <form action="cgi-bin/guestbook.cgi" method="post">

    <!-- form input elements go here -->

    </form>
</html>
```

The value of the `action` attribute is a URL, so you can use absolute or relative URLs to point to a form handler on your site.

Using input elements

The elements you use to solicit input from your site visitors make up the bulk of any form. HTML supports a variety of different input options — from text fields to radio buttons to images. There are three HTML elements that you use to create input controls:

- ✔ `<input>`: Uses the `type` attribute to define several different controls, including text and password fields, check boxes, radio buttons, submit and reset buttons, hidden fields, and images.
- ✔ `<select>` **and** `<option>`: Used together to create drop-down lists.
- ✔ `<textarea>`: Creates a multiline text-input field.

Every input control, regardless of the type, associates some value with a name. When you create the control, you give it a name and the control sends back a value based on what the user does in the form. For example, if you create a text field that collects someone's first name, you might name the field `firstname`. When the user types his or her first name in the field and submits the form, the value associated with `firstname` is whatever name the user typed in the field.

For input elements that require a user to select an option (such as a check box or radio button), rather than typing something into a field, you define both the name and the value. When the user selects a box or a button and hits the submit button, the form returns the name and value assigned to the element.

The whole point of a form is to gather values associated with input controls, so the way you set the name and value for each control is important. The following sections explain how you should work with names and values for each of the various controls.

Text fields

Text fields are single-line fields that users can type information into. You define a text field using the `<input>` element and the `type` attribute with a value of `text`. You use the `name` attribute to give the input field a name, and the user supplies the value when he or she types in the field. This markup creates two text input fields: one for a first name and one for a last name:

```
<form action="cgi-bin/guestbook.cgi" action="post">
<p>First Name: <input type="text" name="firstname"></p>
<p>Last Name: <input type="text" name="lastname"></p>
</form>
```

Notice that in addition to the input elements, the form includes paragraph (<p>) elements and some text to label each of the fields. By themselves, most form elements won't give the user many clues about what kind of information you want him or her to provide. You also have to use HTML block and inline elements to format the display of your form. Figure 10-5 shows how a browser displays this HTML.

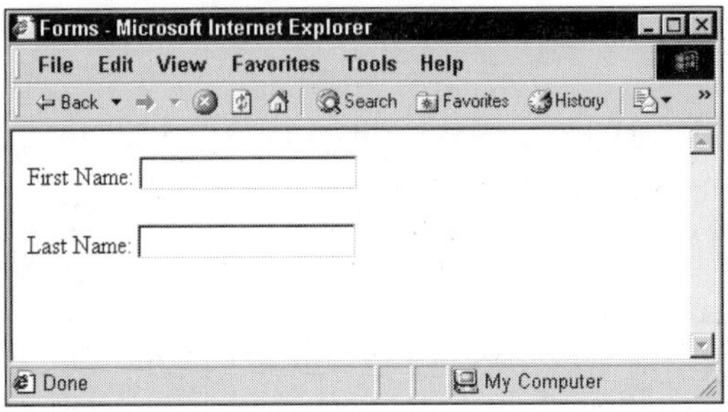

Figure 10-5: Text entry fields in a form.

Notice that the browser makes both text fields the same length. You can control both the length of the text fields and the number of characters the user can type into the field by using the `size` and `maxlength` attributes. The following markup creates a modified version of the form that sets both fields to a size of 30 and sets the `maxlength` to 25.

```
<form action="cgi-bin/guestbook.cgi" action="post">
<p>First Name: <input type="text" name="firstname" size="30" maxlength="25"></p>
<p>Last Name: <input type="text" name="lastname" size="30" maxlength="25"></p>
</form>
```

Each field will be approximately 30 characters wide; even so, a user can only type 25 characters into each field, as shown in Figure 10-6.

Password fields

A password field behaves just like a text field, except that when a user types into the field, the text the user types is obscured by an asterisk, bullet, or other character so someone looking over his or her shoulder can't see what is being typed.

Figure 10-6:
You can
specify
the length
and the
maximum
number of
characters
for a text
field.

You create a password field using the `<input>` element with a `type` attribute set to `password`, as follows:

```
<form action="cgi-bin/guestbook.cgi" action="post">
<p>First Name: <input type="text" name="firstname" size="30" maxlength="25"></p>
<p>Last Name: <input type="text" name="lastname" size="30" maxlength="25"></p>
<p>Password: <input type="password" name="psswd" size="30" maxlength="25"></p>
</form>
```

Figure 10-7 shows how a browser replaces what you type with asterisks.

Figure 10-7:
Password
fields are
like text
fields
except that
the browser
masks the
text a user
enters.

Check boxes and radio buttons

You can use check boxes and radio buttons to give users a collection of possible options they can choose from. When you use check boxes, users can choose more than one option from a collection, but when you use radio buttons they can only choose one option.

To create radio buttons and check boxes, you use the `<input>` element with the `type` set to `radio` or `checkbox`. Because users are simply selecting an option rather than typing text into a field, you use the `name` attribute to give each option a name and the `value` attribute to specify what value is returned if the user selects a particular option. You can also use the `checked` attribute to specify that an option should be already selected when the browser displays the form. This is a good way to specify a default selection in a list. Here's some markup that shows how to format check box and radio button options:

```
<form action="cgi-bin/guestbook.cgi" action="post">
<p>What are some of your favorite foods?</p>
<p><input type="checkbox" name="food" value="pizza" checked>Pizza<br>
    <input type="checkbox" name="food" value="ice cream">Ice Cream<br>
    <input type="checkbox" name="food" value="eggsham">Green Eggs and Ham<br>
</p>

<p>What is your gender?</p>
<p><input type="radio" name="gender" value="male">Male<br>
    <input type="radio" name="gender" value="female" checked>Female
</p>
</form>
```

Notice that each set of options uses the same name for each input control but gives a different value to each option. You give each item in a set of options the same name to let the browser know they are part of a set. Figure 10-8 shows how a browser displays this markup.

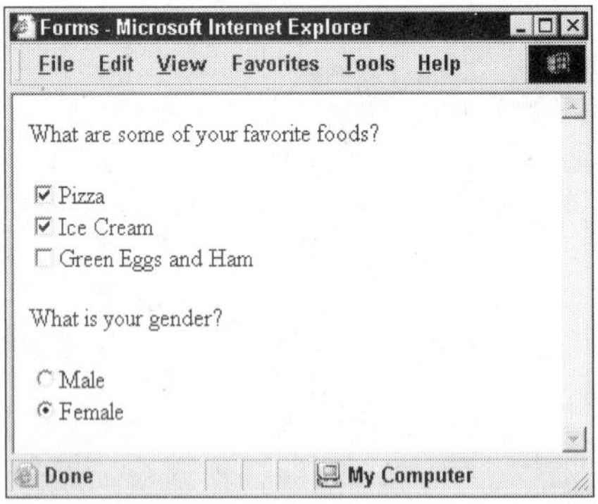

Figure 10-8:
Check boxes and radio buttons.

Hidden fields

A *hidden field* gives you a way to collect name and value information that the user can't see along with the rest of the form data. Hidden fields are useful if you want to keep track of information associated with the form (such as its version or name).

If your ISP provides a generic application for a guest book or feedback form, you may have to supply your name and e-mail address in the form's hidden fields so the application sends your form data specifically to you. To create a

hidden field, you use the `<input>` element with its `type` attribute set to
`hidden`, and then supply the name and value pair you want to send to the
form handler. Here's an example:

```
<form action="cgi-bin/guestbook.cgi" action="post">
<input type="hidden" name="e-mail" value="me@mysite.com">
<p>First Name: <input type="text" name="firstname" size="30" maxlength="25"></p>
<p>Last Name: <input type="text" name="lastname" size="30" maxlength="25"></p>
<p>Password: <input type="password" name="psswd" size="30" maxlength="25"></p>
</form>
```

File upload fields

You can also use a form to give users a way to share documents and other
files with you. When the user submits the form, the browser grabs a copy of
the file and sends it with the other form data. To create this *file upload field,*
you use the `<input>` element with the `type` attribute set to `file`. The file
itself is the form field value; you use the `name` attribute to give the control a
name.

```
<form action="cgi-bin/guestbook.cgi" action="post">
<p>Please submit your resume in Microsoft Word or plain text format:</br>
   <input type="file" name="resume">
</p>
</form>
```

Browsers render a file upload field with a browse button users can use to surf
their local hard drive and select a file to send to you, as shown in Figure 10-9.

Figure 10-9:
A file
upload
field.

When you accept files from users via a form, you open yourself up to receiving extremely large files or files that might be infected by viruses. You should
consult with whoever is programming your form handler to discuss options
for protecting the system files are saved to. You can put several barriers in
place that can help minimize your risks, including virus scanning software,
restrictions on file size, and restrictions on file type.

Drop-down lists

Long lists of radio buttons or check boxes can take up a lot of screen real estate and make your page look cluttered. *Drop-down lists* give you an alternative method for giving users lots of options to choose from. You use two elements to create a drop-down list: `<select>` to hold the list and a collection of `<option>` elements to identify the list options. You use a `name` attribute with the `<select>` element to give the entire list a name, and the `value` attribute with each `<option>` element to assign a unique value for each. Here's an example:

```
<form action="cgi-bin/guestbook.cgi" action="post">
<p>What is your favorite food?</p>
<select name="food">
  <option value="pizza">Pizza</option>
  <option value="ice cream">Ice Cream</option>
  <option value="eggsham">Green Eggs and Ham</option>
</select>
</form>
```

The browser turns this markup into a drop-down list with three items, as shown in Figure 10-10.

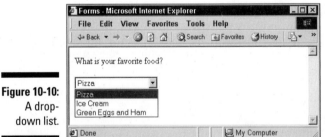

Figure 10-10:
A drop-down list.

As with radio buttons, the default allows a user to choose only one option from your list. If you want your user to choose more than one option (usually by holding down the Alt or Cmd key while clicking options in the list), add the `multiple` attribute to the `<select>` element.

Also, by default, the browser displays only one option until the user clicks the drop-down menu's arrow to display the rest of the list. Use the `size` attribute with the `<select>` element to specify how many of the available options to show. If there are more options than you specify, the browser includes a scroll bar in the drop-down list.

You can specify that one of the options in the drop-down list is already selected when the browser loads the page, just as you can specify a check box or radio button to be checked. Simply add the `selected` attribute to the `<option>` element you want selected.

This modification to the markup given earlier allows the user to choose more than one option from the list and sets the number of options to display to two. Also, the third option in the list is selected by default.

```
<form action="cgi-bin/guestbook.cgi" action="post">
<p>What are some of your favorite foods?</p>
<select name="food" size="2" multiple>
 <option value="pizza">Pizza</option>
 <option value="ice cream">Ice Cream</option>
 <option value="eggsham" selected>Green Eggs and Ham</option>
</select>
</form>
```

Figure 10-11 shows how adding these attributes modifies the display of the list in a browser.

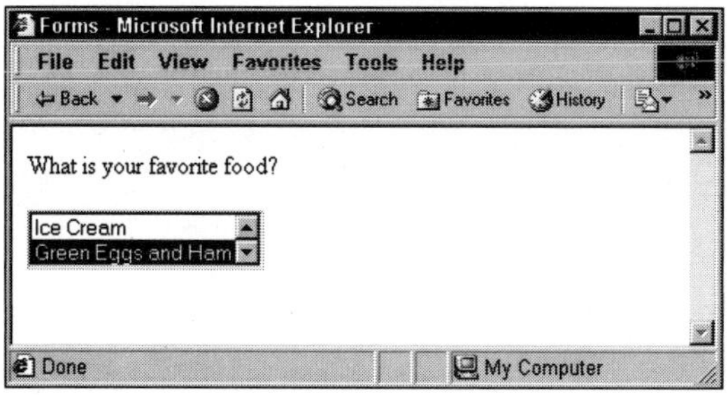

Figure 10-11:
A drop-
down list
with mod-
ifications.

Multiline text boxes

Often, a single-line text field won't provide your users with enough room to include large chunks of text in a form. If you want to create a *text box* instead of a text field, use the `<textarea>` element to define the box and its parameters. Use the `rows` and `columns` attributes to specify the height and width of the box. The text the user types into the box provides the value, so you need only give the box a name with the `name` attribute:

```
<form action="cgi-bin/guestbook.cgi" action="post">
  <textarea rows="10" columns="30" name="comments">
    Please include any comments here.
  </textarea>
</form>
```

Any text you include between the `<textarea>` and `</textarea>` tags displays in the text box in the browser, as shown in Figure 10-12.

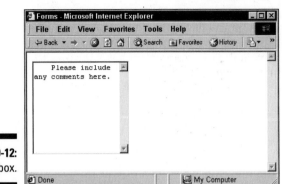

Figure 10-12:
A text box.

Submit and reset buttons

Visitors need a way to let a browser know they are done with a form and are ready to send the contents. They also need a way to clear the form if they want to start all over again or decide not to fill it out after all. You use the `<input>` element with a `type` of `submit` to create a button users can click on to submit the form to you. You use the `<input>` element with a `type` of `reset` to create a button that clears the form. These buttons help the user tell the browser what to do with the form, but don't actually send you any information. This means you don't need to set up name and value labels for them, but you do use the `value` attribute to specify how the browser labels the buttons for display. Here's an example:

```
<form action="cgi-bin/guestbook.cgi" action="post">
<p>First Name: <input type="text" name="firstname" size="30" maxlength="25"></p>
<p>Last Name: <input type="text" name="lastname" size="30" maxlength="25"></p>
<p>Password: <input type="password" name="psswd" size="30" maxlength="25"></p>

<p>What are some of your favorite foods?</p>
<p><input type="checkbox" name="food" value="pizza" checked>Pizza<br>
   <input type="checkbox" name="food" value="ice cream">Ice Cream<br>
   <input type="checkbox" name="food" value="eggsham">Green Eggs and Ham<br>
</p>

<p>What is your gender?</p>
<p><input type="radio" name="gender" value="male">Male<br>
   <input type="radio" name="gender" value="female" checked>Female
</p>

<p><input type="submit" value="Send"> <input type="reset" value="Clear"></p>
</form>
```

Figure 10-13 shows how a browser renders these buttons as part of an overall form.

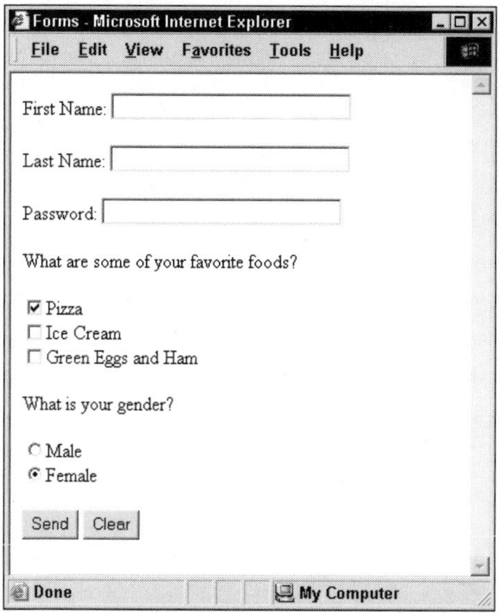

Figure 10-13:
Submit
and reset
buttons.

If you don't like the submit and reset buttons that a browser creates, you can substitute your own graphical buttons by using the <input> element with a type of image and an src attribute that specifies the image's location. For an image that submits the form, set value to submit. For an image that clears the form, set value to reset. Also, use the alt attribute to provide alternative text for browsers that don't show images (or for users who can't see them).

```
<p><input type="image" value="submit" src=" submit_button.gif alt="Submit">
<input type="image" value="reset" src="reset_button.gif" alt="Clear"></p>
```

What Do You Want to Do with Your Form Data?

Getting form data is really only half of the form battle. You create form elements to help users give you a way to provide them with data, but then you need to do something with that data. Of course, your form and your data will be unique every time, so there is no single, generic form handler that can manage the data for every form. Before you can find (or write) a program that handles your form data, you have to know what you want to do with it.

For example, if you have a form that gathers information from users to display in a guest book, you want to add the data to a text file or even a small database that holds the entries, and then create a Web page that displays the guest-book entries. If you want to create a shopping cart, you'll need programs and a database that can handle inventory, customer-order information, shipping data, cost calculations, and more. On the other hand, if you just want to receive comments from a Web form via e-mail, you may need only a simple `mailto:` URL.

Your Web hosting provider — whether it's an internal IT group or an ISP to which you pay a monthly fee — has the final say in what kind of applications you can use on your Web site to handle form data. If you plan to incorporate forms into your site, be sure that your hosting provider supports the applications you need to run on the server in order to process form. Chapter 17 includes more information on finding the right ISP to host your pages.

Using CGI scripts and other programs with form data

Typically, most form data is processed in some way or another by a CGI script written in some programming language. This can be Perl, Java, AppleScript, or one of many other languages that run on Web servers. These scripts take the data from your form and make it useful by putting it into a database, creating customized HTML based on it, writing it to a flat file, or one of thousands of other things.

CGI is much too complicated a topic to cover completely in this book, so if you aren't familiar with CGI scripts and how they work, the "CGI Scripts for Fun and Profit" article on Webmonkey provides an excellent overview:

```
http://hotwired.lycos.com/webmonkey/99/26/index4a.html
```

Chapter 14 also discusses CGI as it relates to creating dynamic Web sites that are integrated with databases.

But don't think that just because you need a program to get the most from your form data that you don't have to become a programmer to make the most of forms. Many ISPs include support for (and access to) standard scripts for processing commonly used forms such as guest books, comment forms, and even shopping carts. Your ISP may give you all the information you need to get the program up and running, and will most likely give you some HTML to include in your pages.

Although you can tweak the markup that manages how the form displays in the canned HTML you get from an ISP, be sure you don't change the form itself — especially the `form` element names and values. The program on the Web server relies on these to make the entire process work.

You can find several large script repositories online that provide free scripts you can download and use along with your forms. Many of these also come with some generic HTML you can dress-up and tweak to fit your Web site. You simply drop the program that processes the form into the folder on your site that holds programs (usually called a *cgi-bin*), add the HTML to your page, and you're good to go. Some choice places on the Web to find scripts you can download and put to work immediately are

  ✔ **Matt's Script archive:** `www.scriptarchive.com/`
  ✔ **The CGI Resource Index:** `http://cgi.resourceindex.com/`
  ✔ **ScriptSearch:** `www.scriptsearch.com`

However, if you want to use programs not provided by your ISP on your Web site, you'll need complete access to your site's cgi-bin folder. Every ISP's setup is a little different, so be sure to read your documentation to find out whether you have support for CGI scripts — and what languages the ISP supports. (Perl is usually a safe bet, but it's even safer to make sure.)

Sending data via e-mail

You can opt to receive your form data via e-mail instead of using a form to process it. You'll just get a collection of name and value pairs in a text file sent to your e-mail address, but that's not necessarily a bad thing. You can include a short contact form on your Web site that asks people to send you feedback (a feature that always looks professional); then you can simply include, in the action URL, the e-mail address you want the data sent to:

```
<form action="mailto:me@mysite.com" action="post">
```

Many spam companies get e-mail addresses by trolling Web sites looking for `mailto` URLs. You might consider setting up a special e-mail account just to receive comments so the e-mail address you use every day won't have yet another way to get pulled onto spam mailing lists.

Designing Forms That Are Easy to Use

Designing *useful* forms is a different undertaking from designing *easy-to-use* forms. Your form may gather the data that you need, but if it's hard for visitors to use, they may abandon it before they're done.

As you use the markup elements you've met in this chapter, along with the other elements that drive page layout, keep the following guidelines in mind:

- **Be sure you provide textual cues for all your forms.** Be clear about what information you're looking for in a particular field and what format you need it in. If you want users to enter a date as `mm/dd/yy`, be sure you tell them that. If you've limited the number of characters a text field can take (using the `maxlength` attribute), let users know so they aren't frustrated trying to enter more characters than your form allows.

- **Use field width and character limits to provide visual clues about the data you need.** For example, if you want users to enter a phone number as *xxx-xxx-xxxx*, consider creating three text fields: one for each segment of the phone number. Doing so helps users understand what kind of information you want.

- **Group like fields together.** A logical grouping of fields makes filling out a form easier for users. If you ask for someone's first name, then his or her birthday, and then his or her last name, it will be confusing. First name, last name, birthday flows more along the lines of the way people think.

- **Break long forms into easy-to-manage sections.** Let's face it; people don't like to fill out forms, even when they're working on a computer. When you break long forms into shorter chunks, people are less intimidated and are more likely to complete the form. Most major online retailers (such as Amazon.com) use this method to help customers provide all the detail the company needs to complete an order without making the buying process seem too arduous.

- **Mark required fields clearly.** If there are certain portions of your form that users must fill out before they can submit it successfully, be sure to mark those fields clearly. You can make them bold, or a different color, or put an asterisk beside them. It doesn't really matter what you do as long as you do something to point out to users how you've marked required fields.

- **Let users know what information they need to complete the form.** If users need to have any information in their hands before they fill out your form, consider adding a form gateway page that details everything users should have in front of them before they proceed on to the form. The RateGenius Apply For a Loan page, shown in Figure 10-14, uses this technique to lay out clearly for visitors about to fill out a long form exactly what information to prepare before starting to fill out the form.

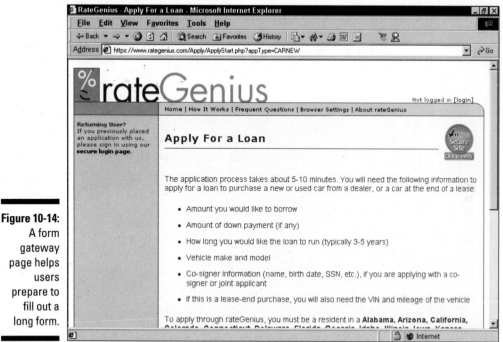

Figure 10-14:
A form
gateway
page helps
users
prepare to
fill out a
long form.

The series of forms RateGenius uses to gather information for car loans and loan refinancing are excellent examples of long forms that collect a variety of different kinds of data using all the available form markup elements. Visit www.rategenius.com to review its form techniques.

Part IV
Extending HTML with Other Technologies

The 5th Wave — By Rich Tennant

"YOU KNOW KIDS – YOU CAN'T BUY THEM JUST ANY WEB AUTHORING SOFTWARE."

In this part . . .

Building attractive, user-friendly Web pages often involves more than HTML markup. In this part, we cover some common and useful tools and techniques that help you extend and expand HTML's capabilities through various add-ons or add-ins. You get a look at Cascading Style Sheets — a markup language designed to let you define and manage how HTML documents look and behave simply and systematically. You also go behind the scenes of scripting languages such as JavaScript and VBScript to see how they can improve not only the way your Web pages interact with your visitors, but also how they can help manage sophisticated display and navigation on your site.

Next, you review the features of various multimedia players and add-ins that can bring sound, video, and animation to your Web pages. You get some hints on how to use such tools to best effect. After that, you explore the complex and interesting relationships that Web pages can create between HTML and databases — and the capabilities you can cultivate through judicious use of such technologies. Finally, you get a sneak preview of the new extended markup languages that may someday replace HTML — how they work, and why you might find them interesting for potential use in your Web sites.

Chapter 11

Getting Stylish with CSS

. . . .

. . . .

*T*he goal of style sheets is to prevent users' whims — as well as misconfigured browsers — from mangling the display of style-dependent Web documents. Style sheets allow authors to specify layout and design elements, such as fonts, colors, and text indentation. Style sheets give you precise control over how elements appear on a Web page. What's even better is that you can create a single style sheet for an entire Web site to ensure that the layout and display of your content is consistent from page to page. And for the last bit of icing on the cake, Web style sheets are easy to build and even easier to integrate into your Web pages.

As HTML has evolved and XHTML looms on the horizon for the future, the goal of the markup powers that be is to eventually remove all formatting markup (such as the `<font>` element) from HTML's collection of elements in lieu of style sheets.

Generally, style sheets give you more flexibility than markup ever will, and the HTML element collection won't grow to include more display-oriented tags. When you want tight control over the display of your Web pages, style sheets are the way to go.

Style sheets aren't well supported in 3.0 and earlier browsers, and aren't even 100 percent supported in even the latest browsers, so you should carefully test your style sheets in a variety of browsers to be sure they don't mangle your page.

Understanding the Problems Style Sheets Solve

HTML was never designed to be a formatting language, and as a result, its formatting capabilities are limited, to say the least. When you try to design a page layout in HTML, you're limited to tables, font controls, and a few other inline styles such as bold and italics. Style sheets give you the tools you need to take your Web page to the next level. With style sheets you can

- ✓ **Carefully control every aspect of the display of your page:** Specify the amount of space between lines, character spacing, page margins, image placement, and more.

- ✓ **Apply changes globally:** You can guarantee consistent design across an entire Web site by applying the same style sheet to every Web page.

  Quickly and easily modify the look and feel of your entire site by changing a single document (the style sheet) instead of the markup on every page.

- ✓ **Instruct browsers to control appearance:** Provide Web browsers with more information about how you want your pages to appear than you can communicate with HTML.

- ✓ **Create dynamic pages:** Use JavaScript or another scripting language along with style sheets to create text and other content that moves, displays, and hides in response to user actions.

Using Style Sheets to Drive the Display of Your HTML

The gist of how style works on the Web is this: You define rules in a style sheet that specify how you want content described by a particular set of markup to display. For example, you could specify that every first-level heading be displayed in purple, Garamond, 24-point type with a yellow background (not that you *would,* but you could). You link style rules to markup, and the browser does the rest.

CSS (for Cascading Style Sheets) is the official name for the HTML style-sheet tool, now in its second version (CSS2). CSS1 was a good, solid shot at building a style-sheet mechanism for the Web. But it *was* only a preliminary shot; the improvements built into CSS2 make CSS more robust. Currently, however, most Web browsers actually offer better support for the first version of CSS (CSS1), which defines some must-have Web features:

✔ Specifying font type, size, color, and effects

✔ Setting background colors and images

✔ Controlling many aspects of text layout, including alignment and spacing

✔ Setting margins and borders

✔ Controlling list display

CSS2 improves the implementation of many CSS1 components and expands on CSS1 with some new definitions:

✔ Defining aural style sheets for text-to-speech browsers

✔ Defining table layout and display

✔ Automatically generating content for counters, footers, and other standard page elements

✔ Controlling cursor display

The next generation of CSS — CSS3 — is a collection of *modules* that address different aspects of Web-page formatting (such as fonts, background colors, lists, text colors, and so on). The first of these modules should become standards (officially called *Candidate Recommendations*) in late 2002, with additional modules becoming final in 2003.

The W3C has devoted an entire section of its Web site to this topic at `www.w3.org/style/css`. You can find general CSS information there, as well as keep up with the status of CSS3. The site links to a number of good CSS references and tutorials, and includes information on software packages that can make your style sheet endeavors easier.

What You Can Do with CSS

You have a healthy collection of properties to work with as you write your style rules. You can control just about every aspect of a page's display — from borders to font sizes and everything in between. The properties fall into several categories:

✔ **Background properties:** These control the background colors associated with blocks of text and with images. You can also use these properties to attach background colors to your page or to individual elements.

- ✔ **Border properties:** These control borders associated with the page, lists, tables, images, and block elements (such as paragraphs). You can specify border width, color, style, distance from the element's content, and so on.

- ✔ **Classification properties:** These control how elements such as images flow on the page relative to other elements. You can use these properties to integrate images and tables with the text on your page.

- ✔ **Font properties:** These control all aspects of the font(s) you use — including font size, family, and height. These properties give you more control over your text with style sheets than the `font` element ever will.

- ✔ **List properties:** These control the way lists appear on your page. You can manage list markers, use images in lieu of bullets, and so on.

- ✔ **Margin properties:** These control the margins of the page, block elements, tables, and images. These properties extend the ultimate control over the white space on your page.

- ✔ **Padding properties:** These control the amount of white space around any block element on the page. When used with margin and border properties, you can create some complex layouts.

- ✔ **Positioning properties:** These control where elements sit on the page. These properties give you the ability to specifically place elements on the page much as you would in a page layout tool.

- ✔ **Size properties:** These control how much space (in height and width) that your elements (both text and images) take up on your page. They're especially handy for limiting the size of text boxes and images.

- ✔ **Table properties:** These control the layout of tables. You can use them to control cell spacing and other table-layout specifics.

- ✔ **Text properties:** These control how text displays on the page. You can set text color, letter and line spacing, alignment, white space, and so on.

A complete description of CSS properties is beyond the scope of this book, but if you'd like to see more about how each property works, there are entire books and Web sites devoted to the fine details of using each and every property in these various categories. If you'd like a print reference, we suggest *Cascading Style Sheets For Dummies* by Damon A. Dean and published by Wiley Publishing. If you'd like a Webified reference, we suggest you visit DevGuru's CSS2 reference at `www.devguru.com/Technologies/css/quickref/css_index.html`.

Although CSS syntax is straightforward, combining CSS styles with markup to fine-tune your page layout can be a little complicated. Fortunately, all you really need do to become a CSS guru is to learn the details of how the different properties work — and then experiment to see how different browsers handle them. As with HTML, practice will give you insight into the right way to use CSS to help convey your message on the Web.

Introducing Basic CSS Syntax

A style sheet is made up of style rules; each style rule has two distinct parts:

- ✔ **Selector:** Specifies the markup element to which you want the style rules to apply.

- ✔ **Declaration:** Specifies how you want the content described by the markup to look.

You use a particular set of punctuation and special characters to define a style rule. The syntax for a style rule always follows this pattern:

```
selector {declaration}
```

A declaration breaks down further into a property and a value. *Properties* are different aspects of how the computer is to display text and graphics (for example, font size or background color). You combine a *value* with a property to specify exactly how you want text and images to look on your page (for example, a 24-point font size or a yellow background). You separate the property from the value in a declaration with a colon, like this:

```
selector {property: value}
```

For example, these three style rules set the colors for first-, second-, and third-level headings respectively:

```
h1 {color: teal}
h2 {color: maroon}
h3 {color: black}
```

The CSS specification lists exactly which properties you can work with in your style rules and the different values that they take. Most are pretty self-explanatory (`color` and `border`, for example). See "What You Can Do with CSS" earlier in this chapter for a quick rundown of what properties the CSS2 specification includes and what values they can take.

Style sheets override a browser's internal display rules; thus your formatting specifications affect *the final display of the page in the user's browser.* This means you can better control how your content looks, and create a more consistent and appropriate experience for visitors to your site. For example, the following style rules specify the font sizes for first-, second-, and third-level headings:

```
h1 {font-size: 16pt}
h2 {font-size: 14pt}
h3 {font-size: 12pt}
```

Figure 11-1 shows a simple HTML page with all three heading levels without the style sheet applied. The browser uses its default settings to display the headings in different font sizes.

Figure 11-1:
An HTML
page
without
style
specifi-
cations.

Figure 11-2, however, shows the Web page with a style sheet applied. Notice that the headings are significantly smaller than in the previous figure. That's because the style-sheet rules override the browser's settings.

Figure 11-2:
An HTML
page with
style
specifi-
cations in
effect.

Users can change their preferences so their browsers ignore your style sheets. Most users don't do so, but some will. It's always a good idea to test your Web page with style sheets turned off to be sure it still looks good (or acceptable, anyway) to those without the benefit of style.

Combining selectors and declarations

Chances are you'll want a style rule to affect the display of more than one property for any given selector. You could create several style rules for a single selector, each with one declaration, like this:

```
h1 {color: teal}
h1 {font-family: Arial}
h1 {font-size: 36pt}
```

After a while, however, such a large collection of style rules becomes difficult to manage. CSS enables you to combine several declarations in a *single* style rule that affects the display characteristics of a single selector, like this:

```
h1 {color: teal;
    font-family: Arial;
    font-size: 36pt;}
```

Notice that all the declarations for the h1 selector are contained within the same set of brackets ({ }) and separated by a semicolon (;). You can put as many declarations as you want in a style rule; just be sure to end each declaration with a semicolon.

From a purely technical standpoint, white space is irrelevant in style sheets (just as it is in HTML), but you should consider some consistent spacing scheme so you can easily read and edit your style sheets.

If you want the same set of declarations to apply to a collection of selectors, you can do that, too: Just separate the selectors with commas. The following style rule (for example) applies the declarations for text color, font family, and font size to the h1, h2, and h3 selectors:

```
h1, h2, h3 {color: teal;
            font-family: Arial;
            font-size: 36pt;}
```

As you can see from the sample style rules included in this section, style sheet syntax relies heavily on punctuation. When you have a style rule that doesn't seem to be working exactly as you anticipated, double-check your syntax to be sure you haven't inadvertently used a semicolon where you should have used a colon, or a parenthesis where you needed a bracket. The W3C's validation service at http://jigsaw.w3.org/css-validator/ can also help you zero in on any problems with your style sheets.

Working with style classes

Sometimes you may want to create style rules that apply only to particular instances of an HTML markup element. For example, if you want to create a style rule that applies only to paragraphs that hold copyright information, you need a way to let the browser know that the rule has a limited scope.

To target a style rule more carefully, you can use the `class` attribute with a markup element. This bit of HTML has two kinds of paragraphs: a regular paragraph (without a `class` attribute) and a `class` attribute with the value of `copyright`:

```
<p>This is a regular paragraph.</p>
<p class="copyright">This is paragraph of class copyright.</p>
```

To create a style rule that only applies to the copyright paragraph, add a period (`.`) and the value of the class attribute (`copyright`) after the paragraph selector in the style rule. The resulting rule looks like this:

```
p.copyright {font-family: Arial;
             font-size: 10pt;
             color: white;
             background: black;}
```

This style rule specifies that all paragraphs of class `copyright` display white text on a black background in 10-point Arial font. Figure 11-3 shows how a browser applies the style rule only to a paragraph that has the proper class attribute defined.

Figure 11-3: Use classes to target your style rules more precisely.

You can also create style-rule classes that aren't associated with any element, as in the following example:

```
.warning {font-family: Arial;
          font-size: 14pt;
          background: white;
          color: white;}
```

You can use this style class with any element by adding `class="warning"` to the element. Figure 11-4 shows how a browser applies the warning style to both the paragraph and heading, but not to the block quote in this HTML:

```
<p class="warning">This is a paragraph of class warning.</p>
<blockquote>This is a block quote without a defined class.</blockquote>
<p class="warning">This is a paragraph of class warning.</p>
```

Figure 11-4:
You can
create style
rules that
work with
any element
by using
classes.

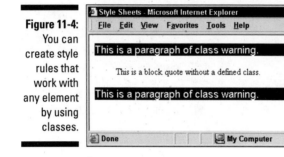

Understanding How Styles Are Inherited

One of the fundamental concepts in HTML (and markup in general) is nesting tags. Your entire HTML document is nested within `<html>` and `</html>` tags, and everything a browser displays in a window is nested within `<body>` and `<body>` tags. (And that's just the beginning, really.) The CSS specification recognizes that you will often nest one element inside another and want to be sure the styles associated with the parent element find their way to the child element.

When you assign a style to an element, all the elements nested inside it have that style applied to them as well. For example, a style rule for the `body` element that sets the page background, text color, font size, font family, and margins looks like this:

```
body {background: black;
      color: white;
      font-size: 14pt;
      font-family: Garamond;
      margin-left: .75in;
      margin-right: .75in;
      margin-top: 1in;}
```

If you want to set style rules for the entire document, be sure to set them in the `body` element. Changing the font for the entire page (for example) is much easier to do that way; it beats changing every single element one at a time.

Paying attention to inheritance

As you begin to build complex style sheets that guide the display of every aspect of a page, you must keep inheritance in mind. For instance, if you set the margins for the page in a body style rule, the margins you set for every other element on the page will build off of the ones you set for the body. As long as you pay close attention to how your style rules work together, you can use inheritance to your advantage to minimize style rule repetition and create a cohesive display for your page.

This chapter covers basic CSS syntax, but if you want to fine-tune your style rules with some advanced techniques, you can get a complete overview of CSS syntax rules in the "CSS Structure and Rules" tutorial put together by the Web Design Group at `www.htmlhelp.com/reference/css/structure.html`.

Even though the style rule is set only for the body element, it applies to all elements in the following HTML (as shown in Figure 11-5):

```
<body>
   <p>This paragraph inherits the page styles.</p>
   <h1>As does this heading</h1>
   <ul>
      <li>As do the items in this list</li>
      <li>Item</li>
      <li>Item</li>
   </ul>
</body>
```

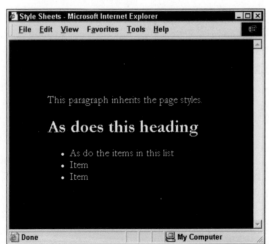

Figure 11-5: Inheritance means style rules apply to nested elements.

Adding Style to Your HTML Page

When you finish creating your style rules, the next step is to connect them to your HTML page. You have three options:

- ✔ Build a style sheet directly into a Web page — called an *internal style sheet* — by using the `<style>` element.
- ✔ Link a style sheet stored outside the Web page — called an *external style sheet* — by using the `<link>` tag.
- ✔ Add style information directly to a tag by using the `style` attribute.

Internal style sheets

An internal style sheet lives within your HTML page. You simply add style rules in a `<style>` element in the document's header and you're done. You can include as many (or as few) style rules as you want in an internal style sheet. (See Listing 11-1.)

Listing 11-1:   Adding an Internal Style Sheet to an HTML Document

```
<html>
<head>
  <title>Internal Style Sheet Example</title>
  <style>
    body {background: black;
          color: white;
          font-size: 14pt;
          font-family: Garamond;
          margin-left: .75in;
          margin-right: .75in;
          margin-top: 1in;}

    h1, h2, h3 {color: teal;
                font-family: Arial;
                font-size: 36pt;}

    p.copyright {font-family: Arial;
                 font-size: 10pt;
                 font-color: white;
                 background: black;}
```

(continued)

Listing 11-1 *(continued)*

```
    warning {font-family: Arial;
             font-size: 14pt;
             font-color: red;}
  </style>
</head>
<body>

<!-- Document content goes here -->

</body>
</html>
```

The main benefit of an internal style sheet is convenience: Your style rules are right there in the page with your markup so you can tweak both quickly. However, if you want to use the same style sheet to control the display of more than one HTML page, make the styles easy to find: Move them out of the individual Web page and into an external style sheet.

External style sheets

An external style sheet holds all your style rules in a separate text document that you can reference from any HTML file on your site. Although you have to maintain a separate style sheet file, the benefits an external style sheet offers for overall site maintenance are significant. If you have 50 pages on your site and they all use the same style sheet, you can change colors, fonts, or any other formatting characteristic on all your pages with a quick change to the style sheet.

To reference an external style sheet, you use the `link` element in the Web page header — like this:

```
<html>
<head>
  <title>External Style Sheet Example</title>
  <link rel="stylesheet" type="text/css" href="styles.css">
<head>
<body>

<!-- Document content goes here -->

</body>
</html>
```

The href attribute in the <link> element can take an absolute or relative link. This means you can choose to link to a style sheet that doesn't even reside on your site! Generally, however, it's best not to do so — after all, you want to control your site's look and feel yourself. However, if you want to quickly add style to your Web page (or experiment to see how browsers handle different styles), you might use an absolute URL to point to one of the W3C's Core style sheets — predefined style sheets you can use by simply linking to a URL. Read more about them at www.w3.org/StyleSheets/ Core/.

When you link to a style sheet that resides on your own site, you create a relative link. When you link to one on someone else's site (such as the W3C's core styles), you create an absolute link. Chapter 5 discusses the difference between the two types of links.

Element-level style rules: Use them with caution

Just so you know, you can attach individual style rules to individual elements in an HTML document. A style rule attached to an element looks like this:

```
<p style="color: green">The paragraph is green.</p>
```

Adding style rules to an element is quick and dirty, but isn't really the best approach. We generally recommend that you choose either internal or external style sheets for your rules instead of attaching the rules to individual elements in your document. Here are a few reasons why:

- Your style rules get mixed up in the page and are difficult to find.
- You have to place the entire rule in the value of the style attribute, which makes complex rules difficult to write and edit.
- You lose all the benefits that come with grouping selectors and reusing style rules in external style sheets.

Chapter 12

HTML and Scripting

● ●

● ●

*H*TML is static. You use it to describe your content and a browser displays that content on the Web. That's it. HTML can't help you create images that magically change when users move mouse pointers over them, cause additional browser windows to pop up when a page loads, or create any of the many other interactive and dynamic effects you see at work regularly on the Web.

So, if HTML can't make this happen, what does? The answer is scripting. When used in conjunction with your HTML markup, *content scripts* — small programs that you add to your Web page — can help your Web pages respond to user actions.

Because scripts are programs, they're written in a programming language and use programming techniques. Therefore, yes, you have to know something about programming if you want to create scripts from scratch. However, you can easily integrate scripts that others have written into your HTML pages without knowing much about programming at all. This chapter focuses on laying out the least you need to know about scripting to integrate pre-written scripts into your Web pages.

If you want to learn the ins and outs of creating scripts yourself, pick up *JavaScript For Dummies,* by Emily A. Vander Veer (Wiley Publishing). This book walks you through the least you need to know about creating scripts for your pages from scratch. Also, many good HTML editors (such as Macromedia Dreamweaver and Adobe GoLive) have built-in toolsets to help you create scripts — even if you don't know anything about programming. This is the route that some developers choose because it's the easiest. Chapter 16 discusses HTML editors like these in more detail.

What Scripts Can Do for Your HTML

In a nutshell, scripts can help you transform static HTML that just sits on the page (an important but dull job) into dynamic HTML that responds to user activities and makes visible or audible changes in the user's experience. For example, if you visit Dummies.com (www.dummies.com) and click the red button next to the search box without entering a term to search on, the browser displays a nice warning box that reminds you to enter a search term before you actually search, as shown in Figure 12-1.

Scripts add programmatic functionality to your Web pages and allow them to respond dynamically to what users do on the page — for example, filling out a form or moving their mouse pointers over an image (called a *mouseover* and covered later). When you add scripts to your page, the page interacts with users and changes its display or its behavior in response to what users do.

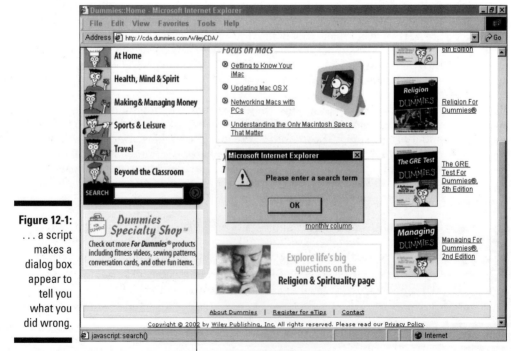

Figure 12-1:
. . . a script makes a dialog box appear to tell you what you did wrong.

If you click this button . . .

A short script verifies whether you've entered a search term before the engine runs the query:

- ✔ If you enter a search term, you don't see the warning.
- ✔ If you don't enter a search term, the script built into the page prompts the warning dialog box to appear.

This bit of scripting makes the page *dynamic,* which means it responds in different ways to how a user interacts with its elements. In effect, the script helps the page respond to what you do with the elements on the page.

Notice that the page URL doesn't change and another browser window doesn't open when you try to search on nothing. The page responds to what you do without sending a request back to the Web server to request a new page. This is why the page is considered *dynamic.*

If you wanted to try this trick without using a script (that is, without the dynamic functionality), the browser would send the empty search string back to the Web browser. Then the server would return a separate warning page reminding the user to enter a search term. All the work would be done on the Web server instead of in the Web browser.

Understanding What Makes Scripts Tick

A *script* is a set of programming instructions that activate when an event that you define occurs. An *event* is most often a user activity, such as moving a mouse pointer over an image, clicking a link, or selecting a drop-down menu.

In your HTML, you specify that a particular script fires off when a particular event occurs on a particular element. For example, the event could be that a user rolls his or her mouse over an image on the page. Of course, you have to specify which element, which event, and which script.

Here's exactly what happens when you activate an *image rollover* (a change in the image triggered when you move the mouse pointer over it):

1. You're browsing the Web and arrive at a really cool Web page that includes some HTML for an image.

   Unbeknownst to you, attached to that image are instructions to call a script named `rollover` that activates both when you move your mouse over and also when you move your mouse off the image.

2. You move your mouse over the image.

   The browser looks for the rollover script and executes the instructions in the script that specify what to do when a mouse pointer moves over the image.

3. The rollover script instructs the browser to replace the original image with a new image.

4. The browser downloads the new image and displays it in place of the original image.

5. You move your mouse off the image.

   The browser looks back at the rollover script and executes the instructions in the script that specify what to do when you move your mouse off the image.

6. The rollover script instructs the browser to display the original graphic again.

7. The browser replaces the new image with the original image and you're back to where you started.

In this example, the only time the browser has to contact the Web server is to get the new image. If you want images to be ready to show if a user event triggers a script, you can have your script instruct the browser to preload and hold onto specific images referenced in the script. They are what the user sees when he or she triggers an event.

Specifying event attributes

Although you write the actual instructions for the script in a scripting language, you still use HTML attributes to specify what script to call for each specific element. The attributes correlate to common user events (such as clicking or moving a mouse) and include the following:

✔ onload: Browser loads an HTML page.

✔ onabort: User cancels a page load.

✔ onunload: Browser stops displaying one Web page because it's about to load another.

✔ onerror: Browser encounters an error in the scripts or other instructions on the page.

✔ onmousemove: User moves the mouse pointer anywhere on the page.

✔ onmouseover: User moves the cursor over an element.

✔ onmouseout: User moves the mouse pointer off of an element.

✔ onmousedown: User moves the mouse pointer over an element, presses the mouse button down, and holds it down.

✔ onmouseup: User releases a held mouse button.

✔ onclick: User clicks an element with the mouse pointer.

✔ ondblclick: User double-clicks an element with the mouse.

✔ onkeypress: User presses and immediately releases a key on the keyboard.

✔ onkeydown: User presses and holds a key on the keyboard.

✔ onkeyup: User releases a depressed key.

✔ onfocus: An element becomes the focus of the user's attention, as a form field might when you begin to type in it.

✔ onblur: An element loses focus because the user chooses to focus on a different element.

✔ onchange: User changes the contents of a form element or selects a different check box, radio button, or menu item.

✔ onselect: User selects a check box, radio button, or menu item from a form.

✔ onsubmit: User clicks a form's Submit button.

✔ onreset: User clicks a form's Reset button.

Not every element supports every event attribute. For example, onsubmit and onreset work with the <input> element in a form because you use that element to create submit and reset buttons. The two attributes don't work with the <p> element because you can't submit or reset a form with a paragraph. Appendix A lists which event attributes work with which elements.

Including scripts in your HTML page

Linking a script to an HTML element that you plan for a user to interact with is simple. You place the script code in the <script> element in the document header. Then you attach the script name to an event attribute in an HTML element. Listing 12-1, for example, specifies that when the user clicks the submit button, the browser should verify that the user filled out both fields in the form.

Listing 12-1: Verifying the User Fills Out Both Form Fields

```html
<html>
<head>
  <title>Linking scripts to HTML pages</title>
  <script language="javascript">
    function checkSubmit ( thisForm ) {
      if ( thisForm.FirstName.value == '' ) {
            alert('Please enter your First Name.');
            return false;
      }

      if ( thisForm.LastName.value == '' ) {
            alert('Please enter your Last Name.');
            return false;
      }

      return true;
    }
</script>
</head>

<body>
  <form method="POST" action="http://www.someURL.com/"
        onsubmit="return checkSubmit(this);">
  <p>
    First Name: <input type="text" name="FirstName"><br>
    Last Name: <input type="text" name="LastName"><br>
    <input type="submit">
  </p>
  </form>
</body>
</html>
```

Notice that the value of the onsubmit attribute, return checkSubmit(this);, includes the name following function in the <script> element, checkSubmit. This tells the browser to run the checkSubmit function in the script on this form. You may want to have several different sets of instructions for the browser to run, depending on what a user does with the page. In that case, store each set of instructions as its own *function,* and link the function to the event attribute.

If this script looks like Greek to you, don't worry. The "Form validation" section later in the chapter walks you through everything going on in this script.

The double parentheses following the name (in both the script and the attribute values) are part of the scripting syntax. You can pass parameters to the script within the parentheses so you can reuse a single script for several elements. When you use someone else's script in your Web page, carefully read any instructions that come with the script. Verify whether you have to put any information in the parentheses or can leave them empty.

You can also put scripts directly into the value of an event attribute (instead of storing them in the document header). This technique works best for short scripts like the one in the "Image rollover" section later in the chapter.

Going with a Client-Side Script

As you might expect, there's more than one way to skin the scripting cat. Because a script is a set of programming instructions, you must have an application that can understand and respond to those instructions. Your two options are the Web browser or the Web server. Scripts that Web browsers read and respond to are called *client-side* scripts. Conversely, scripts that Web servers read and respond to are *server-side* scripts. (All the scripts we discuss in this chapter are client-side scripts.)

Server-side scripts are commonly used with data that users submit through HTML forms. They also help databases and other applications connected to a Web page. You can learn more about the role these scripts — often called CGI scripts — play in a Web site in Chapters 10 and 14.

When you include client-side scripts in your Web pages, the browser handles all script processing after a visitor to your site downloads the page. When you use a client-side script, you rely on the browser to interpret and run the script. That reduces the amount of processing your Web server has to do; it also limits how many times the browser must contact your Web server to change the way a page looks or behaves.

However, different browsers support scripting in slightly different ways; you may have to do a little extra work to make sure your script runs successfully on all browsers. Older versions of the popular browsers (3.0 and earlier), don't handle scripting well — and text-only browsers can't handle it at all — so if you include scripts, remember that their benefit is lost on users who run those older browsers.

When you download a script from the Web or have someone write a script for you, be sure to identify which browsers the script works with. You want scripts that work with as many browsers as possible so you can support as many different users' browser configurations as possible. A good programmer can create scripts that work well in different browsers, and will provide documentation for the script that specifies which browsers it works with. You should also state whether your script encounters any known problems when it runs in particular browsers.

May We Suggest Some Nice JavaScript?

You probably won't be surprised to find out that there's more than one language for writing Web page scripts. JavaScript was created by Netscape to work with the Navigator browser and VBScript was created by Microsoft to work with Internet Explorer. For quite a while, the two scripting languages competed heavily for developer favor, but in the end, JavaScript won and actually became a standard known as ECMAscript (even though everyone calls it JavaScript).

Older browsers (versions 3.0 and earlier) don't work well with scripts written in rival languages. JavaScript scripts don't work nearly as well in Internet Explorer 3.0 as they do in Navigator 3.0. VBScript is even more restrictive; scripts written in it won't run at all on anything but Windows machines using Internet Explorer as the browser.

More recent browsers have all standardized on JavaScript — thus most of the scripts you'll find are written in JavaScript. (So are the ones you'll see later in the chapter.) If you choose to learn a scripting language, choose JavaScript.

You don't need to know much about programming to use scripts in your Web page. All you really have to understand is how to use event attributes to link scripts to common user activities (such as clicking a submit button or changing some text). You can download canned scripts from several different repositories on the Web (look for a list at the end of the chapter) and then slap them into your page. That's really all there is to it.

You can use scripting to create some advanced user interfaces that respond to just about everything a user does. However, such scripts will be particular to your site; you'll have a harder time finding canned scripts that meet your needs. For standard dynamic features (such as form validation and image rollovers), you can find what you need on the Web. For more complicated features (or those specific to your site), you'll need to work with a programmer (or become one yourself) to create the necessary scripts.

Finding scripts online

Here are some good online sources of free scripts to add to your Web pages:

✔ **The JavaScript Source:** http://javascript.internet.com/

✔ **JavaScript Kit:** www.javascriptkit.com/

✔ **Java-Scripts.Net:** www.javascripts.net/

✔ **JavaScript City:** www.javascriptcity.com/

The following three sections look at the kinds of JavaScript scripts you can easily add to your Web pages, even if you don't know much about programming. They illustrate various approaches that programmers use to write scripts — and introduce basic concepts you'll need to work with scripts in your own pages.

Image rollover

Listing 12-2 shows an image rollover — short and sweet, it stores all scripting commands for the browser in the event attributes for the <img> element.

Listing 12-2:   Image Rollover

```
<html>
<head>
  <title>A simple image rollover</title>
</head>

<body>
  <p>
    <img src="image_one.gif" alt="button" border="0"
        onmouseover="this.src = 'image_two.gif';"
        onmouseout="this.src = 'image_one.gif';">
  </p>
</body>
</html>
```

The <img> element initially references image_one.gif, as shown in Figure 12-2.

Figure 12-2: When the page loads, it displays the image referenced in the image src attribute.

The instructions in the `onmouseover` attribute tell the browser to change the source of `this` element (the image element) to `image_two.gif` when a user moves his or her mouse pointer over the image. This effectively rewrites the `<img>` element so it reads `<img src="image_two.gif">`. Figure 12-3 shows that the browser does indeed display a different graphic when the mouse pointer moves over the image.

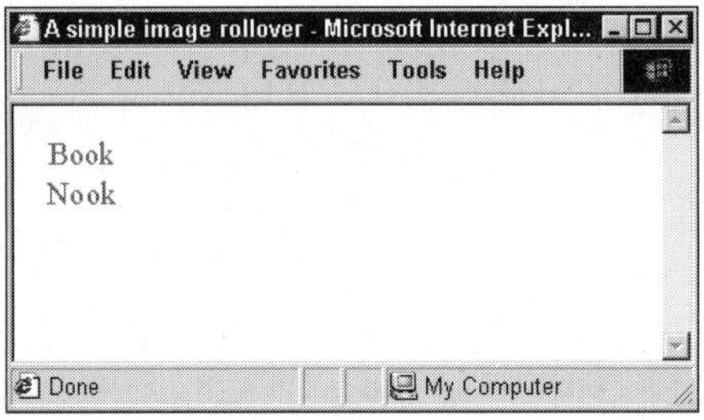

Figure 12-3:
When a
mouse
pointer
moves over
the image,
the browser
displays a
different
graphic.

The instructions in the `onmouseout` attribute tell the browser to change the source of the `<img>` element back to its original value (`image_one.gif`) when the mouse pointer moves off the image.

The URLs in this example are *relative,* which means the images must reside in the same folder as the HTML for this markup and scripting to work. If you want to store your images in a separate directory, you can — just reference the image in the script accordingly. For instance, if all images lived off the main Web server root directory in a directory called `images`, the `<img>` element would change to something like this:

```
<img src="/images/image_one.gif" alt="button" border="0"
     onmouseover="this.src = '/images/image_two.gif';"
     onmouseout="this.src = '/images/image_one.gif';">
```

You can read more about relative URLs in Chapter 3.

There are about as many ways to create image rollovers as there are images. (Okay, maybe not *that* many, but you get the point.) The rollover shown here is just one example; as you search for scripts to use in your page, you may find others. Be sure to read any notes or documentation included with the script you choose; find out where to put image names to make the script work.

Rollovers are an easy way to add some nice effects to your site, but don't overuse them. If images are constantly changing on your site, users may be distracted from the important content. Choose a few places to use rollovers — say, your main navigation — and use them consistently across your site. You'll get the benefit of the effect without making your visitors seasick.

Pop-up windows

A common use for scripting is to open new links in separate windows and manage the size and appearance of the browser window. Listing 12-3 attaches scripting instructions to a link that forces the linked document to open in a new 300 x 200 window that doesn't have a status bar, menu bar, or scroll bars, and that isn't resizable, as shown in Figure 12-4.

Listing 12-3:   Pop-Up Window

```
<html>
<head>
  <title>A pop-up window</title>
</head>

<body>
  <a href="javascript:void(0);"
  onclick="window.open('http://www.dummies.com', 'popupWin',
  'toolbar=0, location=0, status=0, menubar=0, scrollbars=0, resizable=0,
   width=300, height=200, left=20,top=20')">Dummies.com</a>
</body>
</html>
```

Figure 12-4:
You can use JavaScript to open a Web page in a new window and carefully control the display of the window.

The `<a>` element in the preceding code sample is listed across several lines for display purposes; however, you'll need to *remove the line breaks* if you add this code to your HTML pages and *put the entire anchor tag on a single line*. Random line breaks in JavaScript can cause errors on the page.

Notice that the value of `href` is `javascript:void(0);` rather than the actual URL the link points to (`http://www.dummies.com`). The link is part of the JavaScript, but you include the `javascript:void(0);` so the browser knows to move past the `href` attribute value and look to the scripting code to find the URL.

The `onclick` event attribute holds all the instructions the browser needs to open the link in a new window, starting with `window.open` that instructs the browser to pop open a new window. The specifics for the window follow in the parentheses:

- ✔ `http://www.dummies.com`: The URL to display in the window.
- ✔ `popupWin`: A name for the window.
- ✔ `toolbar=0`: Don't display the toolbar.
- ✔ `location=0`: Don't display the location bar.
- ✔ `status=0`: Don't display the status bar.
- ✔ `menubar=0`: Don't display the menu bar.
- ✔ `scrollbars=0`: Don't display the scroll bars.
- ✔ `resizable=0`: Don't allow the window to be resized.
- ✔ `width=300`: Sets the window width to 300 pixels.
- ✔ `height=200`: Sets the window height to 200 pixels.
- ✔ `left=20`: Positions the new window 20 pixels from the left of the parent window.
- ✔ `top=20`: Positions the new windows 20 pixels from the top of the parent window.

This code turns off all the menus and other window features by setting their values to zero (0). You can turn any of them on by changing the zeros to ones (1). Also note that the values for toolbar, location, and other window specifics aren't included in quotation marks. JavaScript doesn't require that you use them. Remember also that even though this code is in an `<a>` element, all these parameters are part of the JavaScript code, not the HTML code; therefore, they must abide by JavaScript rules.

Pop-up windows are helpful if you want to call someone's attention to some special content immediately, but they can backfire on you if you use them too much. Many Web sites use pop-up windows to deliver ads, so users are becoming desensitized (or hostile) to them and simply ignore them (or install software that prevents them). Before you add a pop-up window to your site, be sure it's absolutely necessary; consider how it affects the user experience if it's angrily slammed shut.

Form validation

A common use for JavaScript is to verify that users have filled out all the required fields in a form before the browser actually submits the form to the form-processing program on the Web server. Listing 12-4 stores a form checking function, checkSubmit, in the <script> element of the HTML page, and references it in the form's onsubmit attribute.

Listing 12-4:   Form Validation

```
<html>
<head>
  <title>Linking scripts to HTML pages</title>
  <script language="javascript">
    function checkSubmit ( thisForm ) {
      if ( thisForm.FirstName.value == '' ) {
          alert('Please enter your First Name.');
          return false;
      }

      if ( thisForm.LastName.value == '' ) {
          alert('Please enter your Last Name.');
          return false;
      }

      return true;
    }
</script>
</head>

<body>
  <form method="POST" action="/cgi-bin/form_processor.cgi"
      onsubmit="return checkSubmit(this);">
  <p>
    First Name: <input type="text" name="FirstName"><br>
    Last Name: <input type="text" name="LastName"><br>
    <input type="submit">
  </p>
  </form>
</body>
</html>
```

This script performs one of two operations if either form field isn't filled in when the user clicks the submit button:

✓ It instructs the browser to display a warning (the text is specified in the `alert`) to let the user know he or she forgot to fill in a field.

✓ It returns a value of `false` to the browser, which prevents the browser from actually submitting the form to the form processing application.

If the fields are filled in correctly, the browser doesn't display alerts and returns a value of `true`, which tells the browser that the form is ready to pass on to the Web server. Figure 12-5 shows how the browser displays the alert if the first name field is empty.

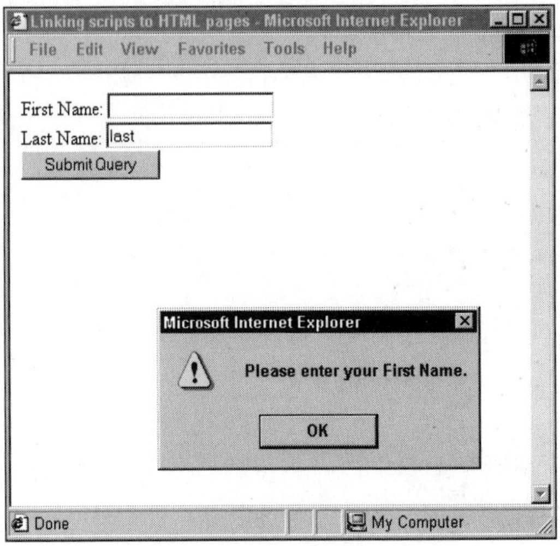

Figure 12-5:
A good
use of
JavaScript
is to validate
form data.

Although this example only verifies whether users filled out the form fields, you can create more advanced scripts that check for particular data formats (such as @ signs in e-mail addresses and only numbers in phone number fields). JavaScript is a robust Web programming language, so your form validation can be as simple (or as complex) as you need it to be.

When you create forms that include required fields, always include client-side scripting validation to catch missing data before the script can even find its way back to the program that processes it on the server. Users get frustrated when they take the time to fill out a form only to be told to click the Back button in their browsers to provide missing information. When you use client-side scripts, the script catches any missing information before the form page disappears so users can quickly make changes and try to submit again.

Chapter 13

Making Multimedia Magic

More and more Web sites are using multimedia. As a developer, you can now integrate different media types, such as audio, video, and/or animation clips, in a Web page to make your pages come alive.

Multimedia has had an interesting evolution. In the beginning, user bandwidth didn't allow multimedia elements to be incorporated; more recently, user bandwidth has increased, and multimedia is being used everywhere. However, in an effort to improve usability and design methodology, designers are being more conservative with their use of multimedia elements.

Many concerns must be addressed before you add media components to your page. For example, will the media type function properly on different platforms, or will the user have to use a plug-in application to see and hear the media? These are only two of the questions this chapter answers.

Although most Web technology has begun to embrace the concept of standards, multimedia is one area that has yet to follow suit. In this chapter, you get a look at some of the diverse audio and video formats, as well as several different players required for users to use these formats. There aren't any consistent standards for embedding these functions (although the W3C uses the <object> element); therefore, browsers use different methods for embedding these functions.

Most methods used by developers (and mentioned in this chapter), do not follow the HTML standard. We rarely break from our dedication to the standard; however, if you're going to work with multimedia, you need to be aware of the most effective use of media — and for now, that means sometimes using non-standard methods.

Using Media Wisely

If you're considering adding multimedia to a Web page, you should be able to identify its function. For example, a band would most likely want to allow users to download an MP3; however, there is little reason for yahoo.com to allow you to play some background music while you search the Web.

If you adhere to a few basic dos and don'ts as you work with multimedia, your Web page will benefit vastly:

- ✔ Understand the role and function of your media — don't just include audio or video for the fun of it.
- ✔ Compress your files — audio and video files can be quite large.
- ✔ Provide an off function for users if a media program starts automatically.
- ✔ Flash intros should allow users to skip them — add a Skip Intro button.
- ✔ Provide a link to all necessary media players.
- ✔ Identify key information about your media, such as file sizes and types — users need to know what they're in for.

Before getting started, you may want to check out some sites to see how other developers are using multimedia elements. The following three are excellent:

- ✔ www.egomedia.com
- ✔ www.cnn.com/
- ✔ www.spoontheband.com

Your Web Multimedia Options

As you select and add multimedia features to your Web page, you have to decide

- ✔ Which file format best suits your needs, as well as which are the most compressed.
- ✔ Whether to use a separate plug-in media player. Remember, not all browsers automatically support every media format.

✔ How to integrate media files into the Web page. You have three basic ways to integrate media files: Link to the external media file, embed and present the clip as an internal file, or *stream* the media.

Audio formats

You've probably heard of the more common formats in the following list, but several other types are also worth looking at. Just remember that when you select the audio format, you should also identify three other crucial factors: your target audience, the players or plug-ins required, and the way you want to present audio on your page.

Check out this list of format options:

✔ **AU (or Sun/NeXT audio):** A compressed audio format defined for Unix.

✔ **AIFF (Audio Interchange File Format):** A common audio format used for the Mac OS. The format does not support any kind of compression, so it tends to produce large files.

✔ **MP3 (MPEG-1, Layer III):** One of the most popular audio formats used on the Web. This format uses a compression ratio that can reduce file sizes to about a megabyte per minute — a drastic reduction in file size — by removing the part of the audio spectrum that is largely beyond the range of human hearing. Because an MP3 file preserves nearly all file contents that the human ear *can* hear, it retains near-CD quality.

✔ **MIDI (Musical Instrument Digital Interface):** The MIDI file format is actually not an audio format, but rather a digital representation of a sound. It was originally created to allow sounds created on one keyboard to be played on another without losing any quality. MIDI is now used to enable electronic instruments and sound cards to communicate with each other. Instead of representations of sounds, a MIDI file contains *instructions* that tell the computer or instrument how to produce the music (which makes the file size remarkably small). The user's sound card reads these instructions and then produces the notes.

✔ **QT (QuickTime) and RA (RealAudio):** The QT format works only with the QuickTime player. Same thing for RA (RealAudio) files. You can find out more about these formats in the section, "Media Players for Audio and Video," later in this chapter.

✔ **RMF (Rich Music Format):** An audio format, defined by Beatnik, that encrypts data and can contain both recorded audio *and* MIDI sequences. RMF file sizes are typically small enough that audio for a Web site's interface can be downloaded *in one file*. This file type requires Beatnik's

Player and JavaScript Music Object to play the files, so it's not used as often as the other types listed here. Check out `www.beatnik.com` for more information.

✔ **SWA (Shockwave Audio):** A compressed audio format, similar to MP3, that produces small files and retains most of the audio integrity. As the author, you can decide the compression ratio: the higher the ratio, the smaller the file. Keep in mind, however, that a smaller audio file also sacrifices some sound quality.

✔ **SWF (Flash):** Animation format with built-in sound capabilities that can also stream files. SWF stands for Shockwave File Extension. Sound can loop in the background of a SWF animation or be triggered by a particular frame or event. As a binary vector format, Flash creates small files that stay small even when they contain sound.

✔ **WAV (RIFF WAVE):** Developed by Microsoft and IBM, this is the common audio file format used for Windows. Even when compressed, WAV files are still comparatively large.

✔ **WMA (Windows Media Audio):** Microsoft format for its new Windows Media Technologies — a suite of utilities for creating, serving up, and viewing streamed multimedia (including high-quality audio).

Video formats

Video publishing on the Web has seen a jump in the last few years. In the past, online video projects cost a lot of money to produce — and even more money to publish. These days, however, anyone with a digital video (DV) camcorder can capture images and publish them on the Web. Video is not yet where developers would like it to be — almost everyone has seen a fuzzy image or two — but if visual quality is not as important (for your purposes) as access, publishing your video on the Web can be relatively easy.

The first step in getting a handle on video is to recognize video formats. The most common are `.mov`, `.avi`, and `.rv`. As the designer, it's your job to include a pointer to the appropriate player; most of the file types in the following list require a specific player to be viewed:

✔ **.avi:** AVI (audio/video interleaved), video format for Windows.

✔ **.dcr:** Movies created with Macromedia Director.

✔ **.mov:** Format for QuickTime movies.

✔ **.mpg:** Created by the Motion Picture Experts Group. This format is a widely used standard for digital compression of moving images.

✔ **.qt:** A QuickTime movie file type from Apple.

✔ **.qt3:** QuickTime 3 provides an advanced compression format for video, audio, MIDI, animation, 3D, and so on.

✔ **.rv:** Real Video, a format for streaming video on the Web, optimized for low-to-medium-speed connections.

✔ **.viv:** VIVO format for the compression of streaming video, particularly over low bandwidth.

Animation

For animation, there's only one superstar. Flash has taken over Web design (no cheap jokes about the Planet Mongo, please). Flash provides movement and images that are sleeker and easier to use than ever before.

For a look at what Flash can do, visit `www.flash99good.com/`. Unlike plain HTML pages, however, Flash-enabled Web pages require a Flash plug-in before visitors can view them. When they've downloaded the player, users don't have to worry about it again until a new version of Flash is unveiled (about every one to two years).

Don't underestimate the amount of time it takes to learn Macromedia's Flash application. Like other graphics applications (such as Photoshop or Dreamweaver), the program can be rather daunting to master and requires dedication.

Most users like Flash animation because the images in Flash movies — which don't look like movies at all, but more like moving Web pages — are clean and smooth. All in all, we like Flash and recommend using it, if you have the time to learn how to use it properly.

Flash is a topic worthy of an entire book. If you would like to explore it more fully, we recommend visiting Macromedia's site at `www.macromedia.com`. If you feel like you *need* an entire book, we suggest the *Flash MX Bible* by Robert Reinhardt and Snow Dowd *Macromedia Flash MX For Dummies* by Gurdy Leete and Ellen Finkelstein (both published by Wiley Publishing, Inc.).

Media Players for Audio and Video

Media can be stored in any number of formats these days; our need to store and transmit information in this form has resulted in numerous *media-rich players* that handle all audio, video, and other media formats. RealOne Player tries to be the player of choice — but with the advent of new compression formats (MP3, MPEG-4, and so on), developers and users alike have to upgrade constantly.

Plug-in applications are programs that users can download, install, and use as a part of their Web browsers. This type of application initially began with Netscape, when users could download, install, and define supplementary programs for audio or video. However, these applications were called "helper applications." This system is still used when you link to a media file.

Now, users can download *plug-in* applications that the browser recognizes automatically — these applications plug in to the browser. Once recognized, the plug-in allows all functions to be integrated into the rendered Web page (for example, when a media file is embedded in a Web page).

Users can download any number of possible plug-ins. Most users, however, wait until they *need* a particular plug-in before they download it.

RealNetworks

RealNetworks (then Progressive Networks) started the streaming audio craze in the mid-1990s — and soon independent players were popping up everywhere. RealNetworks went through a stage of production where versions of its software didn't support older versions of its own media formats — in short, the whole thing was a mess.

Now, however, RealNetworks has released RealOne Player, which provides an all-in-one player — it does streaming audio and video, constructs MP3 libraries, and can be used to burn CDs. You must have the RealOne Player to listen to .ra or .rv files.

Many *experienced* multimedia users prefer MP3 players (such as WinAmp or Sonique— or iTunes for the Mac), and streaming services such as Shoutcast. However, most less-experienced users out there are familiar with the RealOne Player. If you want to reach them where their audio preference lives, you can download the RealOne Player at www.real.com.

QuickTime

We like QuickTime, created by Apple, although it doesn't have the wide range support that the other players have. QuickTime supports most media formats, and supports about the same functionality as the other players mentioned in this section.

The only thing QuickTime can't do is rip MP3s or burn CDs. (That sort of thing is left up to iTunes, another Apple product.) QuickTime is also compatible with Flash, Cakewalk, Premiere, and other multimedia tools. Download a copy of this player at `www.apple.com/quicktime`.

Windows Media Player

The proprietary Windows answer to an all-in-one player has many of the same advantages as the RealOne Player. It supports streaming audio and video, DVD playback, encoding and burning audio files, as well as other multimedia-related functions. You must have the Windows Media Player to listen to `.wmp` files. Download the Windows Media Player at `www.microsoft.com/windows/windowsmedia/players.asp`.

Linking to Audio and Video

One method of getting users to access your multimedia content is by adding a hyperlink that leads to the audio or video file. This method is bar-none the easiest delivery method you can choose.

You can link to most audio and video file types (except for streaming formats). Here's how it works:

1. You use the `<a>` element to provide a link to the media file, like this:

2. When the user clicks the hyperlink, the media file opens in a separate media-player window.

We recommend providing your users with information about what they will be downloading. For example, you could provide the file format, size, and URL location. You should also provide a link to the appropriate media player in case your users have to download it first. Figure 13-1 shows a link to an MP3 file to download.

You cannot link to streaming formats. If linked, a streaming format downloads like any other media file, and will not play until completely downloaded — that is, it won't *stream*.

When you've created a media file, using one of the file types defined in the previous sections, you point to the file by using the `href` attribute, like so:

```
<a href="song.wav">Click Here to listen to a song.</a>
```

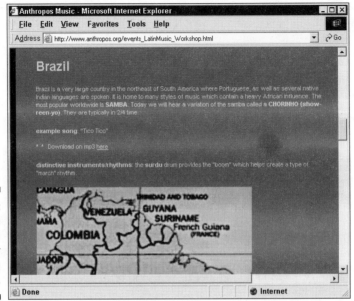

Figure 13-1:
This site
shows a
link for
downloading
an MP3 file.

Because we use a relative address for this audio file, the file must be located in the same directory as the Web page. If you wanted to link to a song not stored on your sever, you could point to the resource by using an absolute address, like this:

```
<a href="http://www.domain.com/song.wav">Click Here to listen to a song.</a>
```

When the user selects the link, the appropriate media player opens, and the audio file plays. The following is a complete example of the markup used to link to an audio file:

```
<html>
<head>
<title>Anthropos Arts</title>
</head>
<body>
<p>One popular form of music in Colombia is the CUMBIA (koom-bee-ya).
   It is typically in 4/4 time.</p>
<p>Example song: "La Piragua" / "The Little Boat"</p>
<p>Download "La Piragua" on mp3
   <a href="http://www.anthropos.org/media/mp3/laPiragua.mp3">here</a></p>
</body>
</html>
```

When the user selects the hyperlink to play an audio file, the browser looks for an appropriate player. If the user doesn't *have* an audio player installed (oops), the browser prompts the user to save the file. A dialog box may also appear, mentioning that the file is being saved to the user's hard drive.

If you're linking to someone else's audio or video file, make sure you have his or her permission to do so. (Look before you link.)

Embedding Audio and Video Files into Your Page

Embedding media components enables you to actually make media an integral part of how your Web page works. When the user activates the media file, it's played as part of the Web page — a separate window is not needed. Here's how it works:

1. You define controls that allow the user to activate the file.

2. The user clicks (for example) a Play button to play file is activated.

   For example, in Figure 13-2, clicking Play activates a song, which plays from within the Web page — no separate window needed.

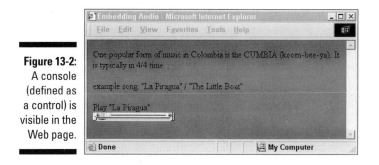

Figure 13-2:
A console (defined as a control) is visible in the Web page.

Although embedding a Flash animation file into your Web page has its own quirks, the concepts remain the same. Once embedded, a Flash movie begins the moment the user accesses its browser window. In this case, the user need not even activate a control.

You can use the `<embed>` or `<object>` element to embed a media file. Originally, developers used the `<embed>` element to embed a media file — not so today. Why? Well, the HTML standard doesn't support the `<embed>`

element (oh, *that*). This state of affairs is difficult for developers because Netscape traditionally supports the <embed> element, whereas Internet Explorer supports the <object> element (which is officially part of the HTML standard). Thus the browser wars continue.

To embed a video, you can use either the <embed> or the <object> element. As with media files, however, neither of these techniques will work in *all* browsers (namely, Netscape, Internet Explorer, and Opera). Such differences in support mean that if you want to reach the widest possible audience, you should provide a link and let the user download (or stream) the video file.

Okay, some of you will have an irresistible craving to embed a media file. Just remember: There are already several different ways to embed media, and we don't have the space to cover each option. To keep from spoiling your fun, however, we can provide you with a few examples.

Using the <embed> element

One of the most common ways to embed media is to use the <embed> element. Here's an example:

```
<html>
<head>
<title>Anthropos Arts</title>
</head>
<body>
<p>One popular form of music in Colombia is the CUMBIA (koom-bee-ya).
  It is typically in 4/4 time.</p>
<p>Example song: "La Piragua" / "The Little Boat"</p>
<p>Play "La Piragua":
  <embed src="http://www.anthropos.org/media/mp3/laPiragua.mp3"
  autostart="false" width="150" height="15"
  controls="smallconsole">here</a></p>
</body>
</html>
```

In this example, we used several attributes to define media properties. In addition to the attributes used in this example, you can add a few more:

✔ src="*filename*": Identifies the source file.

✔ autostart="false | true": Use this attribute to require sound to play automatically when the document renders, or to require users to activate the control.

✔ controls="console | smallconsole | playbutton | pausebutton | stopbutton | volumelever ": The controls attribute defines the type of control that will be displayed and serves as the interactive trigger for the user.

- ✔ width="*pixel*": The width attribute defines the width for the control being used.

- ✔ height="*pixel*": The height attribute defines the height for the control being used.

- ✔ loop="*n*" **or** ="true | false": The loop attribute enables you to specify the number of times an audio file should loop. The default is 1.

- ✔ align="left | right | center | justify": The align attribute functions the same as it does when used with the <img> element. The default is left.

Embedding the Windows Media Player

If you use the <embed> element, Internet Explorer users may not be able to access the media file. Therefore, if you're trying to reach a large audience, another recommended method is to embed the Windows Media Player as a part of Internet Explorer and Netscape. Although doing so won't reach *all* users, it will reach more than you'd reach by using the <embed> element.

Providing a link to the necessary media player helps users access your media.

The Windows Media Player is normally embedded into a page for Internet Explorer as an ActiveX Control using the <object> element (this does not work on Macs). For Netscape, the player is incorporated by using a plug-in defined by the <embed> element. If you use this technique, you can define the <embed> element within the <object> element (is that slick, or what?) — allowing this method to work for both Internet Explorer and Netscape — like this:

```
<object id="mediaplayer" width=320 height=310
  classid="clsid:22d6f312-b0f6-11d0-94ab-0080c74c7e95"
  codebase="http://activex.microsoft.com/activex/controls/mplayer/
  en/nsmp2inf.cab#version=5,1,52,701"
  standby= "loading media player" type="application/x-oleobject">
<param name="filename" value="movie.avi">
<param name="autostart" value="true">
<param name="showcontrols" value="true">
<param name="showstatusbar" value="true">
<embed type="application/x-mplayer2"
  pluginspage="http://www.microsoft.com/windows/mediaplayer/"
  src="video/movie.avi" width="320" height="310" name="mediaplayer"
  autostart="true" showstatusbar="1" showcontrols="1">
</embed>
</object>
```

All the items shown here in bold are variables that you would want to define yourself. The rest you can leave alone. Note, however, that you may want to change a few variables such as autostart.

Defining background audio

Internet Explorer supports a function that allows background music. First, define the Internet Explorer version:

```
<html>
<head>
<title>Anthropos Arts</title>
</head>
<body>
<bgsound src="http://www.anthropos.org/media/mp3/laPiragua.mp3">
<p>One popular form of music in Colombia is the CUMBIA (koom-bee-ya).
   It is typically in 4/4 time.</p>
<p>Example song: "La Piragua" / "The Little Boat"</p>
</body>
</html>
```

The <bgsound> element is not officially part of the HTML standard, so we don't recommend using it. If you do, you have to use the src attribute to define the audio file's location. (The only audio formats recognized with this tag are .wav, .au, and .mid.) You can also use a loop attribute to define how many times the audio file should loop. The values for the loop attribute can be a *number* (loop="5") or infinite (loop="infinite") to loop the audio file until the user leaves the Web page or goes into a deep trance (just kidding).

You can also indirectly define background music for Netscape by using an <embed> attribute. For your users to enjoy some background music, you use the <embed> element and set the autostart attribute to true (<embed autostart="true">).

Keep in mind that these attributes are not a part of the HTML standard. In the future, as Internet Explorer and Netscape provide stable support for the <object> element, you may want to make the switch and use it.

Streaming Audio and Video

To master *streaming media* (audio or video), you must first understand how a Web server, HTTP, and your browser work together. A Web page is stored on the Web server. When you open your browser and request a Web page, that request is sent to a Web server that then sends the information to the browser. The transaction is completed quickly, and then the Web server disconnects and goes on to handle other requests from other users.

On the other end of this transaction, your browser accepts the information from the Web server, renders it on the screen, and then ignores the Web server until you select a link.

On both ends, the server and the browser open and then close the transaction quickly. This scenario makes sense when you're dealing with basic HTML pages or image files, which have no need for a continuous connection.

Audio and video file types, on the other hand, contain an additional variable that affects how they behave: time. Audio and video files are considerably larger than images or HTML files, and take longer to download, so the open-and-shut scenario we just described doesn't work well at all for audio or video; users end up waiting impatiently for the download to complete.

Streaming uses new Internet technology that divides an audio or video file into packets sent continuously to the user. The streaming software on the other end receives these packets and reconstructs the audio file; the streaming player plays the packets as they're received.

One disadvantage to streaming media is that users with dialup connections might have problems with streaming media; the better (faster) the connection, the better the quality.

However, many developers point out that the streaming media option is used more to improve access (because the file can be viewed before the entire file has been downloaded) than to improve delivery quality. The trade-off — in effect, chancy quality for worldwide access — produces a video file that may be fuzzy at times, or an audio file that may occasionally pop or hiss at the user. Of course, streaming technologies are still relatively young; as their popularity grows, the technology will improve.

Streaming video behaves much like streaming audio; however, video has two main types of streaming: *progressive streaming* and *real-time streaming*. Progressive streaming, done on demand, uses HTTP to download a compressed video file from the Internet. Realtime streaming uses Real Time Streaming Protocol (RTSP) to broadcast video to your browser; your browser must access a video-streaming server.

Setting up a streaming media file is similar to linking or embedding it — except the linked or embedded media file is actually a *meta file* that contains the URL *locations* of the media files to be streamed. If a developer wants to set up a system that allows multiple streaming audio files (think online radio), server software must be used. If just want to stream a few audio files, you can use a Web server instead.

When you're creating streaming audio, you need to create three files:

- ✔ **Media file:** As with all other methods, you need the audio file; if you're using RealNetworks, the audio file should be created with RealProducer and have a .rm extension.

- ✔ **Meta file:** This text document points to where the audio file can be found on the server; if you're using RealNetworks, the meta file should be created with a text editor and have a .ram or .rpm extension.

- ✔ **HTML document:** The HTML document should reference the meta file by using the <a> element.

Check with your Internet service provider to see whether it has a streaming-media server in place. If it does, you won't have to use the Web server.

You can also embed a RealMedia file by using the <embed> element. Just remember that the <embed> element is not well supported.

Chapter 14

Integrating a Database into Your HTML

. . . .

In This Chapter

▶ Understanding what a database can add to your HTML

▶ Integrating a database with your Web pages

▶ Finding a host for your database-enabled Web pages

. . . .

Databases can store vast amounts of information — from sales records to baseball statistics and more — that you might want to make available to visitors to your Web site. Although you *could* hand-code hundreds of Web pages with the data in the database, it would take nearly forever to put the site up — and maintenance would be a nightmare. Instead, it makes much more sense to connect your Web site to the database and let them work together to serve information. And that is exactly how thousands of Web developers post and manage complex data on the Web.

Before you actually wrestle your HTML into a working relationship with a database, you need to have some major items already in place. In particular, you need to have a Web server running a program (often a custom-coded CGI script) that tells the database exactly what to do. (CGI stands for Common Gateway Interface; when a Web page needs to connect to a database, the CGI script passes on the instructions to the database.) Even with the most sophisticated techniques, you face a considerable investment of time and work. That's why this chapter gives you an overview of the process, what it can do for you, and what to watch out for — so you can decide for yourself whether the payoff is worth the effort.

Understanding the Advantages of Using Database Technology on the Web

First things first. A *database* is a bunch of data that has been organized in a way that makes it easy for users to find individual pieces of information. You can organize, manage, delete, and add data to the database, and depending on the database's capabilities, you can access data using a variety of methods. You can also store a lot of different kinds of data; pretty much anything that can be categorized can be put into a database.

Oracle, MySQL, Sybase, and SQL Server are just a few of the databases out there, and chances are you've heard of at least one of them. Later in the chapter, we take a look at the different kinds of databases so you can begin to sort through your options and choose the database that is right for you (or know what you're working with if your database has already been chosen for you).

The benefits of integrating a database with your HTML are striking:

- ✔ **Databases hold and organize a great deal of information.** In particular, databases maintain the relationships between different pieces of data (for example, a link between an address and the person who lives there). You can manage and keep track of data in a database more effectively than you can in just about any other format.

- ✔ **Advanced query languages such as SQL extract data from a database according to detailed criteria.** You can build these criteria into your Web page so that the page gets and displays only certain pieces of data (such as all in-stock products immediately available for shipment, or all users who have ordered a product in the last 15 days).

  SQL stands for Structured Query Language, and it's a language for working with databases to make the stored data more accessible.

- ✔ **Your Web site can interact with the data in the database.** For example, it can help people provide you with information to plug into your database, such as product orders or contact information. They don't have to tell you over the phone or have a special application to access your database; all they need is a Web browser and a URL to get to your site.

- ✔ **Your Web site can update itself automatically as the data in the database changes.** In effect, you won't have to update your Web page at all. Each time the page loads, it gets the latest batch of data from the database. All you need do is keep the database up to date.

Linking Databases to Your Web Page: The Basics

Imagine this scenario: You already have a database that catalogs products, prices, availability, and customer data. (Maybe you're using Microsoft Access, SQL Server, Oracle, or FileMakerPro.) You typically use the information in the database to create print catalogs and to manage customer orders you receive in the mail and on the phone. Now you want to move the whole operation to the Web. You have a couple of options:

✔ **Create a static online catalog.** You could use the information in your catalog to create a collection of standard HTML pages with all product information hard-coded into the page. You could create a separate order form that users would fill out and either snail-mail or fax to you. Every time information changes in your actual database, you have to change the data on the Web pages.

✔ **Build an interactive online catalog on-the-fly.** You could connect the database to your Web site and create your catalog on-the-fly by using information pulled from the database in real time (rather than hard-coded into the HTML). Users could place orders online and skip the mailbox, fax, or phone all together.

These two approaches illustrate a tradeoff of know-how versus hassle factor. The first approach requires the least technical know-how but will be (at best) clunky and difficult to maintain. The second takes advantage of HTML and programming techniques to create a Web site that interfaces directly with your database. It's easier to maintain — but it requires more technical know-how.

A bit about SQL

Structured Query Language, or *SQL,* is the syntax you use to work with data in a database. You phrase your communications with a database as *queries.* Queries can be simple (say, searching the database for *all products* without applying any other criteria) or they can bristle with complexity — as when (for example) you search a product database for all products *from a particular manufacturer* that are *in stock* and then do an inventory of *at least ten items* that *weren't* recently purchased *by a particular customer.*

The rules you use to bind your search are called *criteria.* You also use SQL queries to write data into the database, modify data that's already in there, and (of course) delete data when it's outlived its usefulness. If you use a form on a Web page to collect a user's contact information, you have to convert the information the user provides into an SQL query and then feed it into the database (more about how this works in the next section of the chapter).

If you're going to build a Web site that integrates a database with your HTML, it's wise to study up a bit on SQL so you can properly phrase your communications with the database. Every database has its own particular version of SQL, but they're all just slight variations on a theme; SQL itself follows some consistent general rules. Therefore, if you're already familiar with one database's SQL, you can easily pick up another's. If you aren't at all familiar with SQL, no problem — the final section in this chapter points you to some good references.

When you connect a database to your Web site, you essentially link a source of data (the fields in the database) to your markup. When users request Web pages, the final results are a combination of the HTML you've created and the data in the database. (We go into more detail on how this all works in the next section, "What You Need to Add a Database to Your HTML.")

As you might imagine, integrating a database with your Web pages takes a serious commitment, a substantial amount of work, and above-average technical know-how. But that's not an excuse to ignore the possibilities. Change can be good, after all, and as better tools emerge, the possibility that you can link a database to your Web page without having to morph into a complete propeller-head increases. In the long run, if you plan to make a lot of information available to users through your Web site, linking a database to your site is a necessity. If you're not ready to make the leap just yet, the main challenge is to get a strong sense of exactly how the pieces of a database-driven Web site fit together. Then you can scope out not *whether* to link database to your HTML, but *how* you want your site to interact with your database.

What You Need to Add a Database to Your HTML

If you want to integrate a database with your HTML to give your Web pages access to the data in the database, you need the following basics:

- A database program (running on a database server)
- Instructions embedded in your HTML pages that request information from the database
- A set of programming tools that enables you to communicate with both the database *and* your Web server

   Use Figure 14-1 to see how everything fits together to create a complete, data-driven Web solution.

Your Web server, database, and the Web application that interfaces between the Web server and the database can all peacefully coexist on the same system as long as there's enough memory to run all the applications without problems. However, Figure 14-1 shows the Web server on a system that runs an intermediary Web application, and a separate system that houses the database.

The next several sections of this chapter delve into the particulars of each element.

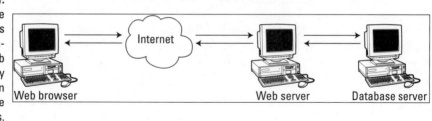

Figure 14-1:
The
components
of a data-
driven Web
solution may
exist on
separate
systems.

Web browser   Web server   Database server

A database

Of course, before you can create a data-driven solution that integrates a database with your HTML, you need a database. Database programs come in all shapes and sizes, with a wide array of features, and to fit all budgets. If you already have a database that you want to connect to a Web site, chances are you won't need to choose a new one. There's no need to reinvent your database just to fit your Web site. In fact, attaching a Web site to an existing database that you already use for (say) taking customer orders or tracking assets, gives you another creative way to work with that data.

If, however, you need to create a database from scratch, you'll need to investigate some of your options to find the database that is right for you. The following sections give you a peek at some of the most popular databases so you can get an idea of where to start looking.

This list of databases isn't exhaustive. There are many other databases you can choose from, and if the database your data is currently housed in isn't on this list, don't panic. The goal of the list is to introduce you to some examples of the types of databases you can choose from. Your Internet Service Provider (ISP) or your company's IT group are good resources to help you get a handle on what databases your Web server can manage and to help you choose the best database for your needs.

Free and powerful: MySQL

MySQL is a free, open-source database that runs on most flavors of Unix (including Linux and Solaris), as well as all versions of Windows from 98 to XP. Best of all, MySQL is available free of charge — and is a robust database for the money (or lack thereof). Did we mention it's free?

If you need to get a database up and running inexpensively (or you're just learning to work with databases), MySQL is a good choice. It runs very well on Unix and Linux — the most popular platforms for serving up Web pages — so it plays well with other major Web applications.

However, MySQL does have its limitations. If your MySQL database crashes (as every database eventually will), you have to put more work into recovering backed up data than you would if you were using a heavier-duty database (such as those we discuss shortly).

Because of its sketchiness in the area of retrieving lost data, this isn't the ideal database for you if your site meets any of the following criteria:

✔ The site has to handle thousands of immediate transactions (as shopping sites or banks might).

✔ The site requires continuous updating.

✔ The site must recover from crashes quickly with minimal interruption of service.

In the real world, MySQL is great for lightweight to medium-weight Web sites. You can definitely run a product catalog with it, or a museum-exhibit tracking site, or a school-attendance and grade-book system.

The only time you should seriously avoid MySQL is when you manage large numbers of financial transactions. Otherwise you can count on MySQL to provide a solid database that will meet just about any Web site need — and do it for free. To learn more about MySQL, visit `www.mysql.com`.

Windows- and user-friendly: Microsoft Access

Microsoft Access has been around for a long time — it's a popular database for storing key business information (such as contact lists, inventory catalogs, and time-tracking systems). Access is a Windows-only application, popular because it offers an easy-to-use system for creating the forms used to access the database. You can run a Microsoft Access database on your company's internal network, create a set of custom forms, and install them on any Windows machine in the company — just as you would any Windows application.

If you've never used a database before, have access to Microsoft Office, and are looking for a good learning tool, Access might be a good candidate. Unlike the databases developed with database experts in mind, Access is designed to be helpful and user-friendly; it plays nicely with other Office products.

Chances are you'll eventually build a Web site database using MySQL, Microsoft SQL Server, or another (more powerful) database product. Because Access is so user-friendly, it tends to be slower than other databases and not as robust.

If you have a legacy Access database and you want to give others access to it via the Web, you can use Microsoft's Active Server Pages (ASP) to do so, as discussed later in this chapter.

To learn more about Microsoft Access, visit www.microsoft.com/office/access/.

The big boys: Oracle, Sybase, and Microsoft SQL Server

Beyond MySQL and Access (and others in the small- to medium-size application world) are the big boys: Oracle, Sybase, and Microsoft SQL Server — to name three of the most popular and well known. These are the most powerful and versatile databases money can buy, and it usually takes quite a bit of money to buy them.

The importance of good database design

If you've never worked with databases before and you're ready to try your hand at Access, MySQL, or another lighter-duty database, be sure to spend some time getting a handle on good database design. Although you must (obviously) learn how to create and manage databases, you'll find that the actual database design is at least as important as whether you can get the thing up and running in the first place.

Database design refers to the way in which you organize that data in the database. You want your organization to make sense from a data perspective, which isn't always the same as from a human perspective. For instance, if you think of a person's name, you most likely think of first name, middle name, and last name as a whole entity. However, when you put together a database, you want to keep each of those names in its own, separate field — doing so gives you more flexibility for searching. Instead of searching for a generic name (which may return more names than you want to sift through), you can search by first name, last name, middle name, or by some combination of the three.

Several general principles of a good database design are worth remembering. A good database

✔ Makes data as useful and accessible as possible *to computer systems* — not necessarily to people, unless they know how to use those systems to best advantage.

✔ Is generic enough to accommodate new types of data.

✔ Is specific enough to manage the details of your data efficiently.

✔ Should be *extensible* so it can grow and change with your data needs. If you know (for example) that presently you need only track products from one manufacturer — but may one day need to track products from several — it makes sense to prepare the database *now* to manage multiple manufacturers later.

The resources at the end of this chapter include books and Web sites that can give you a good look at database-design techniques. Keep in mind, however, that no matter how much you read about good database design, eventually you have to start creating and working with actual databases; there's no substitute for real-world experience.

These databases feature the following:

- ✔ Complete security
- ✔ Immediate recovery from crashes using *transaction rollback* (a feature that restores a database to the way it was right before the crash)
- ✔ Entire suites of plug-ins and applications that integrate seamlessly
- ✔ All the tools you need to create and manage huge databases

If you're just starting out with databases, remember that these products are not designed as learning tools. Their complexity and industrial-strength features are more appropriate to invest in when you need to build a large, robust database. Even then, the best advice we can give you is not to fork over the big bucks until you've consulted with database- and Web-development experts to determine the best collection of technology to meet your needs. If you're even thinking about buying Oracle (for example) or integrating a Web site with an Oracle database, professional help is indispensable.

To learn more about Oracle databases, visit `www.oracle.com`.

To learn more about Sybase databases, visit `www.sybase.com`.

To learn more about Microsoft SQL Server, visit `www.microsoft.com/sql/default.asp`.

Instructions embedded in your HTML pages

Yes, it's true — HTML doesn't include a single element or attribute for querying a database. (Skim Appendix A, the complete listing of elements and attributes in HTML 4.01, if you don't believe us.) There's no mention of the word *database* anywhere in there. Zip. Zilch. Zero. Nada.

Even so, you have to get those instructions for working with a database into your HTML *somehow.* The typical way is to manage all database interaction through a programming or scripting language in conjunction with the HTML in your Web pages. The scripting sits right in your HTML page, and some of it may sit in other scripts that run on your Web server.

The good news is that *you don't have to create these scripts yourself.* Instead, you can choose from a variety of *Web-development* or *Web-application languages* — or is that *solutions?* — the buzz-words for these languages seem to change almost daily. Regardless of nomenclature, all such languages have one thing in common: They help you extend the functionality of your Web page way beyond what HTML can provide.

If you suspect that these languages — and some others covered in the book, such as JavaScript (Chapter 12) and CGI (covered in this chapter) — might just all work together, provided you can guide the display with HTML markup, you're right! This approach can create feature-rich Web sites that border on software applications. Imagine a complicated Web site that manages customers, takes orders, directs shipping, and uses all these technologies, along with database connectivity, to take Web sites far beyond simple text-and-image-driven pages. (But will it make coffee . . . ?)

The next three sections provide an overview of the most popular Web-application development languages. They are intended to give you an overview of what your options are, not present an exhaustive list. The list of resources at the end of the chapter will point you toward Web sites and books that cover other Web development options and solutions.

PHP

PHP (sort of a redundant acronym that stands for *PHP: Hypertext Preprocessor*) uses a set of custom tags that begin with `<?` and end with `?>` that you embed into your HTML. When a user requests a Web page, a PHP processor on the Web server interprets the tags, does things like connects to a database or checks the date and time, and then replaces the PHP tags with the results of the instructions. If the instructions request that the PHP processor query the database for all users named John Doe, the processor does that, and then replaces the request in the HTML with the actual results of the request.

For example, this HTML uses the PHP `echo()` function and the `HTTP_USER_AGENT` variable, along with some HTML, to print the name of the browser (formally called a *user agent*) that the person viewing the PHP-enabled page is using:

```
<html>
  <head>
    <title>A simple PHP example</title>
  </head>

  <body>
    <p>Hello. You are viewing this page with
       <?php echo $_SERVER["HTTP_USER_AGENT"]; ?>.
    </p>
  </body>
</html>
```

And now for some superfluous, geeky information

Message to the geekiest readers of this book (that is, those with a little background in programming): You can integrate ASP.NET with Visual Basic or other Windows applications, and you can integrate JSP with Java applications. This means you can create faster, more powerful applications optimized for a particular operating system in Visual Basic, C++, or Java and use either ASP.NET or JSP to take the information from those applications and feed it to your Web page. (If you have no idea what you have just read, you obviously go out and have fun on Saturday nights.)

When the Web server receives a request for the HTML page, it passes it off to the PHP application that evaluates

```
<?php echo $_SERVER["HTTP_USER_AGENT"]; ?>
```

to get the name of the Web browser and then replaces the function with the actual name of the browser. The PHP application passes the HTML page back to the Web server, which in turn, sends it to the Web browser.

Some JavaScript commands embedded in HTML pages are especially designed for the browser to interpret and use after the page is downloaded. PHP tags, on the other hand, are intended to be evaluated and be replaced *by the PHP application* long before the HTML page even makes its way to the Web browser. Browsers don't understand PHP elements; therefore, the server must process those elements first.

If the user who requested this page were using Netscape Navigator 4.5 on a Macintosh, the results of this HTML/PHP combination would be:

```
Hello. You are viewing this page with Mozilla/4.5 (Macintosh; I; PPC).
```

Obviously, this example is very simplistic and doesn't include any database calls. However, PHP uses this exact same methodology to query databases. After you know PHP syntax and some SQL, the rest is gravy.

PHP is an open-source Web-development application that runs on just about any operating system. You often find it used with MySQL, but you can use it with just about any database. Of course, having some programming experience is a definite plus if you're going to use PHP, but it's a good option if you're just beginning to experiment with Web applications. You can get the goods on PHP at www.php.net.

ASP.NET and JSP

ASP.NET is Microsoft's Web-application language; JSP is Sun's Web-application language (based, of course, on Java). Both work much like PHP; their proprietary tag structures are different, but everything else is the same. When a user requests an ASP or JSP page from the server, the server hands the page to the ASP or JSP processor. Then the processor interprets the custom codes, makes any calls to databases and other applications, replaces the custom codes with text and markup, and sends the page to the Web server to pass along to the Web browser. (Busy, busy, busy.)

The ASP.NET processor isn't free (as you might imagine); however, JSP processors from Sun and other vendors *are* available for free. ASP.NET runs best on Microsoft servers (no surprise there), but can run on Unix and its variations. JSP runs on both Windows and Unix servers with nearly equal ease.

TIP

Do it yourself or hire an expert?

By now you might have noticed that integrating a database with your HTML pages can be a little complex. As we mentioned at the beginning of the chapter, you'll need to acquire some expertise to make databases play well with your HTML. So the question becomes, when should you hire an expert to do your Web development for you? There is no straightforward answer, but in general, you should consider hiring an expert if you don't know much about programming or databases and need to build a mission-critical Web site.

It may seem less expensive in the short term to invest some time and master all the related technologies yourself — but the inevitable beginner's mistakes can prevent your site from working the way you'd like it to, and may not keep it from crashing frequently. However, if you're looking to build a standard application — such as an online store or other e-commerce endeavor — many hosting providers provide access to applications they have already built for the purpose, and are running for a monthly fee. That option means that maybe you can have your site up and running quickly, without learning the details of the technologies yourself, and without having to pay up front for a developer (or team of developers) to build it. Check it out.

The downside to this approach is that you have to live with the functionality that the application comes with; you can't customize it. So, before you make your decision, carefully evaluate what the application offers; be sure it meets your needs adequately. If it doesn't, struggling to make do with the application may make you wish you had built one from scratch to begin with.

If, of course, you're just putting together a small Web site for fun (or have some time to dig into new technologies), then by all means take the time to acquire these skills for yourself. They will be useful in the long run, and you can build an application that fits you to a tee. You might consider having a professional help you with the design, but once you have a good design, you may have the time and energy to finish the implementation yourself.

To learn more about ASP.NET, visit `www.microsoft.com/net/`.

To learn more about JSP, visit `http://java.sun.com/products/jsp/`.

A connection between your Web server and the database

A Web server handles all requests for Web pages and other resources from outside users *and* from your HTML pages themselves. If an HTML page asks for an image, the server serves it up. If an HTML page asks for an audio file, the server serves it up. If an HTML page asks for data from a database, however, the server needs some guidance. Serving images and media are part of what a Web server is designed to do. Serving database connections is a whole other kettle of fish.

To help your Web server (and consequently your HTML) make a connection to the database and fetch data from it, you must have an application that runs on the Web server that can process requests from the PHP, ASP, JSP, or other custom tags you write into your Web pages. As we mention in the previous section, PHP, ASP, and JSP processors interpret the custom tags you use to add commands to HTML. For those processors to interact with the database, you need a database connection, usually an Open Database Connection (ODBC).

Every database has small programs called *drivers* that act as connectors, working with the various Web-application processors so the main processor can connect to the database. When you're choosing a Web-application language, be sure it has a driver available for your database of choice. Chances are you'll find what you need, but it doesn't hurt to double-check.

Finding Database Support from Your ISP or IT Department

As you get ready to integrate a database into your HTML with PHP, ASP, JSP, or some other Web-application language, take the time to find out whether your ISP (or department) actually *supports* the database and language you plan to use. (Details, details . . .)

You need to have a processor and a database driver available on your Web server to add database commands to your HTML — and to have those commands translated in the queries that go to the database.

Although most ISPs let you put just about any collection of text, images, and other media files on your Web site, many have strict rules about what applications and databases you can use. Databases require maintenance, and applications suck up memory and processor speed. Chances are you won't have access to your Web server if an ISP manages your application and database; you'll need to rely on the tech support staff of the ISP to do it. Make sure they can and will.

Many ISPs now offer MySQL and PHP support; some even offer JSP and other database support. If you want to use a database in tandem with a Web-application language, check with the folks at your ISP first to see whether they'll let you use the ones you have in mind. If your ISP doesn't have the support you need, you may have to change ISPs.

If you're working on a Web server hosted by your company's internal IT department, work with them to find out what databases and languages they're willing to support. It won't do you any good to choose a JSP/MySQL solution if your entire IT department runs on Microsoft and wants you to use an ASP/SQL server solution instead.

Find Out More

This chapter outlines the basic options and issues associated with connecting a database to your HTML pages. The more ambitious your vision for an HTML-database pairing, the more you'll need to know about what you're getting yourself into before you, uh, get yourself into it. To find out more about databases and Web applications, you can consult the following Web sites and books (all books published by Wiley Publishing, Inc.):

✔ Builder.com's resources on databases: `http://builder.com/builder/sub_area.jhtml?id=w108`

✔ Builder.com's programming and scripting resources: `http://builder.cnet.com/webbuilding/0-3882.html`

✔ Webmonkey's ASP resources: `http://hotwired.lycos.com/webmonkey/programming/asp/`

✔ Webmonkey's PHP resources: `http://hotwired.lycos.com/webmonkey/programming/php/`

✔ Webmonkey's Database resources: `http://hotwired.lycos.com/webmonkey/backend/databases/`

✔ *ASP.NET For Dummies* by Bill Hatfield

✔ *JavaServer Pages For Dummies* by Mac Rinehart

✔ *SQL For Dummies* by Allen G. Taylor

- *MySQL/PHP Database Applications,* 2nd Edition, by Jay Greenspan and Brad Bulger
- *FileMaker Pro 6 Bible* by Steven A. Schwartz
- *MySQL: Your Visual Blueprint for Creating Open Source Databases* by Michael Moncur
- *PHP Bible,* 2nd Edition, by Tim Converse and Joyce Park
- *MySQL Bible* by Steve Suehring
- *SQL Weekend Crash Course* by Allen G. Taylor
- *MySQL Weekend Crash Course* by Jay Greenspan
- *PHP and MySQL For Dummies* by Janet Valade

Chapter 15

How HTML Relates to Other Markup Languages

*H*TML is a great and wonderful thing — after all, it's the cornerstone of Web pages and has been instrumental in making the Web a prime communications medium. However, HTML does have its limitations (as you've no doubt begun to notice as you create and maintain your own Web pages).

At the heart of these limitations is the finite collection of elements and attributes included in the HTML specification. Even though HTML has evolved over time, and additional elements and attributes have been added, along with support for style sheets, no way can HTML possibly provide every element or attribute you'd like it to have.

HTML was designed to describe text-based documents built primarily of paragraphs, headings, lists, and similar elements, and it does that very well. But there's lots of other kinds of data, such as manufacturer ID numbers, course titles, car parts, recipe ingredients and instructions, and financial data. The idea of using text-based markup to describe that type of data (and a million other kinds) for the Web sure does make sense, so it's not surprising that in the past several years, the need for something different, more extensive, more flexible, and more robust became clear. Enter XML.

Defining Extensibility

The Extensible Markup Language (XML) is the descendent of the mother of all markup languages (literally), Standard Generalized Markup Language (SGML). SGML is a *metalanguage,* a language for creating other markup languages. XHTML is a child of XML that recasts HTML in XML format.

The HTML DTDs are written in SGML, which technically makes HTML an SGML vocabulary, but because HTML is a defined vocabulary with a limited set of elements, it doesn't contain any of SGML's extensibility features.

Here are the differences among HTML, XML, and XHTML, in a nutshell:

- ✔ **HTML:** Designed for describing a specific kind of data (text-based), HTML defines the appearance of text and embedded objects, such as images, ensuring a consistency in data description that browsers can predict and work with. In plain-vanilla HTML markup, a heading is always a heading, and that heading generally looks a certain way in most browsers. The problem is that HTML handles a finite number of elements and attributes, yet there are infinite kinds of data people want to include on Web pages.

- ✔ **XML:** The best way to think of XML is as a set of rules for defining data. What makes XML *extensible* is the fact that, as long as you follow the rules, you can write markup to define data of any type for any kind of output. (Display on the Web is one of a million kinds of output to choose from.) You're in the driver's seat, defining elements and attributes as determined by the needs of your particular project, and you can link your markup to just about any program imaginable.

- ✔ **XHTML:** A reworked version of HTML 4 in XML syntax, XHTML is HTML, The Next Generation. With XHTML, you can use XML rules to define new elements and attributes for display. Theoretically, XHTML is God's gift to the control freak: You can define any kind of data (you're only limited by your imagination), and you can also control its visual display.

Web browsers know and love HTML, so as long as you create Web pages that use good ol' HTML, browsers will know what to do with them. Because XML, and by extension XHTML, allow you to create your own markup, there's no way a Web browser can be prepared to display your custom elements without a little help. If you want to use XHTML to create your own markup, you'll need to use a style sheet to give browsers the help they need to display your own kind of markup.

XML: Extending Your Markup

XML is a pared-down version of SGML with 10 percent of the complexity and 90 percent of its extensibility. XML enables authors to create their own customized markup — and that means extensibility (which HTML, with its predefined element set, can't offer). Whereas HTML took some inspiration from SGML (and maybe even gobbled up some of its aspects), XML is a direct descendent of SGML — which means you can create any set of markup you like with XML — the sky's the limit.

The end-all, be-all resource for information related to XML is the W3C's XML pages, at `www.w3.org/XML`. Another great site is O'Reilly and Seybold's XML.com at `www.xml.com`. This chapter can scratch the surface of what XML is and why you should care — but these sites are chock-full of information and resources to help you get up to speed quickly with XML.

Understanding how XML works

To get a good idea of what XML can do that HTML can't, think about the different items that might be included in the description of a product in a catalog. For each product you might have a name, a short and long description, a picture, a vendor, a price, and more. HTML doesn't really have elements that help you define a product's price any differently from the way you define its name. You can, however, use list items, even paragraphs, to define a product in HTML, like this:

```
<h2>Widget 2345</h2>
<p>This widget makes your business run more smoothly.</p>
<a href="widget_2345_large.gif"><img src="widget_2345_small.gif"></a>
<ol>
    <li><b>Product Number:</b> 11098</li>
    <li><b>Price:</b> $129.95</li>
    <li><b>Vendor:</b> Widgets International</li>
    <li><b>Available:</b> Ships in 24 hours</li>
</ol>
```

Although this HTML is enough to help post information about this widget on a Web page, it doesn't tell much else about the widget. If you tried to send this information to a business partner and use it to share data about your widget stock, the markup wouldn't tell him or her much about the data in the page. However, see how XML can make a difference in how the markup describes information:

```
<product id="11098" available="24">
  <name>Widget 2345</name>
  <description>This widget makes your business run more smoothly.</description>
  <image type="thumbnail" src="widget_2345_small.gif" />
  <image type="large" src="widget_2345_large.gif />
  <price currency="US">129.95</price>
  <vendor>WI</vendor>
</product>
```

Notice how this XML tells you so much more about the product than the HTML did. That's the beauty of XML — you create markup that perfectly describes your content.

Of course, a Web browser wouldn't be able to make much of this XML because browsers can't possibly know how to display every element anyone might come up with. Which leads us to an important bit of information about XML. XML's primary focus is to define content, not display.

When you work with XML, you're working to carefully describe your content, without any regard for how it's displayed. In fact, *display* of content isn't even XML's most significant use. XML has become the de facto method for *describing* content so computers can share it. Web sites and other computer systems pass XML-described data back and forth around the Web because the XML tells those systems all they need to know to work with the data after they've received it.

As you might expect, however, XML can be used with style sheets that help browsers and other clients display your content. Display isn't everything in today's world, but it's still something you often have to attend to.

The XML FAQ at www.ucc.ie/xml/ is a great place to get more information about what XML is and what you can use it for.

Introducing DTDs

The beginnings of your XML endeavor must begin with the XML document. You have to carefully construct the elements to follow the markup syntax rules outlined by the XML specification. Then, you have to create a Document Type Definition (DTD) that defines how these elements interact.

All of the XML behavioral rules are created in a DTD. With HTML, the DTD was created for you, which explains why you have a limited number of predefined elements to work with. With XML, however, you can create your own DTD; therefore, you create your own element set and the rules that govern that element set.

This is where the *extensibility* comes in: You can create your own DTD — and therefore, your own element set, which you can extend whenever you want.

We cannot get to the details of XML because that's a whole other book — no, really, it is! (Check out *XML For Dummies,* 3rd Edition, written by Ed Tittel and Natanya Pitts and published by Wiley Publishing, Inc.)

Introducing XHTML

XHTML is really just HTML reworked to adhere to the rules of the XML specification — the syntax rules for creating XML markup — and associated with the XHTML DTD (which is nothing more than a list of what elements and attributes you'll find in XHTML).

The *X* in XHTML means that not only can you work with the predetermined element set defined in the XHTML DTD (the same elements found in HTML 4.0), but you can also add any other markup you want into the fray — as long as the markup follows XML rules.

If XML is the markup of the future, and XHTML is HTML in XML syntax, then is there any good reason *not* to start using XHTML immediately? Well, probably yes — just as good reasons exist for seriously considering XHTML as your markup of choice for Web pages (those are coming up shortly). Although, if you decide to switch, you'll find it's really not all that hard; however, jumping right into XHTML may not be the best way to accomplish your purposes. It's worth pausing a minute to consider. . . .

Avoiding mutant markup

Although XHTML (and XML in general) enables you to extend the element set with your own markup, always remember that some application somewhere (usually a Web browser when you talk about HTML or XHTML) has to work with your markup. Most Web browsers don't know what to do with the custom elements and attributes that you might throw into the middle of an XHTML document. Browsers may read XHTML, but don't expect them to read Joe's Wildly Customized Mutant Markup Language. Before you start creating your own markup for fun and profit, you should take some time to get firmly grounded in the purpose and rules of XML so you understand exactly how to get results.

Deciding whether to switch to XHTML

XHTML 1.0 and the next version of HTML are one and the same, and there's been a lot of discussion among Web developers recently about the prudence of making an early switch from HTML to XHTML. In the end, the decision is yours, but you'll be better served if you have some information to mull over while you make your decisions.

Here's a sketch of why switching to XHTML may make good sense:

- ✔ XHTML is the future of Web page markup, so you might as well get used to it now.

- ✔ If you're using Web pages as part of a larger XML solution (such as an online catalog, financial-services site, or content-management solution), you'll want all your markup to adhere to the XML specification. If it does, you can include other XML markup in your documents.

- ✔ XHTML leads to cleaner, better-structured Web pages than HTML does simply because the rules of XML demand well-structured documents.

On the other hand, here are some reasons why you might want to hold off on switching to XHTML:

- ✔ Older Web browsers have some problems with documents that adhere to XHTML syntax. For example, in XHTML empty elements like the image element must have a slash (/) before the greater than sign (>), and some old browsers (2.0 versions, mostly) have problems interpreting this markup.

- ✔ You don't really need to make the switch for your pages to work on the Web. If you have hundreds of Web pages already written in functioning HTML, there's no reason to retrofit them with XHTML if your only goal is to present content on the Web.

A good recommendation (going forward, at least) is to get comfortable using HTML — and to keep in mind that yet another level exists, beyond that known to ordinary HTML. When you've mastered HTML, you can begin experimenting with XHTML. The elements and attributes are the same, but the syntax of XHTML is a bit more rigorous (and less forgiving of markup errors).

Tips for switching to XHTML

If you do decide to make the switch to XHTML, this section includes a few practical rules to follow, each one basic to creating markup in XML.

All XML documents (and that means XHTML documents) must be *well-formed* — which means they adhere to all the basic rules outlined here.

Rule 1: Always nest correctly

Overlapping your elements is illegal in XML (and, hence, verboten in XHTML); you must nest your tags correctly. Repeat the following mantra over and over again: *What you open first, you close last.*

If you're shaking your head and saying, "Huh?" here's an example to clear things up — in fact, an incorrect one:

```
<p>What you open <em>first</em>, you must close <em>last</p></em>
```

See that offender in bold? Please don't do that. The following is correct:

```
<p>What you open <em>first</em>, you must close <em>last</em></p>
```

Take a close look at both examples to make sure you're clear.

Rule 2: Always include so-called "optional" ending tags

Although you may be sorely tempted to omit that ending </p> tag, such a deed is a no-no according to the XML Commandments. This rule does not include empty elements (which are *forbidden* to have a closing tag, as decreed in Rule 6).

The current rule goes something like this: If an element has a closing tag, whether optional or required in HTML, you must include it in your XHTML markup.

This is incorrect:

```
<ul>
    <li>list item one
    <li>list item two
</ul>
```

This is correct:

```
<ul>
    <li>list item one</li>
    <li>list item two</li>
</ul>
```

Rule 3: Attribute values must always be quoted

This rule requires a little effort: Attribute values must always be quoted. You can use both single (') or double (") quotation marks. It doesn't matter which ones you choose, as long as you include them. (And, so you don't confuse people who view your source code, be consistent and use one or the other.)

This is incorrect:

```
<colgroup span=40 width=15>
...
</colgroup>
```

This is correct:

```
<colgroup span="40" width="15">
...
</colgroup>
```

Rule 4: All element and attribute names must be lowercase

Unlike HTML, XML and XHTML are case-sensitive. For this reason, you must always use lowercase when naming elements and attributes. This rule doesn't apply to attribute values — only attribute names and element names.

This is incorrect:

```
<INPUT TYPE="CHECKBOX" NAME="PET" VALUE="CAT">
```

This is correct:

```
<input type="CHECKBOX" name="PET" value="CAT">
```

Rule 5: Attribute name-value pairs cannot stand alone

In HTML, you find a couple of instances of attributes as standalone text strings, such as `compact` or `checked`. These standalone strings are not allowed in XML. You can work around this problem by setting standalone attributes as equal to themselves. Silly? Sure, but it's an XHTML rule — and it works.

This is incorrect:

```
<input type="CHECKBOX" name="PET" value="CAT" checked>
```

This is correct:

```
<input type="CHECKBOX" name="PET" value="CAT" checked="checked">
```

Rule 6: Empty elements must end their start tag with />

The easiest way to comply with this rule is to include a `/>` at the end of all your empty elements. To ensure that older browsers can understand this construct, include a space before the trailing `/` and `>`.

You also want to avoid simply adding an end tag (which is legal but not always understood by older browsers).

This is incorrect:

```
<img src="graphic.gif">
```

This is correct:

```
<img src="graphic.gif" />
```

Note the space after the filename and before the trailing />.

Rule 7: You must include a DOCTYPE declaration

The DOCTYPE declaration is what references the DTD. This is not required by browsers, but because you're following XML rules in your XHTML markup, and because you want your page to validate against a DTD, you can't leave it out. The declaration looks like this:

```
<!DOCTYPE html PUBLIC "-//W3C//DTD XHTML 1.0 Strict//EN"
  "DTD/xhtml1-strict.dtd">
```

The DTD must appear before the root element — that is, the <html> tag — and must follow the previous syntax. Here's the declaration broken down:

- **Declaration keyword:** <!DOCTYPE
- **Type of document:** html
- **Identifier keyword:** PUBLIC
- **Public identifier:** "-//W3C//DTD XHTML 1.0 Strict//EN"
- **DTD filename:** "DTD/xhtml1-strict.dtd">

The previous example is one of the three DTDs you may choose from; here are the two other options:

```
<!DOCTYPE html PUBLIC "-//W3C//DTD XHTML 1.0 Transitional//EN"
  "DTD/xhtml1-transitional.dtd">
<!DOCTYPE html PUBLIC "-//W3C//DTD XHTML 1.0 Frameset//EN"
  "DTD/xhtml1-frameset.dtd">
```

The only difference between these other DTDs is the public identifier and filename. To read more about your DTD options, visit the XHTML specification at www.w3.org/TR/xhtml1/#normative.

Rule 8: You must include an XHTML namespace

According to the specification, the root element — <html> — must include the XML namespace that uses an xmlns attribute. A *namespace* is a collection of names used in XML documents as element types and attribute names. XHTML is using the XHTML collection of names and therefore needs a namespace, which looks like this:

```
<html xmlns="http://www.w3.org/1999/xhtml"></html>
```

Keeping markup clean with HTML Tidy

David Raggett, an early developer of HTML (and an active contributor to the development of XHTML), wants to help you out.

We all make mistakes when creating and editing HTML. With this in mind, Raggett created a simple tool to fix these mistakes automatically and tidy up sloppy editing into nicely laid-out markup. His tool is called HTML Tidy — a free utility offered on the W3C Web site. Luckily for us, Raggett added some XHTML features to HTML Tidy; now this tool takes a look at your HTML page, cleans it up, and then outputs it as XHTML. HTML Tidy can even help you identify where you need to pay further attention to making your pages more accessible to people with disabilities.

To read more about Tidy, visit www.w3.org/People/Raggett/tidy.

The program is not currently a Windows program, unless you download the entire HTML kit for editing. If you're familiar with DOS programs, feel free to download just HTML Tidy and get to work. If you're like most of us who are spoiled by the Microsoft Windows interface, you may want to visit a Web front end created by Peter Wiggin. Visit the URL listed here (http://webreview.com/1999/07/16/feature/xhtml.cgi), enter your URL, and then see your page magically convert before your very eyes.

Part V
From Web Page to Web Site

The 5th Wave — By Rich Tennant

"So far our Web presence has been pretty good. We've gotten some orders, a few inquiries, and nine guys who want to date our logo."

In this part . . .

*P*art V is where we change focus from individual HTML documents (or Web pages) to the collections of interlinked, interrelated HTML documents known as Web *sites*. Here we inspect the contents of a typical Web professional's HTML toolbox, and point out why you might find such tools useful. We also provide some examples of how the toolbox functions in the real world. Next, we tackle the practical topics involved in creating a Web presence online — what it takes to host, maintain, and update a Web site of your very own. Whether your Web site serves as a personal hobbyhorse, a greeting to the world, or a managed, professional resource on the job, you'll find this information absolutely invaluable.

Chapter 16

Creating an HTML Toolbox

*H*TML documents are made up of plain old text. To create one all you really need is a simple text editor, such as Notepad — and in the beginning that was all a Web author had available to use. However, as the Web evolved, so did the tools used to create Web pages. Now there's so much more to Web authoring that it's difficult to just use a simple text editor unless you don't care about graphics and HTML validation.

As time passes and you become more comfortable with HTML, you'll build an HTML toolbox. This chapter is dedicated to helping you build that toolbox. From HTML authoring applications to FTP programs, this chapter arms you with what you need to know to make educated decisions about the tools you need.

In addition to an HTML editor, you need an FTP tool to upload files to a Web server, and specific software tools for validation and maintenance so you can check your pages twice and keep them shipshape. This chapter reviews and recommends the latest HTML authoring tools — as well as other tools you'll find in any professional Webmaster's well-stocked toolbox. Some of these tools may already be on your system — quietly waiting to help you create stupendous Web pages.

What You Need

The first step to building your toolbox is identifying the essential components. Although an HTML editor may make your Web pages easier to create, it's not necessarily the only tool you need to publish and maintain your Web site. You need an entire tool collection — a *Webmaster's toolbox.*

This chapter goes into detail about the types of tools you need, and we even go a little further by recommending our favorites. Here's the short version:

- **HTML editor:** Keep in mind that two different kinds of HTML editors exist: helpers and WYSIWYG editors, which we describe in the following section.

- **Graphics applications:** If you plan to use graphics in your Web pages, you need an application to create and edit them.

- **Validators:** *Validation* is the process of comparing a document to a set of document rules, in this context a DTD. Typically, a document author creates an HTML document, submits it for validation, and uses the report to identify errors, correct those errors, and resubmit the document for validation.

There are some occasions when breaking HTML rules is the only way to get your page to render in older Web browsers. Although many browsers will render erroneous HTML, there are reasons for document rules, and be warned that poorly defined HTML might produce unpredictable results.

- **Link checkers:** The Web is based on the concept of linking; therefore, a broken link on your site can be quite embarrassing. Use a link checker before you publish your site (and routinely for maintenance) to verify that your users never get the dreaded `404 Object Not Found` error message.

- **FTP utilities:** After your Web pages are created, validated, and checked in all applicable browsers, you're ready to upload them to your Web server. Until your pages are uploaded to a Web server, only you can see them.

To find out more about ISPs that provide Web hosting, see Chapter 17.

Using Text Editors in the Real World

Text editors come in two flavors: helper and WYSIWYG. The *helper* puts you in the driver's seat; it has fewer capabilities, but it does the job. The *WYSIWYG* editor does everything but your laundry. In reality, if you get serious about creating Web pages, you really won't make a choice between the two flavors. You can have your cake and eat it, too. Here's some more information:

- **The helper editor:** An HTML helper does exactly what it sounds like: It helps you create HTML; it doesn't do all the work for you. Usually, a helper application displays "raw" HTML — tags and all (shocking though this may seem) — and such tools often color tags to help you differentiate them from your content. Helpers usually include an HTML-aware spell checker that knows your tags aren't just misspelled words, and helpers also incorporate other functionality to make HTML development easier and more fun. In our opinion, no Webmaster's toolbox is complete without a good HTML helper.

- **The WYSIWYG editor:** A WYSIWYG editor creates HTML for you, shielding your delicate eyes from naked markup along the way. These tools look much like word processors or page-layout programs; they're designed to do quite a bit of the work for you.

WYSIWYG editors can make your work easier and save hours of endless coding — after all, you do have a life, right? — but we recommend that you limit your use of a WYSIWYG editor to the initial design stage. For example, you can use one to create a complex table in under a minute, and use a helper to refine and tweak your HTML markup directly.

Finding an HTML Editor

Although this book explains how to create and maintain HTML pages with nothing more complicated than a pocketknife and a ball of string, we don't think you should snub all HTML editors.

As mentioned in the previous section, you have helper editors, and WYSI-WYG editors can be divided into two categories. Personally, we think that editors are just tools, and not substitutes for knowledge. Don't be fooled by editors with a lot of bells and whistles. Here are a few tips on how to locate and choose a good editor.

At the very least, an HTML editor needs to

- Be easy to understand and use.
- Comply with HTML 4.
- Upgrade as HTML changes.
- Support image map creation.
- Check local links for accuracy.
- Support HTML validation and spell checking.
- Enable you to see and tweak your HTML code directly.

An exceptional HTML editor also

- ✔ Provides site map information.
- ✔ Provides pixel-level control over object and text placement.
- ✔ Supports style-sheet creation.
- ✔ Supports Extensible Markup Language (XML).
- ✔ Accommodates Common Gateway Interface (CGI) scripts, Java applets, and scripting.

Often the best, most popular, and least expensive HTML editor for a particular platform is neither a helper nor a WYSIWYG editor — it may be a combination of the two. Keep an eye out as you review the selections for each platform in this category; editors and combination editor/helpers may be listed.

Not all WYSIWYG editors can serve as good learning tools. Be warned: If you're using a product such as FrontPage that doesn't create the cleanest code, *don't emulate its example.* Messy markup is a bad habit that leads only to confusion, frustration, and (pardon the expression) awful language.

Dreamweaver

In our opinion, Dreamweaver is the best WYSIWYG Web development tool for both Macintosh and PC systems — and most job postings support this assertion. As an all-in-one product, supporting Web site creation, maintenance, and content management, Dreamweaver is an impressive product used by most Web developers. Dreamweaver has continued to evolve since Macromedia first introduced the product in 1997. Since then, Macromedia has been committed to continued development of this product. The most recent version of the product is called Dreamweaver MX.

Where to go for more information

Although the different tools listed here are of high quality and have a place in many Web-masters' toolboxes, your opinions and experience may differ — no, as hard as we try, we can't read your mind (yet). If you find yourself still looking for bliss, many Web sites offer more information on the latest Web-page-development tools. For example, try TUCOWS — The Ultimate Collection of Winsock Software — at www.tucows. com. The developers of the TUCOWS site review all the tools they list, and if a tool isn't up to snuff, it doesn't get listed; it's as simple as that. TUCOWS has been around for a long time — in Web years — and it's never led us astray.

TRICKS OF THE TRADE

The one-two punch of using a WYSIWYG editor with a helper editor

After you start an HTML document, you can open it in both Dreamweaver and HomeSite (or BBEdit), and the changes you make to your page in one program are automatically registered in the other. This two-in-one combination is a direct reflection of what the pros have figured out: You don't need just one kind of HTML editor — you need both. Finally, Dreamweaver and HomeSite (or BBEdit) create solid HTML that plays by the official HTML 4 rules so you don't have to worry about the quality of your HTML. If you create code by hand, Dreamweaver warns you that you made a mistake and corrects it for you if you choose.

Dreamweaver MX marks a turning point because it belongs to a suite of products, Macromedia's Studio MX, that work together to provide a full spectrum of Internet solutions. Studio MX includes Fireworks MX, Dreamweaver MX, Flash MX, ColdFusion MX, and Freehand 10.

Although Dreamweaver is a WYSIWYG tool, it comes with a helper editor. If you're a PC user, you get HomeSite, a feature-rich helper editor that we discuss in detail later in the chapter. For Macintosh users, Dreamweaver uses the well-known and well-respected BBEdit as its helper HTML editor.

We like Dreamweaver for a handful of reasons, one of which is that it has an easy-to-follow-and-learn dialog box that allows authors to style Web pages using Cascading Style Sheets (CSS) without knowing what a style rule is! Many of the benefits of Dreamweaver stem from its sleek user interface and respect for clean HTML.

Creating an HTML document with Dreamweaver:

1. **Select File⇨New.**

   The New Document dialog box appears (as in Figure 16-1).

2. **Select Basic Page from the Category list and HTML from the Basic Page list and click Create.**

   A basic HTML document appears, ready for changes.

3. **Add elements using Dreamweaver's panels or drop-down menus.**

   For example, you can add a title by entering text in the Title text box in the Document toolbar (see Figure 16-2).

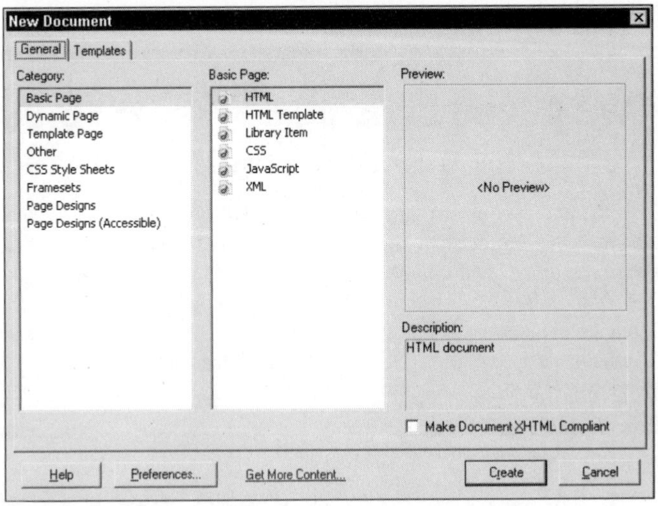

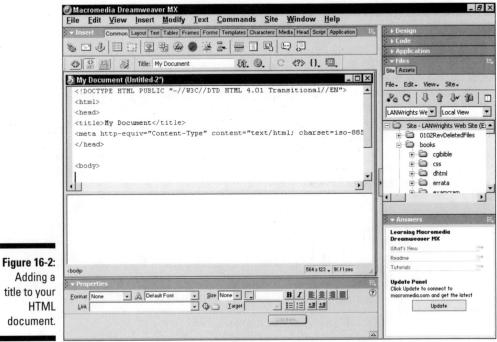

Figure 16-1:
The New
Document
dialog box.

Figure 16-2:
Adding a
title to your
HTML
document.

With all this functionality, rest assured Dreamweaver doesn't come cheap. Dreamweaver is priced in the $300 range, but that price includes a HomeSite license, quality documentation, tutorials, and an all-around tool that you can use for many aspects of Web development. Also, Macromedia is loyal to its customers. After you buy a copy of Dreamweaver, upgrades are available at lower cost. In addition, you have all the power of an established multimedia company behind the product. What more can you ask for?

To find out more about Dreamweaver, visit the Macromedia Web site at `www.macromedia.com/software/dreamweaver`.

FrontPage

FrontPage 2002 is the newest version of the Microsoft commercial Web-authoring system for Windows 95/98/2000/XP and Windows NT/2000 or later. Since Microsoft bought FrontPage from Vermeer Technologies Inc. in January 1996, FrontPage has become a premier personal Web-authoring, publishing, and maintenance tool for Windows users. As we predicted, this product has become the most widely used tool of its kind on the Internet.

FrontPage organizes each Web site in its own project folder so you can develop and manage multiple sites. Enhanced drag-and-drop features let you drag Microsoft Office files into the FrontPage Explorer or move hyperlinks, tables, and images within the FrontPage Editor. The Verify All Links feature automatically verifies that all hyperlinks are valid — within and outside your Web site. This feature even corrects all link errors within your site for you.

FrontPage 2002 also supports database connectivity, ActiveX controls, Java applets, VBScript and JavaScript creation and insertion, tables, frames, and HTML 4.0, plus the Microsoft version of Dynamic HTML. Breathe!

As if all this wasn't enough, the FrontPage Bonus Pack includes an application for creating and editing graphics for your Web documents. The Bonus Pack includes more than 500 tools and effects, and works with PhotoShop-compatible plug-in products, such as Kai's Power Tools from MetaTools, Inc. Image Composer includes more than 600 royalty-free Web-ready images. You may also download the free Microsoft GIF Animator to animate your own Image Composer images and make your Web site really jump on the screen.

The FrontPage interface also enables you to use any document created with Microsoft Office 97 or 2000 because it works like other Office applications. FrontPage uses the shared spell checker, global Find and Replace, and the Microsoft thesaurus.

Now, you can't quite say "FrontPage, create my Web site" into your PC's microphone, walk off, have an espresso, and come back to view the finished work. But, if you apply the knowledge of planning and preparation from earlier chapters in this book, you should be able to have a decent Web site created, tested, and running on your ISP's Web server in little time by using FrontPage.

There are a few disadvantages to using FrontPage, however. To begin with, the HTML markup left in the wake of a FrontPage experience can leave even the savviest of Web gurus scratching their heads. If you're a developer who likes to tweak a few points by hand using your favorite text editor before your Web page goes live, you might be disappointed with FrontPage. However, if you don't mind messy HTML, you'll be fine using FrontPage!

Another notable disadvantage also deals with its output. FrontPage, being a Microsoft product, can be viewed using any version of Internet Explorer; however, it's not as friendly to non-Microsoft browsers. If you choose to use FrontPage, be sure to check your work in multiple browsers before uploading your documents.

FrontPage is not quite as pricey as Dreamweaver, but you can expect to pay just under $200 for a single user license. With that price, comes all the goodies and functionality you would expect of a Microsoft product. Just be warned that you will want to validate your pages before you upload them for all the world to see.

For more information about FrontPage 2002 and to take an interactive tour of the interface, check out the Microsoft Web site at `www.microsoft.com/frontpage`.

HomeSite

HomeSite 5 is the newest version of this software and the first non-WYSIWYG editor for us to look at. It has quickly become the text editor of choice for Windows users. This editor does not have full WYSIWYG capabilities and it does require HTML knowledge. However, it provides assistance at every step. If you recall, this is the editor used for the Windows version of Dreamweaver. So, if you have Dreamweaver, you also have HomeSite.

We like the easy-to-use interface, shown in Figure 16-3. Even with a simple interface, HomeSite is an extremely feature-rich HTML editor for the beginner and professional. Some of our favorite HomeSite features show why:

✔ You can instantly get a browser view by clicking a tab.

✔ The HTML is color-coded to help you with your editing.

✔ You can drag-and-drop and access context menus with a simple right-click of the mouse.

✔ You have access to an integrated spell checker, as well as global search and replace tools that check your spelling and update entire projects, folders, and files simultaneously.

✔ You can use the image and thumbnail viewers to browse image libraries directly in your editor.

✔ You can customize the toolbars and menus to suit your individual needs.

As a further bonus, HomeSite offers extensive online help with accessing documentation on HTML and other popular scripting languages. The result is one impressive system. But there's even more. HomeSite helps you with your project management, provides for link verification, internally validates your HTML, and opens and uploads your files to your remote Web server.

As a standalone product, you can purchase HomeSite for about $100. But remember, if you have Dreamweaver, you already have HomeSite. If you're a Windows user, we highly recommend this editor.

To learn more about HomeSite, visit the Macromedia Web site at `www.macromedia.com/software/homesite`.

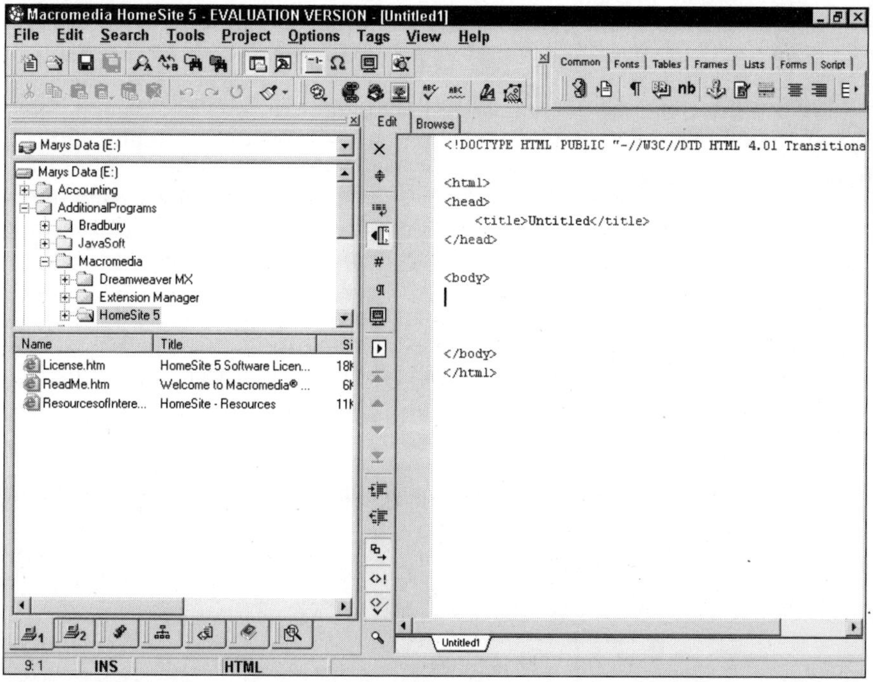

Figure 16-3:
HomeSite's interface displaying a blank HTML document.

BBEdit

BBEdit is for the Mac (PC users don't have to listen!), and like HomeSite, it's a favorite of Web developers. The only difference is that these Web developers use a Macintosh computer. There are two versions of BBEdit to choose from: BBEdit and BBEdit Lite. As its name suggests, BBEdit Lite is a limited version of the BBEdit package that comes in the Macintosh version of the Dreamweaver MX suite, which we rave about earlier in this chapter. From the folks at Bare Bones Software, BBEdit Lite is a Macintosh text editor that comes complete with a set of HTML extensions to make Web page development easier.

These HTML extensions for BBEdit Lite are quite extensive and provide a well-rounded HTML-authoring system. Tools of this kind can (for example) use an editor to open a standard text file and automatically save the file with HTML elements. The two sets of extensions for BBEdit Lite — BBEdit HTML Extensions by Charles Bellver and BBEdit HTML Tools by Lindsay Davies — come with the editor so you don't have to do any extra installation along the way.

Although BBEdit Lite doesn't include all the functionality that its big brother BBEdit does, you find that using BBEdit Lite gives you access to most, if not all, HTML authoring functions you're ever likely to need — even for the most complex Web pages. BBEdit Lite also addicts you to the BBEdit way of life, and we predict that soon you'll be using the full-blown version of BBEdit. It's all a conspiracy, didn't you know? Seriously though, to download a copy of BBEdit Lite, simply point your Web browser at www.barebones.com.

If you opt for the full version of BBEdit, you won't be disappointed. Although you aren't hidden from the markup — remember, BBEdit is not a WYSIWYG editor — BBEdit still makes it easy for you. BBEdit is another one of those all-in-one programs that enables you to create, validate, and upload a Web page using just a few clicks. Creating an HTML document is easy. By selecting File⇨New⇨HTML document, you're already on your way.

When you've created a document shell, you can start adding elements by hand, or you can use BBEdit's Markup drop-down menu to add HTML elements such as lists, tables, and forms. If you're a Mac user, dare we say this application is a must!

Both BBEdit and BBEdit Lite can be found at www.barebones.com. Remember, if you have Dreamweaver for the Mac, you already have BBEdit.

WARNING!

Word processors and HTML

If you're joined at the hip to Microsoft Word or Corel WordPerfect, you can try their built-in HTML-editing and site-management features. These features provide adequate HTML assistance but aren't really in the same ballpark with better standalone WYSIWYG Web development and HTML editing systems. If you already own one of these word-processing programs, however, their Web functionality is free. For now, you may want to use your favorite one for text and for Web development. For example, Word 97/2000/XP for Windows has a WYSIWYG editing window with a good number of functions in its toolbar. This program is adequate for a word processor turned Web document editor. However, who knows what Microsoft will do in the long-term with both Word 97/2000 and FrontPage contending for the role of Web document development systems.

Why worry about that now? If you own one, try it out for Web development. Just keep in mind

that if you create HTML in a word processor, the HTML you get will not be 100-percent standard — resulting in an erratic, clumsy Web page at best. If you have long documents that have been developed in a particular word processor that need to be converted to HTML, doing a first-stage conversion in the processor itself may be easier, but you will have to do any final clean-up and tweaking in a full-fledged HTML editor, and most likely you will have to tackle it by hand as well. Dreamweaver supports the importing of Word documents; however, even using Dreamweaver's cleanup tools, you will have to edit the document by hand before it's ready for the Web.

See the following sites for further information on Microsoft Word 97/2000 for Windows, and Corel WordPerfect 8.0 for Windows, respectively:

```
www.microsoft.com/office
www.corel.com/Office2000/index.
  htm
```

GoLive

Recently, Adobe has been giving Macromedia a run for its money in the Web development department, and GoLive is a part of that game. GoLive doesn't have the popularity among seasoned developers; however, it's gaining popularity.

If you're thinking about delving into the world of WYSIWYG editors, give some consideration to GoLive 6. Although we prefer BBEdit or HomeSite, this is a reputable WYSIWYG editor. So here's the skinny on GoLive.

GoLive, like Dreamweaver, attempts to do it all. It not only creates dazzling pages, but it can also handle multiple display options (for example, handheld devices), site management, maintenance, and even multimedia. One of the features we like about GoLive is its easy site-creation wizard. Using Adobe's trademark floating windows, the site organization is always accessible as the main floater. You can use the GoLive Site wizard to define basic characteristics about HTML documents (whether a single document or a collection), and then create a blueprint for your site structure.

This functionality is similar to the storyboard used to design a Web site. The idea is to get a feel for how the site goes together and spot potential weaknesses in the design — on paper — *before* you have to wrestle with markup. This functionality serves a similar function, so you can get a good working sense of what you need before you start building the pages. (It makes sense; an architect wouldn't start on a house without a blueprint, right?)

You can purchase GoLive 6 for just under $400 for new users and just under $100 for an upgrade. It features full support for Mac OS X, as well as Windows XP, 2000, and 98.

To read more about GoLive and see the interface in action, visit the Adobe Web site at www.adobe.com/products/golive/overview.html.

Graphics Tools

Graphics applications are beasts. They can do marvelous things, but learning how to use them can be a bit overwhelming at first. We wish that we had the space to provide detailed instructions for each product, but that would take an entire book for each product. However, we would like to introduce you to three favorite tools.

We recommend that you also create text-only versions of your site to allow for complete accessibility. To read more about accessibility concerns, see Chapter 18.

You might want to outsource your graphics work because graphics applications can be pricey and complicated; however, it's always good to have a graphics program that you can use to tweak images if need be.

Photoshop

Photoshop is a cross-platform Adobe product that can do just about anything you can think of. It's not cheap; with a price tag reaching $600, you hope it could rebuild the earth if it had to. Well, it comes close to it. Photoshop has something for everyone. It can create simple Web graphics, complex slicing for images pulled together by tables, digital photography, and any other traditional graphic work that it was first designed for. Of course, that doesn't even begin to cover just what Photoshop can do.

First things first, Photoshop is for the pros. However, if you plan to get involved in serious Web graphics, it just might be worth the price tag because it's the best-respected graphics application on the market. Employers expect their graphic artists to know Photoshop from top to bottom, and if you think you might be heading in that direction, you may want to give it a whirl.

Because of the hefty price tag, we recommend downloading a 30-day trial version before you make an actual purchase. It couldn't hurt and will make you an educated consumer. If you're ready to join the big leagues, check out the *Photoshop All-in-One Desk Reference For Dummies,* by Barbara Obermeier, with David Busch, and published by Wiley Publishing, Inc. This desk reference is packed with information on just about every Photoshop tool known to man.

To learn more about Photoshop, visit the Adobe Web site at www.adobe.com.

PaintShop Pro

We like PaintShop Pro because (at right around $100) it's a less expensive, PC-based alternative to Photoshop that provides similar features. (There's no version for Mac users.) If you're just learning HTML, and want to add some graphics, PaintShop Pro is a more reasonable approach. You can do almost anything with PaintShop Pro that would be needed for beginning or intermediate-level graphics editing. We highly recommend this product for Web authors who want to add images to their sites but have no desire to make graphic art their full-time living (or their fulltime hobby).

To learn more about PaintShop Pro, visit www.jasc.com.

Fireworks

Fireworks is a fairly young graphics program from Macromedia. It was designed specifically for Web graphics, and should only be used to create and edit images for the Web. (Photoshop and PaintShop Pro handle every kind of image you can think of, but aren't dedicated, as Fireworks is, to Web graphics.)

Because it's used only for the Web, its interface is less daunting and easier to use. Fireworks is designed to work hand in hand with Dreamweaver — and it does just that. With the new suite of products that make up Macromedia's Studio MX, Fireworks is one of the many products that work seamlessly together to develop complex Web sites with dazzling images. This is a mid-range product, great for smaller graphic projects destined for the Web.

To learn more about this product, visit www.macromedia.com.

Link Checkers

If you think spelling errors are embarrassing, here's something that's even worse: broken hyperlinks. Hyperlinks make the Web what it is; if you have broken links on your site, that's borderline blasphemous. Seriously, if your text promises a link to a great resource or page but produces the dreaded 404 Object Not Found error when users click it, you'll end up with disappointed visitors — who may never surf to your Web address again.

The worst broken link is one that points to a resource in your own pages. You can't be held responsible for what others do to their sites, but you are 100-percent accountable for your own site. Don't let broken links happen to you!

As with the other checks, many HTML editors include built-in local link checkers, and some editors even scour the Web for you to check external links. In addition, the majority of Web servers also offer this feature.

Checking external links isn't as simple as it sounds because a program must work over an active Internet connection to query each link. This checking can be processor intensive, and you should check external links only during off-peak hours, such as early morning, to avoid tying up other Web servers as well.

A number of scripts and utilities are available on the Web to help you test your links. Two personal favorites are the W3C Link Checker and MOMSpider.

W3C Link Checker

First created to check validity of W3C technical reports, the W3C Link Checker utility was written by Renaud Bruyeron and then reworked by Hugo Haas. The same W3C Link Checker utility is available online, for download, or (if you're a savvy programmer), as source code that you can tweak to suit.

The way the Link Checker utility works is it reads the HTML document and grabs all links — this includes named anchors. It first verifies that anchors are not duplicated, and then verifies that all links are pointing to an actual reference. Like all validators, the utility produces a report that warns against HTTP redirects and any duplicated anchors.

To use the online validator, visit http://validator.w3.org/checklink, and then enter the URL of the document you want to check (see Figure 16-4). This does mean that you can only check documents already on the Web. To check documents before they go live, you'll have to use a standalone product. However, many WYSIWYG products provide this functionality already, so check your product before downloading a standalone.

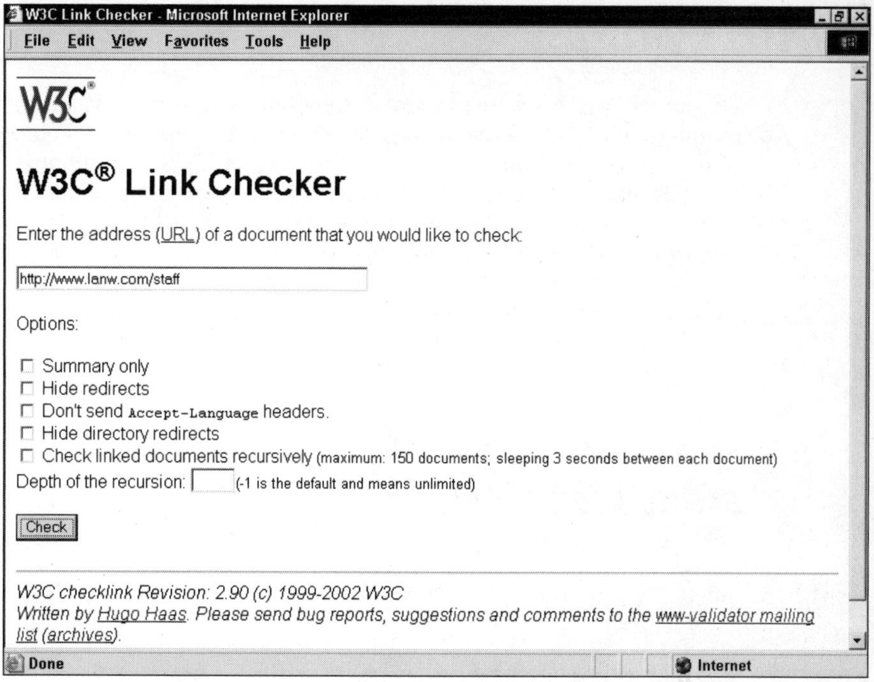

Figure 16-4:
Using the
W3C Link
Checker we
can verify
that all links
found at
www.lanw.
com/staff
are not
broken.

MOMSpider

MOMSpider was one of the first link checkers available to Web developers. This link checker is written in the Perl programming language and runs on virtually any Unix machine. MOMSpider needn't even reside on the same computer as the site it checks — so even if you don't serve your Web site from a Unix machine, you can still check links from MOMSpider on a remote system.

Anyone who has some knowledge of Perl can easily configure MOMSpider to create custom output and to check both internal and external links on a site. Don't fret: If you don't know Perl, you can easily find a programmer who can adjust a MOMSpider in his or her sleep for a nominal fee. Many ISPs run a MOMSpider on your site for a low monthly fee and cheerfully handle the configuration and implementation for you.

To find out more about MOMSpider, visit the official site at http://ftp. ics.uci.edu/pub/websoft/MOMspider/.

HTML Validators

The majority of browsers are forgiving of markup errors. Most don't even require an `<html>` element to identify an HTML page, and instead simply search for recognizable HTML elements to identify a document as readable. Just because the real world is that way, doesn't make inconsistency a good thing. You may see a day when browsers can't afford to be so forgiving, and that day is drawing closer as HTML, Extensible Hypertext Markup Language (XHTML), and other extensible markup languages become more complicated and precise. Get the markup right from the beginning and save yourself a bunch of trouble later on. HTML validation is built into many HTML editors.

Introducing the W3C's standalone validator

Although not many standalone HTML-validation applications exist, the W3C has put together a free, Web-based validation system available at `http://validator.w3.org`.

The W3C validation tool enables you to choose which HTML or XHTML DTD (version) you want to use when you check your document — and you get a variety of different outputs to match your preference. You can choose a terse output that lists only the line numbers in your document, the boo-boos, and a brief description of each — or a verbose output that goes into great detail about why each and every error is an error and even includes links to the relevant information in the HTML specification.

Using the W3C's online validator

Even if you have a validation application in your current text editor, we strongly recommend that you never, ever — What, never? No, *never!* — post a page on the Web without running it through this validator first. If your HTML is correct, your pages will look better on a variety of Web browsers. Your users will also be happier (even if they don't know exactly why).

When you use the online validator, if you're on a network that has a firewall, it may prevent you from uploading your HTML files. This is because the firewall considers online validation applications to be a risk to your computer's security. Although there's certainly nothing wrong with online tools (especially the one supplied by the W3C), there's not much you can do to work around the problem. You have no choice but to use a local tool that you download, such as HTML Kit (also offered by the W3C) or a validator bundled with your text editor, such as HomeSite or BBEdit.

If you're ready to use the W3C's online validator, here's how to get started:

1. **Verify that you included the correct DOCTYPE declaration.**

   To use the W3C validator, you must include a DOCTYPE declaration, or select one from a drop-down menu. If you don't, the validator doesn't know which DTD your document conforms to, and therefore, doesn't know which set of rules to check. So first things first: Be sure to add a DOCTYPE declaration, such as the HTML 4.0 transitional declaration:

```
<!DOCTYPE HTML PUBLIC "-//W3C//DTD HTML 4.01 Transitional//EN"
    "http://www.w3.org/TR/html4/loose.dtd">
```

   If you're validating a frameset document, you must use the frameset DOCTYPE declaration:

```
<!DOCTYPE HTML PUBLIC "-//W3C//DTD HTML 4.0 Frameset//EN"
    "http://www.w3.org/TR/REC-html40/frameset.dtd">
```

2. **Visit http://validator.w3.org.**

3. **Enter the URL of your page in the URI Address text box (as in Figure 16-5).**

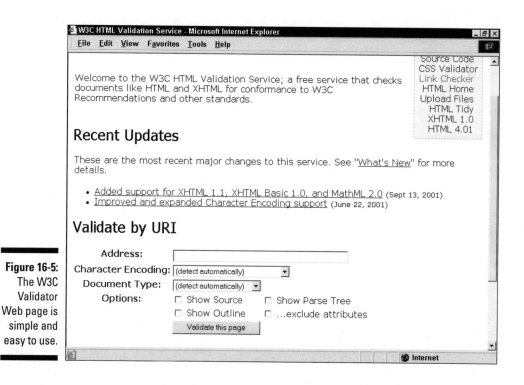

Figure 16-5:
The W3C
Validator
Web page is
simple and
easy to use.

4. Choose from these other options as needed:

- **Character Encoding:** For beginners, we recommend leaving the default setting (detect automatically). If you're not a beginner, choose the appropriate character encoding for your document.

- **Document Type:** Beginners should probably leave the default setting (detect automatically) in place. If you know the version of HTML (or other markup language) you used when you wrote your document, pick it from the list.

- **Options:** You can select the format and type of information defined by the report. You don't have to select any of the options; the default produces error and warning messages with line numbers that tell you where the error is in the original HTML document.

5. Press Enter or click the Validate this page button.

You either receive a Web page that states No Errors Found or you receive a Web page listing any warnings or errors. If errors are found, you may have to take some time to get used to deciphering the murkier error messages. Figure 16-6 shows a sample.

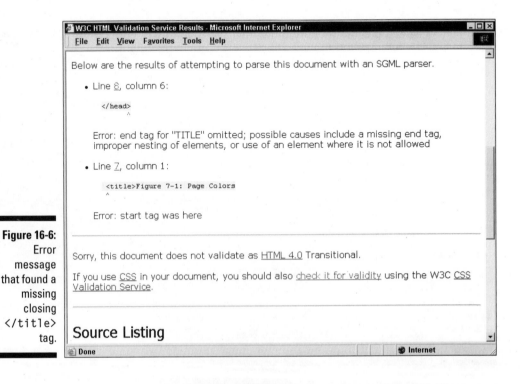

Figure 16-6:
Error message that found a missing closing </title> tag.

6. **Fix the errors and validate your document. Keep doing this until it returns a** `No Errors Found` **message.**

    This process may not be tons of fun, but after one page full of errors, you'll be a real stickler about validating the *next* HTML document.

 Just because your page returns the greatly anticipated `No Errors Found` message doesn't mean you're done. Be sure to check all your Web pages in any browser that your users might use. Netscape and Internet Explorer are known to render pages differently (no big deal in the newest versions, but you can't be sure that all your users update their software every few months).

FTP Clients

After you've created all your pages and you're ready for the world to take notice, you might find yourself scratching your head and wondering what the heck to do next. This is a common phenomenon known as Web fright. Many first-time Web authors get to this point and then stare blankly at their screens.

There is only one cure for Web fright. It's all about the File Transfer Protocol (FTP). *FTP* is a protocol you can use to transfer a file from one machine to another. With FTP, it doesn't matter what platform a machine is running, all will understand, provided each machine has FTP software installed.

Okay, maybe there are *two* cures. Not only do you need a means for transferring your Web page online, but you also need a destination for your Web page. A Web server is used to house the collections of pages for the Web site. You may have your own Web server machine. If you don't know whether you have a Web server, then you don't have one. Don't go run out and buy one, either!

A Web server runs special software that's dedicated to presenting and maintaining Web files (among several other Web-related tasks). If you don't have one of these supercomputers, your local ISP (such as EarthLink or MSN) can host your pages for a fee.

After you've selected the host, and know how to access the Web server (your host will provide you with this information), you upload your pages to the host's server using FTP — for which (yep) you need an FTP program. All such programs are similar, and easy to operate. Two of our personal favorites are WS_FTP Pro for Windows, and Fetch for the Macintosh:

  ✔ WS_FTP Pro can be located at `www.ipswitch.com`.

  ✔ Fetch can be located at `http://fetchsoftworks.com`.

The basic interface for an FTP program consists of dual windows (shown in Figure 16-7). One window provides access to your own hard drive; after you log on to the Web server, the other window provides access to that server. Two arrows usually show up between these two windows: one pointing left and one pointing right. To upload a file from your hard drive to the Web server, you highlight the file in one window and select the appropriate arrow. Using FTP, you can upload or download files to and from the Web server.

For more information on Web servers, Web hosting, and transferring your files, see Chapter 17.

Figure 16-7: The basic WS_FTP Pro interface.

Chapter 17

Setting Up Your Online Presence

. . . .

In This Chapter

▶ Locating a place to host your Web pages

▶ Acquiring a domain name

▶ Moving files to your Web server

▶ Maintaining your site

▶ Promoting your site

. . . .

*Y*ou've built a great Web page, or two, or even a whole Web site, and it's time to get it on the Web for the whole world to see. The actual act of moving your files from one place to another is pretty easy (as you find out a bit later in this chapter), but you have some decisions to make about where to keep those files and if you need your own Web site domain. Also, you should formulate a plan for maintaining your site and promoting it. In this chapter, you find out how to do all these things so you can establish an online presence fit for the excellent HTML you've created.

Hosting Your HTML

The first and most important step in putting your pages online is finding someplace on the Web to put them on display — a host. In general, you have two choices for hosting your pages:

✔ Host them yourself.

✔ Pay someone else to host them.

The word *host* is used throughout the Web industry to mean a Web server set up to hold Web pages (and related files) so they can be accessed by the rest of the world. In this chapter, we use *host* as a noun and as a verb — when you host a Web page, you're running Web-server software on a computer.

As you might expect, setting up and maintaining a Web server has pros and cons, whether you're hosting your own pages or paying someone else a fee to host them for you. The next few sections of this chapter look at both approaches to hosting — and give you the skinny on what's involved with each. You can decide which option works best for you.

Just because you choose one hosting option over the other now doesn't mean you're stuck with it for life. If you find hosting your own pages a little overwhelming, after a while, you can easily move your files to a service provider, or vice versa. When you think about which hosting option is best for you, concentrate on your needs for the next six months to a year; plan to reevaluate your decision in a few months.

Hosting Your Pages Yourself

In this section, we talk about hosting an average-size site (1 to 100 pages or so) that doesn't include more than a couple of multimedia files, and doesn't have any special security or electronic commerce (e-commerce) applications.

If you need to run a large corporate site, an online store, or any other complex site, you'll need more expertise, equipment, and software than what's listed in this section. Books such as *E-Commerce For Dummies* and *Webmastering For Dummies,* 2nd Edition (both from Wiley Publishing, Inc.) can help you get started working with more complex sites. We also recommend that you talk with a Web professional who has practical experience in setting up and maintaining complex Web sites.

You can set up your own Web server and host your Web pages yourself. To do this, you'll need:

- ✔ **A computer designated as your Web server:** Web servers are often *dedicated* to a single task, leaving word-processing and other activities to a different computer.

- ✔ **Web-server software:** Common Web-server software packages include Apache and Microsoft's Internet Information Server (IIS), called Internet Information Services in Windows 2000 and later.

    In this chapter, as in the rest of the Web world, you may see the term *Web server* used to refer to a dedicated computer (that is, the actual hardware) as well as to refer to **Web-server** software. That's because you can't have one without the other.

- ✔ **A dedicated Internet connection:** Your Web server isn't very useful or reliable if it's only connected to the Internet when you fire up a dialup connection.

Introducing Web servers

You might be surprised to find out that the first two items in this list (*Web server* and *Web-server software*) are the easiest to come by. Computers are cheap these days, and a Web server doesn't have to be all that beefy to work efficiently. After all, it's dedicated to performing a single set of functions: accepting and responding to requests for Web pages, and of course holding your Web files.

Unless you're serving multimedia files that can take up gigabytes of space, you'll find that all the files associated with any average Web site only total a few megabytes at best. In fact, an average home desktop computer purchased in the last two or three years will make an acceptable Web server.

There is no shortage of Web-server software for you to choose from, and several very good, free Web servers give you access to programs you can download and install in a matter of minutes. Both Windows and the Apple OS come with Web servers built into them that are designed for personal use — that is, fairly small potatoes Web sites.

If you want something meatier because you're hosting even a medium-size Web site, we recommend that you choose one of the free Web-server software downloads, such as Apache. These applications are designed to handle more server activity than personal Web-server software is.

TUCOWS at `www.tucows.com` is an excellent source for freeware and shareware Web-server software downloads. In addition to links to software downloads, you'll find reviews of different Web-server software so you can gather information and find the right program to meet your needs.

Getting a dedicated Internet connection

The most expensive piece of the host-it-yourself approach is a dedicated Internet connection. Each page on your Web site has a unique Uniform Resource Locator (URL) that is an exact and specific Web address, so your Web server needs to have an Internet connection that never goes down and whose Internet address never changes.

The fact that your connection must be *dedicated,* or constant, puts dialup phone connections and even standard Internet access cable and Digital Subscriber Line (DSL) connections out of the running because their Internet addresses change regularly. Also, most ISPs prohibit you from hosting a Web site on your standard dialup, cable, or DSL connection.

Here's a list of considerations regarding your dedicated connection:

- **It's gonna cost you:** To get a dedicated Internet connection, you'll need to arrange for one from an ISP and pay a special fee (at least $50 a month if not more) to have that dedicated line. If you already have an ISP, you can find out what the ISP offers, as well as how much it charges.

- **Faster is better:** Your dedicated connection needs to have a decent speed. Of course, you can host a Web site over a dialup phone connection, but what would be the point? Your pages would trickle out from your site to your users' browsers so slowly most users simply wouldn't stick around or come back for a second time.

  At a minimum, you need a dedicated cable or DSL line, and even with those, you shouldn't try to host multimedia files simply because they are so large.

  If you already have a cable or DSL line, you're not in the clear. Your computer's IP address (its unique address on the Web) changes regularly because your ISP has a bank of addresses it uses for all connected subscribers. Because your address changes regularly, it's *dynamic.* Your Web server's IP address must be *static,* which means it never changes. This consistency allows other computers to find the server on the Web and request Web pages from it. Your ISP has more flexibility with dynamic addresses, so they cost less than static addresses.

If you're getting the idea that hosting a Web site yourself is a little complicated and expensive, you're right. Not only do you have to pay for the equipment and dedicated Internet connection, but you also have to learn how to set up and administer a Web server and keep all the pieces working 24/7. This is all well and good if you have the time, knowledge, and resources to devote to managing a Web server, but if you don't, consider the more practical option we discuss in the following section, "Using a Hosting Provider."

Using a Hosting Provider

A hosting provider manages all the technical aspects of Web hosting, from hardware to software to Internet connections. All you have to do is manage your HTML pages. Back when the Web was young, hosting provider options were scarce, and what *was* available was expensive. The times have changed, and needs have grown, so reasonably priced hosting providers are abundant these days.

If you decide to let someone else host your pages, you have two choices for how much you pay:

✔ **Nothing:** Some services actually host your pages for free. That's it; you pay zip, zero, nada to get your pages on the Web. What's the catch? You have to pay in other ways, usually with advertising attached to your page.

✔ **Something:** Most Web-hosting services, however, charge you a fee, from a few dollars a month to triple digits a month. The trick to making the most of your hosting funds is to find just the right hosting service to meet your Web site needs.

Web hosting for free

The old saying *There's no such thing as a free lunch* is particularly true in Web-land. A handful of hosting providers offer to house your Web pages for free, but they have to make their money somehow — generally, from advertisements they attach to your Web site.

You don't usually have any control over which ads are attached to your site, and it may look to your visitors like you're promoting a particular product when you really aren't.

So why use a free hosting service if you have to deal with the ads the service attaches? If you're just putting a page up for fun, you're early in the learning process and want to practice with a page or two online, or are willing to live with the ads if it means you don't have to spend money, then free Web hosting may be right for you.

Free Web hosting, however, is not right for any business Web site — small or large — simply because all those ads don't look professional. Visitors to your site will know you're taking the cheap route, and may make some inferences (usually incorrect) about your business.

Also most free Web-hosting services won't let you attach a domain name to your site (covered a little later in the chapter). If you plan on procuring your own domain, or you already have one, free hosting isn't the right option for you.

If you want to investigate your free Web-hosting options, start with these providers:

✔ `www.netfirms.com/`

✔ `http://geocities.yahoo.com/home`

✔ `www.freeservers.com/flash/index_flash.html`

✔ `http://angelfire.lycos.com/`

For a longer list of free hosting providers, search for "free Web hosting" in your favorite search engine.

Web hosting for a fee

If you want complete control over your Web site, you may want to pay a service provider a fee to host your pages. The service provider handles all the infrastructure pieces — such as storage space, software, Internet connections, backups, and such — and you simply manage your files.

When you pay someone to host your Web pages, you want to get all the services you need for your site without paying too much. In addition to hosting your Web pages, most providers offer additional services, including (but not limited to):

- E-mail accounts
- Mailing lists
- Common Gateway Interface (CGI) and other server-side scripting support (so you can add guest books and other neat widgets to your site — see Chapters 10 and 12 for more information)
- Database support
- E-commerce support

Any good provider will also host your pages under your domain name if you have one or want one, and most will even help you purchase a domain and get it up and running.

Finding the right provider

Before you start looking for a hosting provider, think carefully about what you'd like to include in your Web site (other than plain HTML pages). Some things you might want to include are

- E-mail capabilities
- A shopping-cart function
- Page counters, search engines, HTML forms, or other interactivity capabilities

After you have a good idea of what services you need, you can start shopping for hosting providers. Each hosting provider's costs will be different, but it shouldn't cost you more than $10 to $20 per month for a basic Web site that includes a megabyte or two of data storage, one or two e-mail addresses, domain-name hosting, and support for scripts and programs. When you think about it, that's all you really need to get a solid site up and running.

If you plan to include more advanced features on your site (such as a shopping cart or a database), you can expect to pay $30 or $40 a month. Even that's not a huge expense for an online store.

When you look for a provider that has a variety of packages available, be sure it's easy to upgrade from one hosting package to the next as your site's needs grow.

The best answer to the question of who you'll choose to host your site may be right under your nose. If you're happy with your current ISP, why not check to see if it offers Web-hosting services. You may find out that your ISP services has a Web-hosting option already included with it, which means you won't have to fork over extra money (over and above what you're already paying) for an Internet connection. If your connectivity plan doesn't include hosting, you may be able to add it for a small fee, instead of starting all over again with a new provider.

If you haven't chosen a hosting provider yet, you might find out if potential providers have a Web interface you can use to manage your Web site. Is there a demo of the interface available? Does it look easy to use? Although the availability of such an interface shouldn't be your only criteria for a good hosting provider, it might sway you in favor of one provider over another.

The Web Hosting Ratings site (`www.webhostingratings.com/`) is a good place to start if your own ISP doesn't pan out as a good hosting provider for your needs. This site includes a search engine you can use to search for hosting plans, and a reviews section where you can read what others have to say about potential hosting providers.

Getting Your Own Domain

As detailed in Chapter 1, a *domain name* is the high-level address for any given Web site. Some examples of domain names are `microsoft.com`, `apple.com`, `w3c.org`, and `dummies.com`.

You may want your own domain name (hence domain) that reflects your business name (or even your personality). If you don't get a domain name of your own, your pages will be part of someone else's domain name — usually your hosting provider's domain name. For example, a personal Web site hosted without a domain name at `io.com` has a top-level URL of

```
http://www.io.com/~natanya
```

With a domain name of `natanya.com`, the same Web site would be hosted at

```
http://www.natanya.com
```

One is, of course, easier to remember than the other, but is that a good enough reason to have your own domain? Maybe — but then again, maybe not.

Deciding whether you need a domain name

Domain names are cool to have, but they aren't free. To get a domain name, you have to register it and pay to use it (more about the exact process in the following section, "Getting a domain name"), and some hosting providers charge you extra to attach your domain name to your Web site. So how do you know whether you need a domain name?

Although there's no simple answer to this question, it's safe to say that a business should invest in a domain name because a Web site is part of a business image. A business that has a unique domain just looks more professional than one that doesn't. Imagine if Microsoft's domain name was `http://www.io.com/~microsoft`? How seriously would you take them?

However, for a personal site or even for a small consulting site, a domain name is really optional. You don't need one to run your site, so it's really up to you if you choose to spend the money. Many individuals have their own sites, as do many families, and you can decide if it's a worthwhile expenditure for you.

One benefit of having your own domain name is that you can change hosting providers without affecting the domain for your Web site. When you pay for a domain name, it's yours; you can move it from one hosting provider to another at will. Without the domain name, you can't change hosting providers without changing your site's URL.

Getting a domain name

If you decide that you want to get a domain name, you have to do two things:

✔ **Find a domain name that you like that isn't taken.** To find out whether a domain name is taken, visit VeriSign at `www.netsol.com` (the keeper of domain names in the United States) and search for the name.

Domain names can be harder to come by than you might imagine, especially ones that include common words in their names (for example, `www.computer.com` or `www.car.com`). You might need to get creative as you look for a domain name. The VeriSign search engine helps you out a bit by suggesting some alternatives to your original choice.

✓ **Register that domain name.** After you find a domain name that you like, you have to register it as belonging to you. Most domain names are registered for two years, and after those two years are up, you can re-register the name. In effect, after you've registered a domain name, it's yours to keep for as long as you're willing to pay for it.

You can register and pay for your domain right on the VeriSign site, but before you do so, check with your site's hosting provider to see whether a better registration deal is available. For example, VeriSign usually charges $70 for a two-year registration, whereas the hosting provider World Wide Mart (www.worldwidemart.com) only charges you $17 a year for the same service (saving you $36).

If you don't have a hosting provider already set up, you have to pay VeriSign for the domain name so you don't run the risk of losing the domain. The cost difference between what VeriSign charges and any deal you'll get with your hosting provider isn't so significant that you may want to lose a domain name over it.

If you're thinking you can register a domain name long before you have a Web site to hook it to, you're correct. In fact, many people have domain names registered that they never put Web sites up for. Some people have great plans for Web sites that never come to fruition, whereas others register domains just to keep competitors from registering them. When you register a domain, VeriSign simply keeps the site in your name until you're ready to use it.

Linking your domain to your Web site

Attaching your domain name to your Web site after you have a hosting provider (or have your own Web server up and running, for that matter) is pretty easy. If you've registered your domain through your hosting provider, you don't actually have to do anything; the hosting provider takes care of everything for you — except the actual care and feeding of your individual pages.

If you have a domain that VeriSign is holding for you, you simply log in to VeriSign with the account you set up when you purchased the domain name, and provide the new nameserver information you received from your hosting provider.

Nameservers are computers on the Internet that translate domain names into the actual Internet location for your computer. Your Web-hosting provider's nameservers know that your domain name matches a specific site listed on their Web servers. That means you need to let VeriSign know the names of those nameservers at your hosting provider. It's really that simple.

Any good hosting provider can give you detailed instructions on how to register a domain name in the provider's system or attach your domain name to your Web site on its computers. If you're changing from one hosting provider to another, your new provider should help you transfer your domain. Most providers give you this information up front or have online help that will walk you through it. If it's not immediately clear how to get your domain set up, be sure to ask for help. If you don't get it, change providers.

Transferring Files to Your Web Site

After you've secured a Web site host, or decided to put up your own Web server, you'll need a way to move the HTML pages you created on your local computer to the Web server. This isn't a one-time activity either. As you maintain your Web site, you'll need to move files you've built on your local computer to the Web server to refresh your site.

The way you move files to your Web server depends entirely on how your Web server is set up. Normally you have a couple of transfer options:

- The File Transfer Protocol (FTP)
- A Web interface for moving and managing files provided by your hosting provider

Via FTP

Of these two options, FTP is almost, without exception, always a possibility. FTP is the standard for transferring files on the Internet, and any hosting provider should give you FTP access to your Web server. When you set up your Web site with your hosting provider, the provider usually gives you written documentation (either in print or on the Web) that tells you exactly how to transfer files to your Web server. Included in that information is an FTP URL that usually takes the form `ftp://ftp.domain.com`.

You can use an FTP client such as WS_FTP (`www.ipswitch.com/Products/WS_FTP/`) or CuteFTP (`www.globalscape.com/products/cuteftp/index.asp`) to open a connection to this URL. Your provider will give you a username and password to use to access your Web-server directory on the FTP site. Then you can move files to your Web site using the client's interface. It's really that easy. If you want to grab a copy of a file from your Web site and modify it, you simply download a copy, make your modification, and re-upload it — all through the FTP client's interface.

Each FTP client's interface is different, but they're all pretty straightforward. Chapter 16 includes more information on finding a good FTP client, so when you find one, spend a few minutes reading its documentation.

You may not need a separate FTP client to move your files to your Web server. Most newer Web browsers (such as Internet Explorer 5.5 and higher and Netscape 6 and higher) have limited FTP capabilities built in. You can easily upload and download files, but you may not be able to make or delete directories. Also, many Web utilities (such as Dreamweaver) have file-management capabilities. Find out more in Chapter 16.

Via your hosting provider's Web site

In the interest of usability and reducing technical support calls, many Web hosting providers have built Web pages that help you upload and manage your Web site files without using a separate FTP utility or even the FTP tools inside HTML editors. The majority of these tools enable you to manage your site, such as uploading and downloading files, creating and deleting directories, moving files around, and deleting files. If you already have a hosting provider, find out if it has a set of Web-based tools for managing your site.

Every provider's interface is different, so be sure to read the provider's documentation before you start to transfer your files. Also remember that most providers who have these Web interfaces won't stop you from managing your site via FTP as well. If you find the interface too cumbersome, or you like the way FTP works better, by all means use it.

Maintaining and Updating Your Site

In many ways, putting a Web site up is only half the battle. Maintaining your site after it's up is as important as getting it up in the first place. Think about your own Web surfing experiences for a moment. How happy are you to come across a site that is obviously outdated and full of stale information? Don't you expect the Web to have the most up-to-date information available? After all, updating a page is as easy as copying a file to your Web server. It's not like you're publishing a book.

How often you update your site information depends entirely on the kind of site you're running and the information you include in it. A news site needs updating every few minutes (as news breaks), but a consulting site might only need updating every few weeks or even every few months (as projects are completed and résumés change).

You may also find that some portions of your site need updating more frequently than others. Thinking back to the news site, the world and national news sections might update many times a day, but living or health sections may need attention every one or two days.

As you begin to move from building phase to maintenance phase for your site, start to think about how frequently each piece of your site will need to be updated or changed. You'll then get an idea of what kind of maintenance schedule and process you're looking at.

Creating a site that is easy to maintain

The best way to help make your maintenance process easier is to build a site that is easy to maintain in the first place. You can put a variety of measures in place to make this happen:

- ✔ **Organize your HTML files, images, and multimedia into folders on your site.** Put all your images in one folder, your multimedia in another, and then divide your pages into folders that reflect the different sections in your site. When you organize your pages and collateral well, you can quickly find files when you update or change them.

- ✔ **Use templates for site navigation and other chunks of commonly used data on your site.** You can save these templates as snippets of HTML in a text file somewhere, and when you create a new page, you can just drop the text into that template. If you use the same HTML for certain elements of your site (for example, a copyright statement) and you make a change to that element (change the copyright date, for example), you can do a search and replace on all the files on your site to make the change quickly.

- ✔ **Keep an updated visual map of your site in electronic or print form.** You can go so far as to use Visio or some other charting tool, or simply sketch the map on a piece of paper. If you have a map you can turn to when you make a change, you can easily see the relationships between the different pages on your site and quickly create links and references on the relevant pages.

  Some HTML software, such as Dreamweaver, has mapping features built into the interface and can generate site maps for you at the click of a button.

- ✔ **Create a mini-style guide that lists the basic design elements you use in all your pages.** Include the background, text, and linking colors you always use, the fonts for each kind of content (headings, body, lists, and so on), graphics you use in particular places, and any other design-related information so it's always at your fingertips.

Getting (and staying) organized

One of the keys to making site maintenance as hassle-free as possible is to get — and stay — organized. The sad truth is that you need to get a handle on your files and information so you always know where everything is. Or you could stay sloppy and disorganized. The choice is yours, but we guarantee that your updates will be more painful if you organize your files the way you organize your junk drawer. Regardless of your organizational style, the following tips can help you get and stay organized as you prepare to maintain your site:

- **Keep everything in one place:** Put all of your Web site files and collateral, both electronic and otherwise, in one place so you can always find the information related to your site. Set aside a folder on your computer's hard drive to store all things Web related and then further subdivide the folder into working directories, images, the actual HTML files that drive your current site, and so on.

- **Decide on a maintenance schedule:** Analyze the data on your site and make a plan for how often each piece of your site needs to be updated. You might consider making a chart and actually scheduling tasks in your calendar so you're sure you have time set aside to update your site.

- **Keep a tickler file:** Create an electronic or paper folder to hold pending Web site information, so you can quickly lay your hands on the data necessary for updating your site when the time comes. As you go about your daily work and find something that you know needs to go into the site, simply throw a copy of it into your Web site folder. For example, if you put press releases on your site once a month, but issue them several times a month, toss an electronic copy of new press releases into a "Web pending" folder as they are released. That way you know right away which ones to add to your site when the time comes.

- **Maintain a separate to-do list:** Keep a running list of things to do to your site, with a deadline for each one. As you get closer to a scheduled site maintenance day, you can look at your list and have a good idea of how much work you'll need to do to make the update and how long it will take you.

- **Get others involved — and keep them on task:** If you rely on others to provide you with information for your Web site, work with them in the early stages of the site to set up a process for scheduling updates and communicating information. Find easy and efficient ways for those people to deliver information to you, and set expectations for how long it will take for you to update the site. Keep in mind that the process you set up will evolve over time, but you've got to start somewhere.

✔ **Do a post mortem:** After your site has been up for six months or so, step back and evaluate your organization and update schedule to see how well it's working for you. You'll have some experience with the site and its information, and you may find a different or better way to organize your data or schedule your updates. Periodic checks like this can help you adjust to your site's needs and adjust your site to your needs.

Running regular checks

In addition to updating your site regularly with new and changed information, it's a good idea to check two key elements of information on your site at least once a month:

✔ Links

✔ Content not scheduled for an update

Looking for broken links

The links you make to the pages within your site shouldn't break unless you move or delete a page from your site. The links you make to other people's sites, on the other hand, are beyond your control and can change or break any time. If there's one thing users hate to find on a site it's a broken link, so take the time at least once a month to scan your site for broken links and either remove or fix them.

You have a variety of options for running link checks. Many higher-end Web development tools include *link checkers* that walk your site and report any broken links. Check out Chapter 16 for more information, or visit TUCOWS (`www.tucows.com`) to download freeware and shareware versions of standalone link checkers. You can also use the W3C's online link checker (`http://validator.w3.org/checklink`) for a free, Web-based link check.

Checking content

Checking content isn't as straightforward as link checking because you won't find software that will troll your Web site and tell you if your content is stale or otherwise broken. Instead, it's up to you to make a monthly quick pass over all the content that didn't show up on your radar when you did updates to other parts of the site. You're basically just checking to make sure that the content's still good. For example, if your site includes bios of key staff, information about them might change over time, but you won't necessarily update individual bios when you add new ones or remove old ones. A regular check of all bios (regardless of staff additions or attrition) will help you be sure all of the information is up to date.

If this task seems daunting, consider dividing your site into sections, filtering out the content you know you'll update regularly, and scheduling each section for a quick review every week. If you use this approach, you never have to review your entire site at once (which can make you tired and cause you to miss errors anyway), and maintenance becomes a manageable activity that you attend to for a few minutes once a week. It's good to get into the habit of regularly reviewing your site anyway, and this is a good way to form that habit.

Obviously, if your site is large or you have several different content contributors, the weekly content checks can get out of hand. However, if people contribute content to your site, they should also contribute time to keeping that content relevant and fresh. Work with your content contributors to set up a regular schedule for reviewing content that isn't slated for a regular update. You can expect them to find things that need to change, but such is the reality of running a Web site.

Expanding Your Site

The day may come when you want to expand your Web site. Maybe you've added a new department to your business, you want to post some of your favorite resources on your consulting site, or there's been a new addition to your family. Whatever the reason, you should carefully plan the expansion before you actually do the work. A little work up front can save you from many headaches once you get started.

The first thing to do is decide on the scope of your expansion. Typically, you'll find that expansion work that you need to do to your site falls into one of these three categories:

✓ **Adding a new page or two:** As you might imagine, adding a new page or two to your site is the easiest work you'll do because you can model the new page or pages on pages that already exist on your site.

When you add a new page, just be sure that it fits into the general flow of your site, and don't forget to link to it from another page on your site — especially the home page and the site map, if you have one. You might also put a note on your site's home page to let visitors know about the new information on the site. This helps those who are familiar with your site find the new pages, and shows everyone that you're keeping your site fresh.

✓ **Adding a new set of pages (or section):** When you add a new section to your site, things get a little more complicated because your site's navigation system can be greatly (and negatively) impacted by the change. If you want every page of the site to refer to the new section, you'll need to change the navigation for the entire site after the new section is complete.

Before you begin the addition, be sure to think through very carefully how the map of your site will change and make a list of all the pages on your site that will need an updated reference to the new section. If you have a checklist laid out before you begin the update, your chances of missing any pages decrease considerably.

✔ **Completely reconfiguring the site:** We're going to level with you right off the bat: When you redesign your entire Web site (as everyone does at least once during the lifetime of a site), it's like starting all over again from scratch. Of course, you do have existing information, images, and even some HTML to work with. You also know more about how your site needs to function and whether you need to improve your methods since first creating the site. Even so, take the time to make a plan for redesign that includes:

   • A revised site map that lists all the sections and pages you plan to include in your new site.

   • A list of the information you can reuse, and which pages you plan to reuse it on.

   • A list of new information that you need and where you plan to get it.

   • A design plan that outlines the general look and feel for each of your pages.

   • A checklist of everything to do to get the site up and running.

Whether you add a section or substantially change the navigation of the site, it's a good idea to run a link checker on your site to find any stray links that you forgot to update during the expansion. You'll be much happier if you find and fix broken links than if a visitor finds the problem and reports it to you.

Along the same lines, if you drastically change the organization of your site, links *from* other sites (like the all-important search engines) to yours may no longer work. For a while, you might keep your old pages in place and include referrer links (discussed in Chapter 5) that help visitors to your old pages find the new pages.

This list may seem a little involved, but if your site has more than ten pages or so, building Web pages without a plan is going off half-cocked. Such folly results in a disconnected mishmash of pages instead of a cohesive Web site.

Getting Your Site Noticed

After you have your site up and running and have a maintenance plan in place, you need to make sure that the rest of the world knows about it. After all, what good is a site if no one visits it? *If you build it they will come* is a nice idea, but don't expect it to apply on the Web.

A search engine is a *crawler,* which is simply a piece of software that wanders the Web collecting information about pages. Each engine works differently and collects different information about a given Web page, but in general, each gathers the URL, the page title (from the `<title>` element), and often the entire text from the page. If you give the engine your top-level URL, the engine crawls from that URL to every page on the site that you link to, and every page those pages link to, and on and on until your entire site is in the engine's database of URLs.

When someone searches for keywords in a page, the engine compares his or her search request with the information in all the pages in the database, and lists the most relevant links first in the results. This means the best way you can help people find you is to make sure the guts of your page are included in text (minus the graphics because the engines can't read the text in graphics) and that the information on your page is as clear and concise as possible.

Step back and think about what terms you would use to search for your page, and be sure those words are on your home page. For example, if you sell widgets at a discount, be sure to include the words *widgets* and *discount* in the text of your home page.

Registering with search engines

The first thing you can do to help get your site noticed is to register with search engines. Although some online services say they will do this for you, you're better off spending a little time doing it yourself for free. Just provide the search engine with the top-level URL for your site, and the engine will do the rest. There's no need to pay to register all 100 pages of your site.

The easiest way to register with a search engine is to visit that search engine and look for its "register" or "add URL" link. Each engine has a form you can fill out to submit your URL to the engine.

Before you start registering, take some time to write up a short description of your site. Some engines ask for this information, and it's better to provide a prepared (and spell-checked) description that you've thought through completely than it is to add one that you created off the top of your head.

Not all search engines use the keywords stored in a page's metadata as part of the search, but some do, which means it never hurts to include keyword `<meta>` elements in your document headers. Read more about metadata in Chapter 4.

Crafting useful page titles

Have you ever noticed that the first thing you see about a page in a search engine's results listing is its title? The title of your page often makes the first impression, so you want it to be a good one. When you craft titles for your pages, be sure that they remain meaningful and intriguing when viewed outside the context of your Web site.

For example, the title "My Home Page" is not a very helpful title because it doesn't say who you are and why potential visitors should care. However, the title "John Doe, MCSE and Network Guru for Hire" tells people a lot more about you and may generate more visits to your page.

You want the titles of your pages to be descriptive but concise, which can be tricky, but you get the hang of it after a while. Consider including the same basic information at the start of each title, followed by a short descriptor of the page. The résumé page on a consulting site might be titled "John Doe, Networking Guru — Résumé and Curriculum Vita" while the recent projects page might be "John Doe, Networking Guru — Recent Projects."

Promoting your site offline

As important as it is for you to register and promote your site online, you should be sure to promote it offline as well. Print the URL on your business cards and other marketing materials. Include it on your correspondence and in your e-mail signature (okay, so that's technically online) and any other place that you think people will see it. Just think of your Web site as an extension of your identity (corporate or otherwise) and promote it as such.

Chapter 18

Creating a Great User Interface

● ●

In This Chapter

▶ Understanding why your UI matters

▶ Using site maps during site development and on your site

▶ Practicing good linking

▶ Choosing media well

▶ Creating an accessible site

▶ Reviewing some excellent user interfaces

● ●

*T*he overall design of your site is called the *user interface* (or UI) — and when you design a good UI, you give users the tools they need to move about your site with minimum fuss. This chapter outlines some standard Web-site design principles to follow as you create your HTML; they can ensure a usable and effective UI.

As its name implies, a UI is the mechanism provided to give a user access to the information on your Web site. Although each UI is unique, they're all made up of the same components: text, graphics, and media files, all held together with HTML. If your site is difficult to navigate, cluttered with flashing text and rampant colors — and generally doesn't help people find what they're looking for — then your visitors probably won't find their way to your site more than once. Why should they bother?

However, if your site's navigation is intuitive, you use images and media to accent your design without overpowering it, and you do all you can to help people locate the information they're looking for, you've created a solid UI and can expect visitors to return time and again.

Defining the Scope and Goals for Your Site

An important first step in creating an effective UI for your site doesn't have anything to do with markup, but instead has everything to do with planning.

Before your site grows too large (or before you even build your site if you haven't started yet), carefully identify the exact purpose of your site and the goals you want it to meet. When you have a good understanding of your site's scope and goals, you can better create an interface that accomplishes them. For example, an online store might have goals like these:

✔ Allow visitors to browse an online catalog and put items in a shopping cart.

✔ Provide visitors with a way to purchase the items in their cart online.

✔ Help users make smart purchasing decisions.

✔ Facilitate merchandise returns and exchanges.

✔ Solicit feedback from users about products they want to see in the catalog or ways to make the site better.

This short list of goals is also an indicator of the areas your site may include — and the kinds of activities it will need to support. Instead of having just a single area (such as a product catalog), the site needs some specialized areas like these:

✔ Online catalog and shopping cart

✔ Buying guides or other information that can help users make better purchasing decisions

✔ A help-and-feedback section

✔ A set of tools to expedite returns and exchanges

When you've established the goals for your site, you can identify the elements best suited for the site:

✔ A navigation system that identifies the major areas of the site helps users quickly identify what part they're in, and helps them move from one part of the site to others without getting lost.

✔ A set of standard design elements (such as buttons, page-title styles, and color specifications) to keep the users oriented as they move from page to page in the same site.

✔ A standard display for items in the catalog, including product-related information such as product images and descriptions, prices, and availability.

✔ Well-designed forms to help users search for products in the catalog, purchase the items in their shopping carts, request a refund or help returning an item, and submit comments to the site.

✔ Long text pages that offer extensive information on purchasing options, product returns, and other helpful information — but are still easy to read and navigate.

TRICKS OF THE TRADE

Design matters

You'll notice that this chapter doesn't lay down the law about exactly what makes a Web page pretty or ugly. We include discussions of good design principles, but it's up to you to choose color schemes and the overall look-and-feel for the site. Always remember that what looks great to one person may be ugly to someone else. That said; keep in mind that design does matter when you're building your Web site.

If you're building a site for your business, that site may provide the first impression for potential customers or clients. The site should reflect your business style. If you run an architecture firm, for example, strong lines and a clean look may be the best way to present your company image. If you run a flower shop, your site may be a bit more organic and decorated (well, okay, *flowery*) to remind visitors of what they might expect if they walked into your store.

If you're new to Web design or graphics and you need a site that marks your business presence on the Web, consider getting help from a Web-design professional to create a general look-and-feel for the site, and then use the images, layouts, and navigational aids they create to build and manage the site yourself. Once established, a distinctive and consistent look-and-feel of your site is relatively easy to maintain.

Regardless of who designs your site, be sure you take the time to get a critique of it from peers, friends, family members, and anyone else who is willing to be brutally honest with you about how good (or even bad) it really looks. A negative-but-constructive critique from someone who knows and respects you beats a "Gee, that's ugly" from someone whose business you are trying to acquire.

REMEMBER

The final section of this chapter, "Some Excellent User Interfaces," takes a look at how Amazon.com's UI matches the online store's goals.

Bottom line: The final UI elements you include in your site — and how you design and organize them — should all flow from the site's goals. Even when you add to an existing site, you should start by considering the goals of the new section of the site, and then identifying the UI elements you need to meet those goals. Of course, by that time you'll have an existing UI to use as a guide, so the UI for the new section should facilitate the original goals of the section and fit your site's overall design.

Mapping Your Site

It's often easier to get to where you're going if you know how to get there. Mapping your Web site can be a vital step in planning — and later running — the site. This process involves two creative phases:

✔ Creating a visual guide on paper or electronically that you can use to guide the development of your site.

✔ Creating a visual guide on your Web site to help visitors find their way around.

Both have their place in good UI design, so each gets its own section.

Using a map for site development

When you use a site map during the development of a Web site — even one that includes a few pages — you know what pages you need to build and how they relate to each other. The map can help you identify the navigation elements you'll need to include — and as a bonus, it provides you with a checklist of pages. These are two ways a site map can help ensure that you've built everything your site needs before you put it on the Web for the world to see.

For example, the visual map of the *XML Dummies,* 3rd Edition Web site (`www.lanw.com/books/xmlfd3e/default.htm`) is shown in Figure 18-1.

This map tells us that the site has four main sections, and three of those sections — chapter contents, chapter URLs, and chapter examples — are each further divided by chapter. Each chapter page then lists the contents, URLs, or examples for a particular chapter in the book.

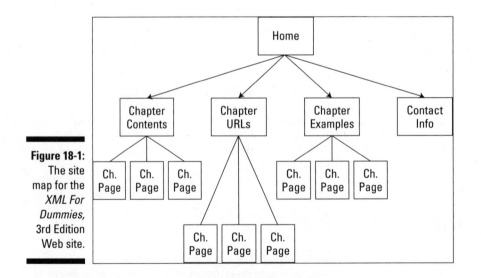

Figure 18-1: The site map for the *XML For Dummies,* 3rd Edition Web site.

Building the site one piece at a time

If you plan to build your Web site a page or section at a time, you can create a map of the final site and then decide which pages it makes the most sense to build first. When you have a good working idea of how your site is going to expand, you can plan for it during each stage. For example, suppose you have created a site map for the *XML For Dummies,* 3rd Edition Web site — and the site needs a Book Examples section. If that section isn't quite finished when the site launches, disaster need not ensue — provided the designer planned ahead to accommodate new sections, and built that capability into the site. You simply leave out any links to that section of the site (as shown in Figure 18-2) when you launch.

When the book examples section is ready, you simply add it to the site and add a link to the main navigation elements, as shown in Figure 18-3.

As long as you know the resources are coming, you can create a navigation scheme that easily accommodates the book examples section when it's ready to add. Without a site map and a complete plan for the site, however, integrating new sections can suck up way too much time and effort.

Figure 18-2:
The *XML For Dummies* site without the book examples.

Figure 18-3:
The *XML*
For
Dummies
site with
the book
examples.

Although you want visitors to your site to know that you plan on expanding it over time, it's not a good idea to create "under construction" sections that don't include much of anything except the hint that they will contain something someday. Instead, consider having a small section of your home page highlight some things coming soon so visitors know new information will be available later. Users are disappointed if your site design merely hints at information it doesn't really have yet.

Using a map as a visual guide for your users

Site maps aren't just for site developers. Even when you devise a solid navigation scheme that leads people to the exact information they need to find, a site map can be a supplemental navigational tool that gives them a different way to find what they're looking for.

Unlike a series of navigation menus or links, a site map lays out all contents of your site so visitors can see all their options at once.

Everyone approaches finding information in a different way. It's up to you to give visitors as many options as you can (realistically) for navigating your site. Some people like to be led; others like to rummage around; still others like to see every possible option and choose the one they like best.

The downside to site maps is that *they grow as your site grows*. Depending on the size and complexity of your site, your map may take several screens to display. When you surf the Web, you'll notice that massive sites such as Microsoft.com, HP.com, and Amazon.com don't offer site maps because maps of their sites would be huge and unwieldy. However, medium and large sites (such as Symantec.com) use them effectively.

In the end, only you can decide whether a site map is a good navigation tool for your site. If you only have a few pages, a site map might be overkill. However, if your site has several sections and you can think of different ways to access your content, a site map might be the best choice.

You can design your site map however you'd like and use any combination of text, graphics, and links. Many maps are just a simple collection of links. Remember that you don't want the map to take too long to download or to be too hard to read. The map is a navigational tool; it should be simple and easy to use. Chapter 5 includes information on how to create and manage hyperlinks.

Establishing Solid Navigation

The navigation you use on your site can make or break it. If visitors can't find what they're looking for on your site, chances are they will leave and never come back. The type of navigation you use on your site depends on how many pages you put on it — and on how you organize them. If you only have a few pages, your navigation may be a simple collection of links on the home page that help users jump to each page. However, if your site has many pages organized into different sections, your home page may only link to those sections and not to each page.

For example, the Dummies.com site houses a large collection of pages organized as a variety of sections; it would be impractical to link to all the pages in any navigation scheme. Also, the site includes articles on a wide variety of topics, as well as book information. The site could be organized into books and articles, but visitors are likelier to be looking for information on a particular subject, so the site is organized by topic. The home page, shown in Figure 18-4, prominently displays these different topic areas on the left.

When you click into one of these topic areas, the remaining topic areas are available in a navigation bar across the top of the page (as shown in Figure 18-5). You don't have to return to the home page to jump from topic to topic.

Figure 18-4:
The
Dummies.
com site is
organized
by topic.

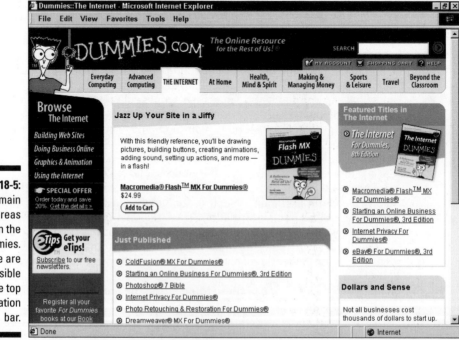

Figure 18-5:
The main
topic areas
on the
Dummies.
com site are
accessible
from the top
navigation
bar.

As you can also see from Figure 18-5, each topic has its own sub-navigation area (at left, echoing the layout the home page) that lists sub-topics within the topic. Although the links are different, the general navigation scheme is consistent throughout the site. Thus visitors know what to expect as they navigate around the site.

Finally, the topmost navigation area of each page includes a regular collection of links that appear on every page of the site to help visitors quickly access important areas from anywhere: a site search, help, account information, and a shopping cart. Every page has the same set of links to information about Dummies, the form to register for eTips, how to contact Dummies, the site copyright statement, and the site privacy policy. Like the shopping cart and help links, these links have to be on every page, but need not be displayed as prominently. Adding them to a consistent site footer keeps them accessible to visitors without obscuring key content for any given topic or sub-topic.

If you create a map to aid site development, you can also use it as a guide for the kind of navigational tools you need to create for your site. Consider each page on the map in turn; list the links that each page must include. A pattern normally emerges that can help you identify the main navigation tools your site needs (such as links to all main topic areas and copyright information, as on the Dummies site), as well as sub-navigation tools (such as links to sub-topics on the topic pages).

After you know what tools you need, you can begin to design the visual scheme for your UI. Do you want to use buttons across the top, buttons down the side, or both? Do you need a footer that links to copyright or privacy information? If you have sections within sections within sections, how can you best help people navigate through them? Answering questions like these is the route to a solid navigation system that helps users find their way around your site — letting them focus on what they came for rather than on how to get there.

Whatever navigation scheme you finally devise, always give your visitors a way to get back to your home page from wherever they are on the site. Your site's home page is the gateway to the rest of the site, and if visitors get lost or want to start again, make sure they can get back to Square One with no trouble.

After you design your site navigation scheme and put together a few pages, ask someone who isn't familiar with your site to review it and try to use it. To help them with their testing, give them a list of three or four tasks you'd like them to complete — pages to visit or a form to fill out, for example. If your test visitor gets lost or has lots of questions about how to navigate the site, you may need to revisit your scheme. Your reviewer may also have suggestions on ways to make the navigation features clearer and easier to use. Remember, you know your site and its content like the back of your hand — in effect, you know too much. You may not see gaps in the navigation system that a first-time user will probably turn up right away. It's better to find those gaps during site development than to be pelted with complaints after the site goes live.

Good Linking Practices

The Web wouldn't be the Web without hyperlinks — after all, they can connect your site to the rest of the Web and turn a collection of pages into a cohesive site. But overusing or misusing links can detract from your site and even lose you some business.

Choose your off-site links wisely

Internal linking is almost a walk in the park compared to external linking — after all, when you link to pages on your own site, the pages those links point to are *under your control.* You know what's on them today and what will be on them tomorrow, and even whether they will exist tomorrow. When you link to resources on someone else's site, however, all bets are off. You don't maintain those pages, you can't modify their content , and you certainly won't know when they disappear. Neither will your visitors — till they slam into a `404 Page not found` message (the usual sign of a *broken link* that now goes nowhere).

Links to other sites are more useful when they're relatively stable and have less chance of breaking. Consider these suggestions:

- ✔ Link to a particular section of a site rather than a specific page on the site. Pages come and go on sites, especially large ones, but the general organization typically stays the same, making sections a better linking bet.

- ✔ Carefully choose what sites you link to. Sites maintained by companies don't usually go away, but those maintained by individuals do so more often.

- ✔ Rather than linking directly to PDFs or images or other media files on a site, link to the pages on the site that link to those resources. Sites often update the resources and give them new names. The page that links to the resource will almost always be updated to reflect new names, so the page is a safer linking bet.

Good linking practices are not a substitute for regular site maintenance. You should regularly check (once a week if possible, once a month at least) all links from your site to external sites to be sure they're still working. A good Web editor will do the checking for you, as will other site utilities as described in Chapter 16.

Even though you don't control the content on the Web sites you link to, providing links to them *implies your support or endorsement of those sites.* When a visitor follows a link from your site to someone else's site, he or she thinks you approve of the content on that new site. That human quirk makes a couple of guidelines necessary:

✔ **If you don't want to be associated with content on a particular external site, don't link to the site.** Seems obvious, doesn't it? But the only way to find out whether you approve of a seemingly relevant site is to visit it and check it out *before* you link.

✔ **Periodically review your links to be sure the sites' owners are still the same — and that the content is still appropriate.** When domain names expire, new owners may take them over and create new content that's completely irrelevant — or, worse, damaging to your image (think pornography).

Craft useful link text

The text you associate with links is just as important as the links you choose to use on your site. The text gives users a hint about where the link is taking them so they can decide whether to go along for the ride. For example, `Visit Dummies.com to read more about this book` is much more helpful than `Read more about this book`.

The first bit of text tells visitors they're going to leave the current site to visit `Dummies.com` and read more about a book there. The second just tells them they're going to read more about the book — and they might be surprised to find themselves flung off one site and onto another.

Generally, when you create link text, let users know the following:

✔ Whether they're leaving your site.

✔ What kind of information the page they're linking to contains.

✔ How the linked site relates to the current content or page on your site

The goal of your link text should be to inform users and build their trust. If your link text doesn't give them solid clues about what to expect from your links, they simply won't trust your links — and won't follow them.

Always avoid the use of "click here" in any link you create. If you link text is well crafted, you don't need the extra words to prompt the user to click on a link. The link text should speak for itself.

Choosing the Right Bells and Whistles

Media can offer a huge boon for your Web site, adding interactivity and some pizzazz to text and static graphics. However, you should only use media that make your site work better (and/or support the information on it). As a general rule, gratuitously slathering a site with media is bad media. When you choose media for your site, ask yourself the following questions:

- ✔ **Why are you adding these particular media to your site?** For example, an audio clip of an interview may be less effective than a transcript. An interactive Flash presentation can demonstrate how a product works or teach someone how to do something — but Flash-enabled content can take longer to download. If a medium doesn't have a clear purpose, you may want to rethink its integration into your site.

- ✔ **What are some alternatives to the chosen media?** Not everyone is equipped to view (or listen to) all media formats. Therefore make sure the information offered in your media is also available in an alternative format. For example, if visitors to your site don't have Flash and can't interact with your Flash navigation, how do they get around your site?

- ✔ **How large is the media file?** Large files may take a long time to download, so make sure the download is well worth the wait for users. When you do choose to include large files, be sure to let users know *how* large so they can choose whether to download. Also see whether you can split large files into smaller files that visitors can access one at a time.

- ✔ **Will visitors need a special plug-in or application to access the media file?** If users aren't set up to play a particular media format, they may skip using the media (or drum their fingers while the application downloads). Be sure you let visitors know exactly what formats your media files are saved in — and the tools needed to view those files — so they can decide whether they want to download the media. (The wise Web-site designer also includes a way for users to bypass the media, which helps to ensure the widest possible audience for the content. More about that in a moment.)

Working with media on the Web is a significant topic in itself. The Resources section at the end of this chapter includes information on Web sites and books that cover media in more detail. Chapter 13 is a good starting point for using media in your Web pages.

Making Your Site Accessible to Everyone

If you optimize your Web site for users with fast Internet connections, large monitors, the latest browsers, and every plug-in known to humanity, you'll be severely limiting the audience for your site. Instead, you should design your site to accommodate as many users as possible with the widest variety of equipment.

The short list of things you can do to make your site accessible includes:

✔ Providing alternative text for all images and alternative content formats for all media.

✔ Using Cascading Style Sheets where possible for styling (instead of `<font>` and other markup) when you apply formatting to your documents.

✔ Reviewing your pages in as many browsers as possible, including a text-only browser so you can get an idea of how the various browsers handle your combination of text and markup.

✔ Following Web Accessibility Guidelines wherever possible, as outlined by the W3C's Web Content Accessibility Guidelines at `www.w3.org/TR/WCAG`.

 Bobby is a Web-based tool that evaluates your Web page and lets you know exactly how accessible it really is. We strongly suggest that you check all your pages with Bobby to find any accessibility problems you might have overlooked. To run a Bobby scan, visit

```
http://bobby.watchfire.com/
```

and type the URL of the page you want to check in the URL: box.

Some Excellent User Interfaces

Spend a few minutes browsing the Web and you'll be bombarded with excellent (and not-so-excellent) examples of user interfaces. How do you know whether an interface *is* excellent? Simple: If you can find what you need on a site with relatively little trouble, and you come away feeling like you had a good experience, you've used a good interface. Two examples of excellent user interfaces are the Amazon.com site and (believe it or not) the IRS site.

Amazon.com

Earlier on, the chapter looked at how a site's goals directly affect its user interface, with an online store as the prime example of defining a site's goals and then designing an appropriate UI. Well, behold a sterling example: Everything about Amazon.com is designed to facilitate the buying experience. This site is divided into sections, each represented by a different color tab across the top. Visit `www.amazon.com` to see what we're referring to.

Regardless of where you are in the site, you can get to any other section — you can always search, access your shopping cart and account, get help, and (of course) check out to buy. The site's system for checking out is broken into easy-to-manage screens, so purchasing isn't intimidating.

Every product page follows the same basic format, whether you're shopping for a book or for a garden hose, large amounts of help and FAQ text are well divided and easy to navigate. Simply click on the HELP link in the upper-right corner.

There isn't anything on the Amazon.com site that doesn't have to do with selling products online. You won't find any gratuitous media, but you will find a special feature that enables you to preview book contents right on the page. The goals of the site are well reflected in its organization and design.

The IRS

The IRS Web site contains a great deal of important information relevant to everyone in the United States. That means the site has to be easily navigable and well organized so users can find what they're looking for. The site is divided into sections, each of which is linked from a persistent navigation bar at the top of the UI, as shown in Figure 18-6.

Each main area of the site uses the same layout, including a left column of fields for searching both the site in general and specific IRS forms. Then there's a list of contents for the site, links to relevant resources, and access to topics of discussion. Although the actual content, resources, and topics change from section to section, they are accessible on all pages from the same spot, as shown in Figure 18-7.

Figure 18-6:
Main areas
on the IRS
site are
accessible
from a
persistent
navigation
bar.

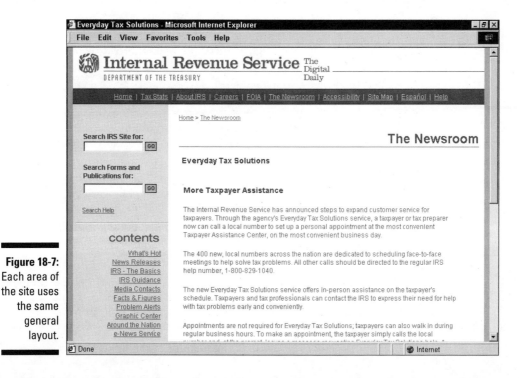

Figure 18-7:
Each area of
the site uses
the same
general
layout.

The inclusion of a persistent link enables a visitor to search for a publication from any page. Such features contribute significantly to one of the site's primary goals: making publications easily available. If you're doing research on a particular tax topic and realize you need a particular publication, you can search for it right from the page that let you know you needed it in the first place. You don't have to jump to a search page first, which saves steps and makes publications that much more accessible.

In general, the IRS site is a great example of making information that users will need most (like publications) immediately accessible. The information on the site is well organized — and it's obvious the site designers work diligently to create a UI that supports users in their search for tax information.

More Resources on UI Design

We've barely scratched the surface of Web and UI design in this chapter, but we're confident it's enough to get you started. We also recommend the following Web sites and books on site and interface design if you want to dig deeper into creating great UIs:

- For a crash course on Web design basics read Design Basics from Webmonkey at

  ```
  http://hotwired.lycos.com/webmonkey/html/97/05/index2a.html
  ```

  In addition, its Site Redesign Tutorial offers an interesting perspective on what it takes to rework a site's design. Read it at

  ```
  http://hotwired.lycos.com/webmonkey/design/site_building/tutorials/
        tutorial4.html
  ```

- Jakob Nielsen is committed to creating accessible Web content. His Web site, `http://useit.com`, is chock-full of resources and articles on creating accessible sites.

- Hey, negative examples are useful too. Web Pages That Suck helps you learn about good design by evaluating bad design. Be sure your site doesn't look like any of those featured at `www.webpagesthatsuck.com/`.

- *Web Design For Dummies* by Lisa Lopuck (Wiley Publishing, Inc.) is another step in the direction of a sophisticated Web site with a knockout look.

- *Web Usability For Dummies* by Richard Mander and Bud Smith (Wiley Publishing, Inc.) can help you fine-tune your site to make it amazingly easy to use (which is a great help in keeping your visitors coming back for more).

Part VI
The Part of Tens

The 5th Wave   By Rich Tennant

"Just how accurately should my Web site reflect my place of business?"

In this part . . .

Here we help you catch potential bugs and errors in your Web pages, cover top do's and don'ts for HTML markup, and point out key HTML resources you can use to extend your knowledge, skills, and sources of inspiration. Enjoy!

Chapter 19

Ten Ways to Exterminate Web Bugs

In This Chapter

▶ Avoiding markup and spelling faux pas

▶ Keeping links hot and fresh

▶ Gathering beta testers to check, double-check, and triple-check your site

▶ Applying user feedback to your site

*A*fter you put the finishing touches on a set of pages (but before you post them on the Web for the world to see) is the time to put them through their paces. Testing is the best way to control your site's quality.

Thorough testing *must* include content review, analysis of HTML syntax and semantics, link checks, and various sanity checks to make doubly sure that what you built is what you really wanted. Read this chapter for some gems of testing wisdom (learned from a lifetime of Web adventures) — as we seek to rid your Web pages of bugs, errors, gaucheries, and lurking infelicities.

Make a List and Check It — Twice

Your design should include a road map (often called a *site map*) that tells you what's where in every individual HTML document in your site, and the relationships among these pages. If you're really smart, you've kept this map up-to-date as you moved from design to implementation. (In our experience, things always change when you go down this path.) If you're merely as smart as the rest of us, don't berate yourself — update that map *now.* Be sure to include all intra- and inter-document links.

A site map provides the foundation for a test plan. Yep, that's right — effective testing isn't random. Use the map to

✔ Investigate and check every page and every link systematically.

✔ Make sure everything works as you think it should — and that what you built has some relationship (however surprising) to your design.

✔ Define the list of things to check as you go through the testing process.

✔ Check everything (at least) twice. (Red suit and reindeer harness optional.)

Master Text Mechanics

By the time any collection of Web pages comes together, you're looking at thousands of words, if not more. Yet many Web pages get published without even a cursory spell check, which is why we suggest — no, demand — that you include a spell check as a step when testing and checking your materials. (Okay, we don't have a gun to your head, but you *know* it's for your own good.) Many HTML tools, such as FrontPage, HomeSite, and Dreamweaver, include built-in spell checkers and that's the first spell-check method you should use. These HTML tools also know how to ignore the HTML markup and just check your text.

Even if you only use HTML tools occasionally and hack out the majority of your HTML by hand, perform a spell check before posting your documents to the Web. (For a handy illustration of why this step matters, try keeping a log of spelling and grammar errors you find during your Web travels. Be sure to include a note on how those gaffes reflect on the people who created the pages involved. Get the message?)

 You can use your favorite word processor to spell check your pages. Before you check them, add HTML markup to your custom dictionary, and pretty soon, the spell checker runs more smoothly — getting stuck only on URLs and other strange strings that occur from time to time in HTML files.

If you'd prefer a different approach, try any of the many HTML-based spell-checking services now available on the Web. We like the one at the Doctor HTML site, which you can find online at www2.imagiware.com/RxHTML/.

If Doctor HTML's spell checker doesn't float your boat, visit a search engine, such as www.yahoo.com, and use web page spell check as a search string. Doing so can help you produce a list of spell-check tools made specifically for Web pages. Poke around www.webreference.com for more pointed pointers, if you feel so inclined!

One way or another, persist until you root out all typos and misspellings. Your users may not know to thank you for your impeccable use of language — but if they don't trip over any errors while exploring your work, they'll have a higher opinion of your pages (and of their creator). Even if they don't know why. Call it stealth diplomacy.

Lack of Live Links — A Loathsome Legacy

We performed an unscientific, random sample to double-check our own suspicions; users told us that positive impressions of a particular site are proportional to how many working links they find there. The moral of this survey: Always check your links. This step is as true after you publish your pages as it is before they're made public. Nothing irritates users more than a link that produces the dreaded `404 Server not found` error instead of the good stuff they seek! Remember, too, that link checks are as indispensable to page maintenance as they are to testing.

If you're long on twenty-first-century street smarts, hire a robot to do the job for you: They work really long hours (no coffee breaks), don't charge much, and faithfully check every last link in your site (or beyond, if you let them). The best thing about robots is that you can schedule them to do their jobs at regular intervals: They always show up on time, always do a good job, and never complain (though we haven't yet found one that brings homemade cookies or remembers birthdays). All you have to do is search online for words such as *link check* or *robot*. You'll find lots to choose from!

We're rather fond of a robot named MOMspider, created by Roy Fielding of the W3C. Visit the MOMspider site at `http://ftp.ics.uci.edu/pub/websoft/MOMspider/`. This spider takes some work to use, but you can set it to check only local links, and it does a bang-up job of catching stale links before users do. (Note that some HTML software, such as HomeSite, comes with a built-in link checker so you can check your links before you post your pages.)

If a URL points to one page that immediately points to another (a pointer), you're not entitled to just leave the link alone. Sure, it technically works, but for how long? And how annoying! So if your link checking shows a pointer that points to a pointer (yikes), do yourself (and your users) a favor by updating the URL to point *directly* to the content's real location. You save users time, reduce bogus traffic on the Internet, and generate good cyberkarma.

If you must leave a URL active even after it has become passé to give your users time to bookmark your new location, you can instruct newer browsers to jump straight from the old page to the new one by including the following HTML command in the old document's <head> section:

```
<meta http-equiv="refresh" content="0"; url="newurlhere">
```

This nifty line of code tells a browser (if sufficiently new) that it should refresh the page. The delay before switching to the new page is specified by the value of the content attribute, and the destination URL by the value of the url attribute. If you must build such a page, be sure to include a plain-vanilla link in its <body> section, too, so users with older browsers can follow the link manually, instead of automatically. You may also want to add some text that tells the visitors to update their bookmarks with the new URL. Getting there may not be half the fun, but it's the whole objective.

Look for Trouble in All the Right Places

You and a limited group of users should test your site well before you share it with the rest of the world — and more than once. This process is called *beta testing,* and it's a bona fide, five-star *must* for a well-built Web site, especially if you intend it for business use. When the time comes to beta-test a site, bring in as rowdy and refractory a crowd as you can find. If you have picky customers (or colleagues who are pushy, opinionated, or argumentative), be comforted to know that you have found a higher calling for them: Such people make ideal beta-testers — if you can get them to cooperate.

Don't wait till the very last minute to test your Web site. Sometimes the glitches found during the beta-test phase can take weeks to fix. Take heed: Test early and test often, and you'll thank us in the long run!

Beta-testers use your pages in ways you never imagined possible. They interpret your content to mean things you never intended in a million years. They drive you crazy and crawl all over your cherished beliefs and principles. And they do all this before your users do! Trust us, it's a blessing in disguise.

These colleagues also find gotchas, big and small, that you never knew existed. They catch typos that word processors couldn't. They tell you things you left out and things that you should have omitted. They give you a fresh perspective on your Web pages, and they help you to see them from extreme points of view.

The results of all this suffering, believe it or not, are positive. Your pages emerge clearer, more direct, and more correct than they would have if you tried to test them by yourself. (If you don't believe us, of course, you *could* try skipping this step. And when real users start banging on your site, forgive us if we don't watch.)

Cover All the Bases with Peer Reviews

If you're a user with a simple home page or a collection of facts and figures about your private obsession, this particular tip may not apply to you. But feel free to read along anyway — it just might come in handy down the road.

If your pages express views and content that represent an organization, chances are oh, *about 100 percent* that you should subject your pages to some kind of peer-and-management review before publishing them to the world. In fact, we recommend that you build reviews into each step along the way as you build your site — starting by getting knowledgeable feedback on such basic aspects as the overall design, writing copy for each page, and the final assembly of your pages into a functioning site. These reviews help you avoid potential stumbling blocks, such as unintentional off-color humor or unintended political statements. If you have any doubts about copyright matters, references, logo usage, or other important details, get the legal department involved (if you don't have one, you may want to consider a little consulting help for this purpose).

Building a sign-off process into reviews so you can prove that responsible parties reviewed and approved your materials may be a good idea. We hope you don't have to be that formal about publishing your Web pages, but it's far, far better to be safe than sorry. (So is this process best called *covering the bases,* or covering, ah, something else? You decide.)

Use the Best Tools of the Testing Trade

When you grind through your completed Web pages, checking your links and your HTML, remember that automated help is available. If you visit the W3C HTML validator at `http://validator.w3.org`, you'll be well on your way to finding computerized assistance to make your HTML pure as air, clean as the driven snow, and standards-compliant as, ah, *really well-written HTML.* (Do we know how to mix a metaphor, or what?)

Likewise, investigating the Web spiders discussed earlier in the chapter is a good idea; use them regularly to check links on your pages. These faithful creatures tell you if something isn't current, so you know where to start looking for links that need fixing.

Foster Feedback

Even after you publish your site, testing never ends. (Are you having flash-backs to high school or college yet? We know we are.) You may not think of user feedback as a form (or consequence) of testing, but it represents the best reality-check that your Web pages are ever likely to get, which is why doing everything you can — including offering prizes or other tangible inducements — to get users to fill out HTML forms on your Web site is a good idea.

This reality-check is also why reading *all* the feedback you get is even better. Go out and solicit as much as you can handle (don't worry; you'll soon have more). But the best idea of all is to carefully consider the feedback that you read and then implement the ideas that actually bid fair to improve your Web offerings. Oh, and it's a really good idea to respond to feedback with personal e-mail, to make sure your users know you're reading what they're saying. If you don't have time to do so, make some!

Even the most finicky and picky of users can be an incredible asset: Who better to pick over your newest pages and to point out those small, subtle errors or flaws that they revel in finding? Your pages will have contributed mightily to the advance of human society by actually finding a legitimate use for the universal human delight in nitpicking. And your users develop a real stake in boosting the success of your site. Working with your users can mean that some become more involved in your work, helping guide the content of your Web pages (if not the rest of your professional or obsessional life). Who could ask for more? Put it this way: You may yet find out, and it could be remarkably helpful.

If You Give to Them, They'll Give to You!

Sometimes, simply asking for feedback or providing surveys for users to fill out won't produce the results you might be seeking — either in quality or in volume. Remember the old days when you'd occasionally get a dollar bill in the mail, to encourage you to fill out a survey? It's hard to deliver cold, hard cash via the Internet, but a little creative action on your part should make it easy for you to offer your users something of value in exchange for their time and input. It could be an extra month on a subscription, discounts on products or services, or some kind of freebie by mail. (Maybe now you can finally unload those stuffed Gila Monsters you bought for that trade show last year. . . .)

But there's another way you can give back to your users that might not even cost you too much. An offer to send participants the results of your survey, or to otherwise share what you learn, may be all the incentive participants need to take the time to tell you what they think, or to answer your questions. Just remember that you're asking your users to give of their time and energy, so it's only polite to offer something in return.

Schedule Site Reviews

Okay, you probably understand that every time you change or update your Web site, you should test its functionality, run a spell check, perform a beta test, and otherwise jump through important hoops to put your best foot forward online. But sometimes, you'll make just a small change — a new phone number or address, a single product listing, a change of name or title to reflect a promotion and so on — and you won't go through the whole formal testing process for "just one little thing."

That's perfectly understandable, but one thing inevitably leads to another, and so on. Plus, if you solicit feedback, the chances are good that you'll get something back that points out a problem you'd never noticed or considered before. It's essential to schedule periodic Web site reviews, even if you've made no big changes or updates since your last review. Information grows stale, things change, and tiny errors have a way of creeping in as one small change succeeds another.

Just as you take your car in for an oil change, or swap out your air-conditioning filter, you should plan to check out your Web site regularly. Most big organizations we talk to do this every three months or so; others do it more often. Even when you think you have no bugs to catch, errors to fix, or outdated information to refresh, you'll often be surprised by what a review turns up. Make this part of your routine, and your surprises will be less painful — and require less work to remedy!

Chapter 20

Ten HTML Do's and Don'ts

*B*y itself, HTML is neither excessively complex nor overwhelmingly difficult. As some high-tech wags (including a few rocket scientists) have put it, *HTML ain't rocket science!* Nevertheless, a few important do's and don'ts can make or break the Web pages you build with HTML. Consider these humble admonishments as guidelines to help you make the most of HTML without losing touch with your users or watching your page blow up on its launch pad.

If some fundamental points that we made throughout this book seem to crop up here too (especially regarding proper and improper use of HTML), it's no accident. Heed ye well the prescriptions and avoid ye the maledictions. But hey, we know they're your pages and you can do what you want with them. Your users will decide the ultimate outcome. (We'd *never* say, "We told you so!" Nope. Not us.)

Never Lose Sight of Your Content

So we return to the crucial question of payload: the content of your page. Why? Well, as Darrell Royal (legendary football coach of the University of Texas Longhorns in the '60s and '70s) is rumored to have said to his players, "Dance with who brung ya." In normal English (as opposed to Texan), we think this means that you should stick with the people who've supported you all along and give your loyalty to those who've given it to you.

We're not sure what this means for football, but for Web pages it means keeping faith with your users and keeping content paramount. If you don't have strong, solid, informative content, users quickly get that empty feeling that starts to gnaw when a Web page is content-free. Then they'll be off to richer hunting grounds on the Web, looking for content.

To satisfy their hunger, place your most important content on your site's major pages. Save the frills and supplementary materials for secondary pages. The short statement of this principle for HTML is, "Tags are important, but what's between the tags — the content — is what really counts." For a refresher course on making your content the best it can possibly be, take a spin through Chapter 2.

Structure Your Documents and Your Site

Providing users with a clear road map and guiding them through your content is as important for a single home page as it is for an online encyclopedia. When longer or more complex documents grow into a full-fledged Web site, a road map becomes even more important. This map ideally takes the form of (yep, you guessed it) a flow chart that shows page organization and links. If you like pictures with a purpose, the chart could appear in graphic form in an explicitly labeled "site map."

We're strong advocates of top-down page design: Don't start writing content or placing tags until you understand what you want to say and how you want to organize your material. Then start building your HTML document or collection of documents with paper and pencil (or whatever modeling tool you like best). Sketch out relationships within the content and among your pages. Know where you're building before you roll out the heavy equipment.

Good content flows from good organization. It helps you stay on track during page design, testing, delivery, and maintenance. And organization helps your users find their way through your site. Need we say more? Well, yes: Don't forget that *organization changes with time*. Revisit and critique your organization and structure on a regular basis, and don't be afraid to change either one to keep up with changes in your content or focus.

Keep Track of Those Tags

Although you're building documents, it's often easy to forget to use closing tags, even when they're required (for example, the `</a>` that closes the opening anchor tag `<a>`). Even when you're testing your pages, some browsers can be a little too forgiving; they compensate for your errors, leaving you with a false sense of security.

The Web is no place to depend on the kindness of strangers; scrutinize your tags to head off possible problems from other browsers that may not be quite so understanding (or lax, as the case may be).

As for the claims that some vendors of HTML authoring tools make ("You don't even have to know any HTML!"), all we can say is, *Uh-huh, surrre*. HTML itself is still a big part of what makes Web pages work; if you understand it, you can troubleshoot with minimum fuss. Also, ensuring that your page's inner workings are correct and complete is something only *you* can do for your documents, whether you build them yourself or a program builds them for you.

We could go on ad infinitum about this, but we'll exercise some mercy and confine our remarks to the most pertinent:

✔ **Keep track of tags yourself while you write or edit HTML by hand.** If you open a tag — be it an anchor, a text area, or whatever — create the closing tag for it right then and there, even if you have content to add. Most HTML editors do this for you.

✔ **Use a syntax checker to validate your work during the testing process.** Syntax checkers are automatic tools that find missing tags — and other ways to drive you crazy! Use these whether you build pages by hand or with software assistance. Here's the URL for the W3C's HTML validator: `http://validator.w3.org/`.

✔ **Obtain and use as many browsers as you can when testing pages.** This not only alerts you to missing tags; it can also point out potential design flaws or browser dependencies (covered in a section later in this chapter). This exercise also emphasizes the importance of alternate text information. That's why we always check our pages with Lynx (a character-only browser).

✔ **Always follow HTML document syntax and layout rules.** Just because most browsers don't require elements such as `<html>`, `<head>`, and `<body>` doesn't mean you can omit them; it just means that browsers don't give a hoot if you do. But browsers per se are not your audience. Your users (and, for that matter, future browsers) may indeed care.

Although HTML isn't exactly a programming language, it still makes sense to treat it like one. Following formats and syntax helps you avoid trouble, and careful testing and rechecking of your work ensures a high degree of quality, compliance with standards, and a relatively trouble-free Web site.

Make the Most from the Least

More is not always better, especially when it comes to Web pages. Try to design and build your pages using minimal ornaments and simple layouts.

Don't overload pages with graphics; add as many levels of headings as you can fit, and make sure your content is easy to read and follow. Make sure any hyperlinks you include add real value to your site.

Gratuitous links to useless information are nobody's friend; if you're tempted to link to a Web cam that shows a dripping faucet, resist, resist, resist!

Structure and images exist to *highlight* content. The more bells, whistles, and dinosaur growls dominate a page, the more distracted from your content visitors will be. Use structure and graphics sparingly, wisely, and as carefully as possible. Anything more can be an obstacle to content delivery. Go easy on the animations, links, and layout tags, or risk having your message (even your page) devoured by a hungry T. Rex.

Build Attractive Pages

When users visit Web pages with a consistent framework that focuses on content, they're likely to feel welcome. The important thing is to *supplement* content with graphics and links — not to trample users with an onslaught of pictures and links. Making Web pages pretty and easy to navigate only adds to a site's basic appeal, and makes your cyber-campers even happier.

If you need inspiration, cruise the Web and look for layouts and graphics that work for you. If you take the time to analyze what you like, you can work from other people's design principles without having to steal details from their layouts or looks (which isn't a good idea anyway).

As you design your Web documents, start with a basic, standard page layout. Pick a small but interesting set of graphical symbols or icons and adopt a consistent navigation style. Use graphics sparingly (yes, you've heard this before); make them as small as possible — limit size, number of colors, shading, and so on, while retaining eye appeal. When you build simple, consistent navigation tools for your site, label them clearly and use them everywhere. You can make your pages appealing, informative, and inviting if you invest the time and effort.

Avoid Browser Dependencies

When you're building Web pages, the temptation to view the Web in terms of your favorite browser is hard to avoid. That's why you should always remember that users view the Web in general (and your pages in particular) from many perspectives — through many different browsers.

During the design and writing phases, you'll probably ping-pong between HTML and a browser's-eye view of your work. At this point in the process, we recommend switching from one browser to another, testing your pages among a group of browsers (including at least one character-mode browser). This helps balance how you imagine your pages and helps keep you focused on content.

There are public telnet servers with Lynx (a character-mode browser) installed that you can use for free and don't require software installation. Visit `www.trill-home.com/lynx/public_lynx.html` for a good list of telnet servers featuring Lynx.

During testing and maintenance, you must browse your pages from many different points of view. Work from multiple platforms; try both graphical and character-mode browsers on each page. Such testing takes time but repays that investment with pages that are easy for everyone to read and follow. It also helps viewers who come at your materials from platforms other than your own, and helps your pages achieve true independence from any single viewpoint. Why limit your options?

If several pages on your site use the same basic HTML, create a single template for those pages. Test the template with as many browsers as you can find. When you're sure the template is browser-independent, use it to create other pages. This helps you ensure that every page looks good, regardless of which browser a visitor might be using, and puts you on your way to real HTML enlightenment.

Think Evolution, Not Revolution

Over time, Web pages change and grow. Keep a fresh eye on your work, and keep recruiting fresh eyes from the ranks of those who haven't seen your work before, to avoid what we call "organic acceptance."

This concept is best explained by the analogy of your face and the mirror: You see it every day; you know it intimately, so you aren't as sensitive as someone else to the impact of changes over time. Then you see yourself on video, or in a photograph, or through the eyes of an old friend. At that point, changes obvious to the world reveal themselves to you as you exclaim, "I've gone completely gray!" or "My spare tire could mount on a semi!" or "Who the heck is *that?*"

As with the rest of life, changes to Web pages are usually evolutionary, not revolutionary. They proceed with small daily steps; big radical leaps are rare. Nevertheless, you must stay sensitive to the supporting infrastructure and readability of your content as pages evolve. Maybe the lack of on-screen links to each section of your Product Catalog didn't matter when you had only three products — but now that you offer 25, it's a different story. You've heard that form follows function; in Web terms, the structure of your site needs to follow changes in its content. If you regularly reevaluate your site's effectiveness at communicating its contents, you'll know when it's time to make changes, whether large or small.

This is why user feedback is crucial. If you don't get feedback through forms or other means, go out and aggressively solicit info from your users. If you're not sure how you're doing, then consider: If you don't ask for feedback, how can you tell?

Navigating Your Wild and Woolly Web

Users who view the splendor of your site don't want to be told *you can't get there from here.* Aids to navigation are vital amenities on a quality Web site. In Chapter 9, for example, we introduce the concept of a *navigation bar* — a consistent graphical place to put buttons that help users get from A to B. By judicious use of links and careful observation of what constitutes a complete screen (or screenful) of text, you can help your users minimize (or even avoid) scrolling. Text anchors make it easy to move to the previous and or next screens, as well as to the top, index, and bottom in any document. Just that easy, just that simple, or so it appears to the user.

We believe pretty strongly in the *low scroll* rule: That is, users should have to scroll *no more than one* screenful in either direction from a point of focus or entry without finding a navigation aid to let them jump (not scroll) to the next point of interest.

We don't believe that navigation bars are required, or that the names for controls should always be the same. We do believe that the more control you give users over their reading, the better they like it. The longer a document gets, the more important such controls become; they work best if they occur about every 30 lines in longer documents (or in a separate, always-visible frame if you use HTML frames).

Beating the Two-Dimensional Text Trap

Conditioned by centuries of printed material and the linear nature of books, our mindsets can use an adjustment. The nonlinear potentials of hypermedia give the Web a new definition for the term *document.* Of course, it's tempting to pack your pages full of hyper-capabilities until it resembles a Pony Express dynamite shipment and gallops off in many directions at once. To avoid this, judge your hypermedia according to whether it (1) adds interest, (2) expands on your content, or (3) makes a serious — and relevant — impact on the user.

Within these constraints, such material can vastly improve any user's experience of your site.

Stepping intelligently outside old-fashioned linear thinking can improve your users' experience of your site and make your information more accessible to your audience. That's why we encourage careful use of document indexes, cross-references, links to related documents, and other tools to help users navigate within your site. Keep thinking about the impact of links as you look at other people's Web materials; it's the quickest way to shake free of the linear-text trap. (The printing press was high-tech for its day, but that *was* 500 years ago!) If you're looking for a model for your site's behavior, don't think about your new trifold four-color brochure, however eye-popping; think about how your customer-service people interact with new customers on the telephone. (*What can I do to help you today?*)

Overcome Inertia through Constant Vigilance

When you're dealing with your Web materials post-publication, remember that it's only human to goof off after finishing a big job. Maintenance may not be nearly as heroic, inspiring, or remarkable as creation, yet it represents most of the activity that's needed to keep any document alive and well. Sites that aren't maintained often become ghost sites; users stop visiting sites when developers stop working on them. Never fear — a little work and attention to detail keeps your pages fresh. If you start with something valuable and keep adding value, a site's value appreciates over time — just like any other artistic masterpiece. Start with something valuable and leave it alone, and it soon becomes stale and loses value.

Consider your site from the viewpoint of a master aircraft mechanic: Correct maintenance is a real, vital, and ongoing accomplishment, without which you risk a crash. A Web site, as a vehicle for important information, deserves regular attention; maintaining a Web site requires discipline and respect. See `www.disobey.com/ghostsites/index.shtml` for a humorous look at ghost sites.

Keeping up with constant change translates into creating (and adhering to) a regular maintenance schedule. Make it somebody's job to spend time on a site regularly; check to make sure the job's getting done. If someone is set to handle regular site updates, changes, and improvements, normally they start flogging other participants to give them things to do when scheduled site maintenance rolls around. Next thing you know, everybody's involved in keeping information fresh — just as they should be. This keeps your visitors coming back for more!

Chapter 21

Ten Great HTML Resources

*B*uilding Web pages or sites is like any other avocation — or should that be "obsession?" — no matter how much you know or can do, you can still always learn and do more. This book only scratches the surface of an entire world of details, tips, tricks, and nuts-and-bolts topics relevant to creating an interesting and exciting Web presence. In this chapter, we look at just ten (or so) HTML and Web design resources in the vast world of information available online. Use these pointers to explore topics or details that interest you, but don't say we didn't warn you — you can get completely *lost* in here!

Accessing the Mother of All HTML Resources

The World Wide Web Consortium (W3C) is the industry group responsible for Web technologies and markup languages — from the Hypertext Transfer Protocol (HTTP) to the Common Gateway Interface (CGI), to markup languages from HTML to XHTML, XML, and beyond. To keep abreast of the latest rules and regulations governing markup languages, drop in on www.w3.org from time to time.

Here you'll find formal specifications — known on the W3C pages as *recommendations* — for past and current markup languages, as well as information about work underway to define new markup capabilities. Presently the W3C's HTML home page resides at www.w3.org/markup/. From there you can

- Read news and recommendations.
- Access tutorials and guidelines.
- Use HTML validation services (http://validator.w3.org/).
- Dig into all kind of other interesting official views and documents about HTML.

Finding Out About Usable and Accessible HTML

Though the adjectives that embellish this section heading may seem pretty innocuous, they're actually subjects of tremendous interest, discussion, and sometimes even controversy.

Usability represents a belief system as much as it represents a collection of best practices for constructing effective HTML documents that are easy to use and follow.

Two high priests of usability are Jakob Nielsen and Steve Krug; their Web sites (and their many books and publications) represent some of the best thinking and discussion on this topic.

- **Useit.com:** Visit Jakob Nielsen's site at www.useit.com (and be sure to check out www.useit.com/alertbox/ for access to a broad range of articles, musings, and information on usability topics).
- **Sensible.com:** Steve Krug's public face is aptly named Advanced Common Sense and is available online at www.sensible.com; be sure to check out his "This Month's Tip" feature.

Accessibility, on the other hand, relates to making Web site content available to those who may not be otherwise able to absorb it. For example, accessibility issues may address ways to describe images verbally or make text-to-speech translations for those who might not be able to see because of vision impairment or for some other reason. Similar consideration for those with other disabilities turns this topic into a fascinating discussion of how to reach all members of a possible audience fairly and equally.

You may not think accessibility is important to your site or Web pages, but if your organization does business with local, municipal, state, or federal governments, you may be required to conform to accessibility guidelines.

For more information on the accessibility topics, pointers to all kinds of documentation and guidelines, and so forth, check out the Web Accessibility

Initiative (WAI) page at `www.w3.org/WAI/`. Please note the handy Resources area on this page, where you'll find links to all kinds of useful and relevant information on the topic.

Visiting the Web Developer's Library

One of our all-time favorite online resources for HTML- and Web-related development tools, topics, tutorials, and a whole bunch more is at the Web Developer's Library. Visit `www.wdvl.com` to see what we mean. You can spend months digging around here and never even come close to exhausting all the thousands upon thousands of treasures contained herein.

The HTML Authoring page at `www.wdvl.com/authoring/html/` is likely to be of great interest to many readers of this book. There, you'll find online courses, reference information about HTML elements and tools, and some great tips and pointers on building good Web page navigation controls.

When you're trying to remember arcane details or techniques, or looking for input and advice on best design and implementation practices, the Web Developer's Library is almost always a good bet!

Need HTML Help?

Although the content at the Web Design Group's HTMLhelp site (`www.htmlhelp.com`) is kind of dated — the site's owners pretty much stopped updating it when HTML 4 was forever frozen in 1999, and XHTML became the new "big thing" for leading-edge Web developers — this remains a useful site nevertheless.

For one thing, the HTMLhelp BBS, or Bulletin Board Service (`www.htmlhelp.com/bbs/`), remains active and widely used. On the day we updated this chapter, there were nearly 70 postings, and over 3,000 postings spread across nearly 800 message threads available. This is a busy, active site and a great place to ask for HTML advice, usage details, or clarification of things you may not fully understand or know how to use.

Likewise, the FAQ (with answers, of course) on Web authoring also remains a useful and popular resource. Check it out at `www.htmlhelp.com/faq/html`.

Joining the HTML Writers Guild

The HTML Writers Guild is a worldwide educational organization for Web developers. With nearly 150,000 registered members, it's certainly attracted plenty of interest and attention from Web developers, HTML hackers, and content creators from many walks of life. Visit www.hwg.org to check out its offerings. We predict you'll find the Resources area particularly worthy because it indexes and annotates lots of useful sites and information available online.

Visit the organization's eClass Catalog for a taste of the online training the Writers Guild makes available to members. Topics covered include Dreamweaver, Microsoft FrontPage, Flash, Fireworks, and a host of other Web tools and development environments. From the home page at www.hwg.org, click eClasses, and then click Course Catalog, for a current list of offerings. As we write this, 47 online classes are available; by the time you read this, that number may be higher!

You can obtain a free trial membership, which lasts up to a full year, simply by clicking the Join! button on the home page. Individuals pay just $49 a year thereafter, for access to a great collection of resources, information, and training.

Checking a Web Reference

Although you can find many good references about the Web on the Web, the one at www.webreference.com is particularly worth investigating. The experts at the HTML Writers Guild (see the previous section) are also involved in this site, which provides advertising-supported pointers to all kinds of resources that offer help with HTML and Web development.

The site also offers access to information from a whole host of expert gurus, who respond to public questions from site visitors in the form of tutorials, articles, and other helpful forms of exposition. You can also sign up for newsletters to keep abreast of news and site changes. Definitely worth a visit!

The HTML With Style area on the site at http://webreference.com/html/ is particularly noteworthy because it includes a whole slew of tutorials on topics like Cascading Style Sheets (CSS), HTTP controls in Web document headers, character and color references, and much, much more. Be sure to check the bottom of this page for pointers to tons of additional tutorials, style-sheet information, and tool notes.

Checking Out Toolboxes

The Bravenet home page (www.bravenet.com) offers all kinds of useful, free Web tools to registered members. From polls, to message boards, to hit counters and site statistics, to search engines and e-mail forms, you'll find lots of useful widgets here.

Kira's Web Toolbox is a long-time source of information and inspiration for HTML developers and aficionados. Worth rummaging around in, you'll find this toolbox at http://lightsphere.com/dev/. It contains great information about CGI programming, passwords, icons, and Web templates.

WebAttack (www.webattack.com) offers pointers to beaucoups of freeware and shareware Web tools and utilities. It also includes useful search and personalization utilities that let you concentrate on what's new each time you visit this helpful site.

The Web Developer's Journal site includes an area titled New and Cool Web Tools (www.webdevelopersjournal.com/software/webtools.html). Dig around to find all kinds of interesting editors, design tools, utilities, and plug-ins.

Mega Web Tools (www.megawebtools.com) is a metatoolbox. That is, it's a source of pointers to hundreds of other toolbox sites online. Nicely categorized and annotated, this is a great clearinghouse to go looking for more widgets and frammistats for your Web toolbox.

WebMonkey Rules

The folks at WebMonkey (http://hotwired.lycos.com/webmonkey/) are part of the HotWired family of Web sites, hosted at Lycos and heir to the ever-so-trendy *WIRED* magazine. Despite (or maybe because of) its ultra-cool pedigree, this site is a treasure trove of facts, best practices, and strong opinions on just about any Web topic you might care to investigate. The Quick Reference section is also pretty dandy, with some of the best browser-compatibility information available anywhere, great style-sheet information, and more. It's one of our favorite sources for well-crafted opinions and good advice.

Finding HTML Goodies

Although we're not completely sure we've saved the best resources for the tenth and final spot in this chapter, HTML Goodies (www.htmlgoodies.com) definitely lives up to its name. Starting with a set of great primers on HTML, JavaScript, Active Server Pages (ASP), and other HTML-related topics, you'll find lots of great information here. Check out the Tutorials and Beyond HTML hyperlinks for pointers to all kinds of useful information, examples, and more. Also, take a look at its discussion groups and newsletters: All are chock-full of useful and timely information.

Part VII
Appendixes

The 5th Wave   By Rich Tennant

Gil Haffass DMD

"Good news, honey! No one's registered our last name as a domain name yet! Hellooo Haffassoralsurgery.com!"

In this part . . .

This part of the book supplements the main text with useful resources and summary information. It includes a complete list of HTML elements, with syntax and brief explanations, a reasonably complete listing of common HTML character codes, a glossary of technical terms found elsewhere in the book, and an index you can use to find your way around the text. We hope you'll not only get to know these supporting members of our cast, but that you'll also use them often and well!

Appendix A

HTML 4 Tags

*K*eeping track of the bountiful bevy of HTML elements can often be tricky, even for experienced Webmasters. To make your HTML life a bit easier, we created this appendix, which includes a table that lists the following information for each element:

- **Name:** The name of the element.
- **Chapter number:** The chapter(s) in which you can find information about the element.

   Some of the more complicated, less frequently used, or deprecated elements are not discussed in detail in this book. Please visit the W3C site at www.w3.org/TR/html4/index/elements.html for more information on these elements.

- **Empty:** If the tag is listed with the letter *E,* the tag is an empty tag and is forbidden to have an end tag.
- **Deprecated:** If the tag is listed with a *D,* then the tag is deprecated, and you should consider using a style sheet rule in its place.
- **Description:** A description of the tag.
- **Attributes:** This list includes the attributes that can be used with the element. When the element takes the common attributes, also called core attributes, we simply say "All core attributes." (As a reminder, those attributes are id, class, style, and title.)

  There are also language and event attributes that can be used with most elements. Likewise, when these attributes apply to elements, we simply say "language attributes" and/or "event attributes," respectively. The language attributes are dir and lang. The event attributes are onclick, ondblclick, onmousedown, onmouseup, onmouseover, onmousemove, onmouseout, onkeypress, onkeydown, and onkeyup. See Chapter 12 for more information on what these attributes do. If an element can only use some of these event attributes, we list them individually. If we just say "event attributes," the element uses all of them.

Table A-1   **HTML Tags**

Name	Ch #	Empty?	Deprecated	Description	Attributes
a	5, 13	N		Anchor	All core attributes, language attributes, event attributes, `accesskey`, `charset`, `coords`, `href`, `hreflang`, `name`, `onblur`, `onfocus`, `rel`, `rev`, `shape`, `tabindex`, `type`
abbr	7	N		Abbreviated form (for example, WWW, HTTP)	All core attributes, language attributes, event attributes
acronym	7	N		Indicates an acronym	All core attributes, language attributes, event attributes
address	N/A	N		Information on author	All core attributes, language attributes, event attributes
applet	N/A	N	D	Java applet	All core attributes, `align`, `alt`, `archive`, `class`, `code`, `codebase`, `height`, `hspace`, `id`, `name`, `object`, `style`, `title`, `vspace`, `width`
area	6	Y		Client-side image map area	All core attributes, language attributes, event attributes, `accesskey`, `alt`, `coords`, `href`, `nohref`, `onblur`, `onfocus`, `shape`, `tabindex`
b	7	N		Bold text style	All core attributes, language attributes, event attributes
base	N/A	Y		Document base URI	`href`, `target`
basefont	N/A	Y	D	Base font size	`color`, `face`, `id`, `size`
bdo	N/A	N		I18N BiDi override	All core attributes, language attributes
big	7	N		Large text style	All core attributes, language attributes, event attributes

Name	*Ch #*	*Empty?*	*Deprecated*	*Description*	*Attributes*
blockquote	4	N		Long quotation	All core attributes, language attributes, event attributes, `cite`
body	4, 7	N		Document body	All core attributes, language attributes, event attributes, `alink`, `background`, `link`, `onload`, `onunload`, `text`, `vlink`
br	4	Y		Forced line break	All core attributes
button	N/A	N		Push button	All core attributes, language attributes, event attributes, `accesskey`, `disabled`, `name`, `onblur`, `onfocus`, `tabindex`, `type`, `value`
caption	N/A	N		Table caption	All core attributes, language attributes, event attributes
center	8	N	D	Use `div align="center"` instead	
cite	7	N		Citation	All core attributes, language attributes, event attributes
code	7	N		Computer code fragment	All core attributes, language attributes, event attributes
col	8	Y		Table column	All core attributes, language attributes, event attributes, `align`, `char`, `charoff`, `span`, `valign`, `width`
colgroup	8	N		Table column group	All core attributes, language attributes, event attributes, `align`, `char`, `charoff`, `span`, `valign`, `width`
dd	4	N		Definition description	All core attributes, language attributes, event attributes
del	7	N		Deleted text	All core attributes, language attributes, event attributes, `cite`, `datetime`

(continued)

Table A-1 *(continued)*

Name	Ch #	Empty?	Deprecated	Description	Attributes
dfn	7	N		Instance definition	All core attributes, language attributes, event attributes
dir	N/A	N	D	Directory list	All core attributes, language attributes, event attributes, `compact`
div	11	N		Generic language/ style container	All core attributes, language attributes, event attributes
dl	4	N		Definition list	All core attributes, language attributes, event attributes
dt	4	N		Definition term	All core attributes, language attributes, event attributes
em	7	N		Emphasis	All core attributes, language attributes, event attributes
fieldset	N/A	N		Form control group	All core attributes, language attributes, event attributes, `accesskey`, `align`
font	7	N	D	Local change to font	All core attributes, language attributes, `face`, `color`, `size`
form	10	N		Interactive form	All core attributes, language attributes, event attributes, `accept`, `accept-charset`, `action`, `enctype`, `method`, `name`, `onreset`, `onsubmit`
frame	9	Y		Subwindow	All core attributes, `frameborder`, `longdesc`, `marginheight`, `marginwidth`, `name`, `noresize`, `scrolling`, `src`
frameset	9	N		Window subdivision	All core attributes, `cols`, `onload`, `onunload`, `rows`
h1-h6	4	N		Heading 1-6	All core attributes, language attributes, event attributes

Name	Ch #	Empty?	Deprecated	Description	Attributes
head	4	N		Document head	language attributes, `profile`
hr	4	Y		Horizontal rule	All core attributes, language attributes, event attributes
html	4	N		Document root element	Language attributes
i	7	N		Italic text style	All core attributes, language attributes, event attributes
iframe	N/A	N		Inline subwindow	All core attributes, `align`, `frameborder`, `height`, `longdesc`, `marginheight`, `marginwidth`, `name`, `scrolling`, `src`, `width`
img	6	Y		Embedded image	All core attributes, language attributes, event attributes, `alt`, `height`, `ismap`, `longdesc`, `name`, `src`, `usemap`, `width`
input	10, 12, 15	Y		Form control	All core attributes, language attributes, event attributes, `accept`, `accesskey`, `alt`, `checked`, `disabled`, `ismap`, `maxlength`, `name`, `onblur`, `onchange`, `onfocus`, `onselect`, `readonly`, `size`, `src`, `tabindex`, `type`, `usemap`, `value`
ins	7	N		Inserted text	All core attributes, language attributes, event attributes, `cite`, `datetime`
isindex	N/A	Y	D	Single line prompt	All core attributes, language attributes, `prompt`
kbd	7	N		Text to be entered by the user	All core attributes, language attributes, event attributes

(continued)

Table A-1 *(continued)*

Name	Ch #	Empty?	Deprecated	Description	Attributes
label	N/A	N		Form field label text	All core attributes, language attributes, event attributes, `accesskey`, `onblur`, `onfocus`
legend	N/A	N		Fieldset legend	All core attributes, language attributes, event attributes, `accesskey`
li	4	N		List item	All core attributes, language attributes, event attributes
link	11	Y		A media-independent link	All core attributes, language attributes, event attributes, `charset`, `href`, `hreflang`, `media`, `rel`, `rev`, `type`
map	6	N		Client-side image map	All core attributes, language attributes, event attributes, `name`
menu	N/A	N	D	Menu list	All core attributes, language attributes, event attributes, `compact`
meta	4	Y		Generic meta-information	Language attributes, `http-equiv`, `name`, `content`, `scheme`
noframes	9	N		Alternate content container for non frame-based rendering	All core attributes, language attributes, event attributes
noscript	N/A	N		Alternate content container for non script-based rendering	All core attributes, language attributes, event attributes

Name	Ch #	Empty?	Deprecated	Description	Attributes
object	13	N		Generic embedded object	All core attributes, language attributes, event attributes, `archive`, `classid`, `codebase`, `codetype`, `data`, `declare`, `height`, `name`, `standby`, `tabindex`, `type`, `usemap`, `width`
ol	4	N		Ordered list	All core attributes, language attributes, event attributes
optgroup	N/A	N		Option group	All core attributes, language attributes, event attributes, `disabled`, `multiple`, `name`, `onblur`, `onchange`, `onfocus`, `size`, `tabindex`
option	10	N		Selectable choice	All core attributes, language attributes, event attributes, `disabled`, `multiple`, `name`, `onblur`, `onchange`, `onfocus`, `size`, `tabindex`
p	4	N		Paragraph	All core attributes, language attributes, event attributes, `align`
param	13	Y		Named property value	`id`, `name`, `type`, `value`, `valuetype`
pre	4	N		Preformatted text	All core attributes, language attributes, event attributes, `width`
q	N/A	N		Short inline quotation	All core attributes, language attributes, event attributes, `cite`
s	7	N	D	Strikethrough text style	All core attributes, language attributes, event attributes

(continued)

Table A-1 *(continued)*

Name	Ch #	Empty?	Deprecated	Description	Attributes
samp	7	N		Sample program output, scripts, and so on	All core attributes, language attributes, event attributes
script	12	N		Script statements	`charset`, `defer`, `language`, `src`, `type`
select	10	N		Option selector	All core attributes, language attributes, event attributes, `disabled`, `multiple`, `name`, `onblur`, `onchange`, `onfocus`, `size`, `tabindex`
small	7	N		Small text style	All core attributes, language attributes, event attributes
span	11	N		Generic language/ style container	All core attributes, language attributes, event attributes
strike	7	N	D	Strikethrough text	All core attributes, language attributes, event attributes
strong	7	N		Strong emphasis	All core attributes, language attributes, event attributes
style	11	N		Style info	language attributes, `media`, `title`, `type`
sub	N/A	N		Subscript	All core attributes, language attributes, event attributes
sup	N/A	N		Superscript	All core attributes, language attributes, event attributes
table	8	N		Table	All core attributes, language attributes, event attributes, `align`, `border`, `cellpadding`, `cellspacing`, `frame`, `rules`, `summary`, `width`
tbody	8	N		Table body	All core attributes, language attributes, event attributes, `align`, `char`, `charoff`, `valign`

Name	Ch #	Empty?	Deprecated	Description	Attributes
td	8	N		Table data cell	All core attributes, language attributes, event attributes, `abbr`, `align`, `axis`, `char`, `charoff`, `colspan`, `headers`, `rowspan`, `scope`, `valign`
textarea	10	N		Multi-line text field	All core attributes, language attributes, event attributes, `accesskey`, `cols`, `disabled`, `name`, `onblur`, `onchange`, `onfocus`, `onselect`, `readonly`, `rows`, `tabindex`
tfoot	8	N		Table footer	All core attributes, language attributes, event attributes, `align`, `char`, `charoff`, `valign`
th	8	N		Table header cell	All core attributes, language attributes, event attributes, `abbr`, `align`, `axis`, `char`, `charoff`, `colspan`, `headers`, `rowspan`, `scope`, `valign`
thead	8	N		Table header	All core attributes, language attributes, event attributes, `align`, `char`, `charoff`, `valign`
title	4	N		Document title	Language attributes
tr	8	N		Table row	All core attributes, language attributes, event attributes, `align`, `bgcolor`, `char`, `charoff`, `valign`
tt	7	N		Teletype or monospaced text style	All core attributes, language attributes, event attributes

(continued)

Table A-1 *(continued)*

Name	Ch #	Empty?	Deprecated	Description	Attributes
u	7	N	D	Underlined text style	All core attributes, language attributes, event attributes
ul	4	N		Unordered list	All core attributes, language attributes, event attributes
var	7	N		Instance of a variable or program argument	All core attributes, language attributes, event attributes

Appendix B

HTML Character Codes

*T*his appendix includes listings for all the character sets supported by HTML 4.0 (and consequently HTML 4.01). Use the nine tables here to find out what you have to type in order to get HTML to output characters that aren't part of the ASCII character set. Each table includes:

✔ The character

✔ The character's numeric entity

✔ The character's character entity

Chapter 1 details why you might want to use any of these entities and how you use them with your markup.

Keep in mind that we couldn't get some characters to display correctly because of font restrictions, so be sure to try using the entity and displaying it in your browser to see what symbol appears.

Even though everything listed here is part of the HTML 4.01 standard, *not all browsers support these characters.* Even if you test your code on your favorite browser before you consider it ready for action, such testing is no guarantee of universal usability. As a general rule, the character shortcuts are least supported and the numeric characters are most supported.

ISO-Latin-1

ISO-Latin-1 is fully supported by all current and most older browsers. Review Table B-1 to find out what you need to know. Check out Table B-9 in the section "More ISO Character Sets Than You Can Shake a Stick At," later in this appendix.

Table B-1	The ISO-Latin-1 Character Set	
Character/Description	*Numeric Entity*	*Character Entity*
Em space, not collapsed	None	
En space	None	
Em space	&#00; – &#08;	
Horizontal tab	&#09;	
Line feed or new line	&#10;	
Unused	&#11; – &#31;	
Space	&#32;	
!	&#33;	
"	&#34;	&quot;
#	&#35;	
$	&#36;	
%	&#37;	
&	&#38;	&amp;
' (Apostrophe)	&#39;	
(	&#40;	
)	&#41;	
*	&#42;	
+	&#43;	
, (Comma)	&#44;	
– (Minus sign)	&#45;	
. (Period)	&#46;	
/	&#47;	

Character/Description	*Numeric Entity*	*Character Entity*
0-9 (Numerals, where 0 is 0, 1 is 1, and so on)	0 - 9	None
:	&#58;	
;	&#59;	
<	&#60;	&lt;
=	&#61;	
>	&#62;	&gt;
?	&#63;	
@	&#64;	
A-Z (Capitals, where A is A, B is B, and so on)	A - Z	None
[	&#91;	
\	&#92;	
]	&#93;	
^	&#94;	
_ (Underscore)	&#95;	
` (Grave accent)	&#96;	
a-z (Lowercase, where a is a, b is b, and so on)	a - z	None
{	&#123;	
|	|	
}	&#125;	
~	&#126;	
Unused	&#127; - Ÿ	
Nonbreaking space		
¡	&#161;	&iexcl;
¢	&#162;	&cent;

(continued)

Table B-1 *(continued)*

Character/Description	Numeric Entity	Character Entity
£	&#163;	&pound;
¤	&#164;	&curren;
¥	&#165;	&yen;
¦	&#166;	&brvbar;
§	&#167;	&sect;
¨	&#168;	&uml;
©	&#169;	&copy;
ª	&#170;	&ordf;
«	&#171	&laquo;
¬	&#172;	&not;
- (Soft hyphen)	&#173;	&shy;
®	&#174;	&reg;
¯	&#175;	&macr;
°	&#176;	&deg;
±	&#177;	&plusmn;
²	&#178;	&sup2;
³	&#179;	&sup3;
´ (Acute accent)	&#180;	&acute;
µ	&#181;	&micro;
¶	&#182;	&para;
•	&#183;	&middot;
¸ (Cedilla)	&#184;	&cedil;
¹	&#185;	&sup1;
º	&#186;	&ordm;
»	&#187;	&raquo;
¼	&#188;	&frac14;
½	&#189;	&frac12;

Character/Description	Numeric Entity	Character Entity
3/4	&#190;	&frac34;
¿	&#191;	&iquest;
À	&#192;	&Agrave;
Á	&#193;	&Aacute;
Â	&#194;	&Acirc;
Ã	&#195;	&Atilde;
Ä	&#196;	&Auml;
Å	&#197;	&Aring;
Æ	&#198;	&AElig;
Ç	&#199;	&Ccedil;
È	&#200;	&Egrave;
É	&#201;	&Eacute;
Ê	&#202;	&Ecirc;
Ë	&#203;	&Euml;
Ì	&#204;	&Igrave;
Í	&#205;	&Iacute;
Î	&#206;	&Icirc;
Ï	&#207;	&Iuml;
Ð	&#208;	&ETH;
Ñ	&#209;	&Ntilde;
Ò	&#210;	&Ograve;
Ó	&#211;	&Oacute;
Ô	&#212;	&Ocirc;
Õ	&#213;	&Otilde;
Ö	&#214;	&Ouml;
×	&#215;	&times;
Ø	&#216;	&Oslash;
Ù	&#217;	&Ugrave;

(continued)

Table B-1 *(continued)*

Character/Description	Numeric Entity	Character Entity
Ú	`&#218;`	`&Uacute;`
Û	`&#219;`	`&Ucirc;`
Ü	`&#220;`	`&Uuml;`
Ý	`&#221;`	`&Yacute;`
þ	`&#222;`	`&THORN;`
ß	`&#223;`	`&szlig;`
à	`&#224;`	`&agrave;`
á	`&#225;`	`&aacute;`
â	`&#226;`	`&acirc;`
ã	`&#227;`	`&atilde;`
ä	`&#228;`	`&auml;`
å	`&#229;`	`&aring;`
æ	`&#230;`	`&aelig;`
ç	`&#231;`	`&ccedil;`
è	`&#232;`	`&egrave;`
é	`&#233;`	`&eacute;`
ê	`&#234;`	`&ecirc;`
ë	`&#235;`	`&euml;`
ì	`&#236;`	`&igrave;`
í	`&#237;`	`&iacute;`
î	`&#238;`	`&icirc;`
ï	`&#239;`	`&iuml;`
ð	`&#240;`	`&eth;`
ñ	`&#241;`	`&ntilde;`
ò	`&#242;`	`&ograve;`
ó	`&#243;`	`&oacute;`
ô	`&#244;`	`&ocirc;`
õ	`&#245;`	`&otilde;`

Character/Description	Numeric Entity	Character Entity
ö	&#246;	&ouml;
÷	&#247;	&divide;
ø	&#248;	&oslash;
ù	&#249;	&ugrave;
ú	&#250;	&uacute;
û	&#251;	&ucirc;
ü	&#252;	&uuml;
ý	&#253;	&yacute;
þ	&#254;	&thorn;
ÿ	&#255;	&yuml;

Greek Characters

If you have a need to use Greek characters, Table B-2 gives you everything you need to know.

Table B-2	Greek Characters	
Character	**Numeric Entity**	**Character Entity**
A	&#913;	&Alpha;
B	&#914;	&Beta;
Γ	&#915;	&Gamma;
Δ	&#916;	&Delta;
E	&#917;	&Epsilon;
Z	&#918;	&Zeta;
H	&#919;	&Eta;
Θ	&#920;	&Theta;
I	&#921;	&Iota;
K	&#922;	&Kappa;

(continued)

Table B-2 *(continued)*

Character	Numeric Entity	Character Entity
Λ	`&#923;`	`&Lambda;`
Μ	`&#924;`	`&Mu;`
Ν	`&#925;`	`&Nu;`
Ξ	`&#926;`	`&Xi;`
Ο	`&#927;`	`&Omicron;`
Π	`&#928;`	`&Pi;`
Ρ	`&#929;`	`&Rho;`
Σ	`&#931;`	`&Sigma;`
Τ	`&#932;`	`&Tau;`
Υ	`&#933;`	`&Upsilon;`
Φ	`&#934;`	`&Phi;`
Χ	`&#935;`	`&Chi;`
Ψ	`&#936;`	`&Psi;`
Ω	`&#937;`	`&Omega;`
α	`&#945;`	`&alpha;`
β	`&#946;`	`&beta;`
γ	`&#947;`	`&gamma;`
δ	`&#948;`	`&delta;`
ε	`&#949;`	`&epsilon;`
ζ	`&#950;`	`&zeta;`
η	`&#951;`	`&eta;`
θ	`&#952;`	`&theta;`
ι	`&#953;`	`&iota;`
κ	`&#954;`	`&kappa;`
λ	`&#955;`	`&lambda;`
μ	`&#956;`	`&mu;`
ν	`&#957;`	`&nu;`
ξ	`&#958;`	`&xi;`

Character	Numeric Entity	Character Entity
o	ο	ο
π	π	π
ρ	ρ	ρ
ς	ς	ς
σ	σ	σ
τ	τ	τ
υ	υ	υ
φ	φ	φ
χ	χ	χ
ψ	ψ	ψ
ω	ω	ω
θ	ϑ	ϑ
ϒ	ϒ	ϒ
π	ϖ	ϖ

Special Punctuation

Use the information in Table B-3 to help format bullets, horizontal ellipsis, and other special punctuation.

Table B-3	Special Punctuation	
Character	*Numeric Entity*	*Character Entity*
•	•	•
...	…	…
′	′	′
″	″	″
‾	‾	‾
⁄	⁄	⁄

Characters That Could Be Letters

Maybe in a parallel universe, these characters might be letters. We're not sure why you'd need to use these characters, but they are laid out for you in Table B-4.

Table B-4	Letter-like Characters	
Character	*Numeric Entity*	*Character Entity*
℘	`&#8472;`	`&weierp;`
ℑ	`&#8465;`	`&image;`
ℜ	`&#8476;`	`&real;`
™	`&#8482;`	`&trade;`
ℵ	`&#8501;`	`&alefsym;`

Characters That Point

We never really knew how many ways you can make an arrow until we learned HTML. Now we pass on this wisdom to you in Table B-5.

Table B-5	Arrow Characters	
Character	*Numeric Entity*	*Character Entity*
←	`&#8592;`	`&larr;`
↑	`&#8593;`	`&uarr;`
→	`&#8594;`	`&rarr;`
↓	`&#8595;`	`&darr;`
↔	`&#8596;`	`&harr;`
↵	`&#8629;`	`&crarr;`
⇐	`&#8656;`	`&lArr;`
⇑	`&#8657;`	`&uArr;`

Character	Numeric Entity	Character Entity
⇒	⇒	⇒
⇓	⇓	⇓
⇔	⇔	⇔

Heavy-Duty Mathematical Characters

Get out your pocket protector. If you're in a technical or scientific field, the characters in Table B-6 might be right up your subset.

Table B-6	Mathematical Characters	
Character	*Numeric Entity*	*Character Entity*
∀	∀	∀
∂	∂	∂
∃	∃	∃
∅	∅	∅
∆	∇	∇
∈	∈	∈
∉	∉	∉
∋	∋	∋
∏	∏	∏
Σ	∑	∑
−	−	−
∗	∗	∗
√	√	√
∝	∝	∝
∞	∞	∞

(continued)

Table B-6 (continued)

Character	Numeric Entity	Character Entity
∠	`&#8736;`	`&ang;`
∧	`&#2227;`	`&and;`
∨	`&#2228;`	`&or;`
∪	`&#8746;`	`&cup;`
∫	`&#8747;`	`&int;`
∴	`&#8756;`	`&there4;`
∼	`&#8764;`	`&sim;`
≅	`&#8773;`	`&cong;`
≈	`&#8776;`	`&asymp;`
≠	`&#8800;`	`&ne;`
≡	`&#8801;`	`&equiv;`
≤	`&#8804;`	`&le;`
≥	`&#8805;`	`&ge;`
⊂	`&#8834;`	`&sub;`
⊃	`&#8835;`	`&sup;`
⊄	`&#8836;`	`&nsub;`
⊆	`&#8838;`	`&sube;`
⊇	`&#8839;`	`&supe;`
⊕	`&#8853;`	`&oplus;`
⊗	`&#8855;`	`&otimes;`
⊥	`&#8869;`	`&perp;`
•	`&#8901;`	`&sdot;`

Technical Characters

The technical characters in Table B-7 are funky-looking brackets. Do with them what you will, and rest easy knowing that they exist.

Table B-7	Technical Characters	
Character	*Numeric Entity*	*Character Entity*
⌈	`&#8968;`	`&lceil;`
⌉	`&#8969;`	`&rceil;`
⌊	`&#8970;`	`&lfloor;`
⌋	`&#8971;`	`&rfloor;`
⟨	`&#9001;`	`&lang;`
⟩	`&#9002;`	`&rang;`

Hearts, Spades, Clubs, and Diamonds

Card fiend? Check out Table B-8.

Table B-8	Playing Card Symbols	
Character	*Numeric Entity*	*Character Entity*
♠	`&#9824;`	`&spades;`
♣	`&#9827;`	`&clubs;`
♥	`&#9829;`	`&hearts;`
♦	`&#9830;`	`&diams;`

More ISO Character Sets Than You Can Shake a Stick At

Not that you would shake a stick at anything. Ever. Who shakes sticks? Anyway, in addition to the various characters shown in this appendix, numerous variants of the ISO-Latin character set have been created, primarily to support developers (and users) who want to read Web pages in languages other than English. As Table B-9 shows, there are 10 named versions of the ISO-Latin character sets, and 15 versions of ISO-Latin itself, each of which is aimed at a separate collection of languages. If you want to service readers in languages other than English, these character sets will be important to you.

Table B-9		ISO 8859 Character Sets
Character Set	*Script*	*Languages*
ISO-8859-1	Latin-1	ASCII plus most Western European languages, including Albanian, Afrikaans, Basque, Catalan, Danish, Dutch, English, Faroese, Finnish, Flemish, Galician, German, Icelandic, Irish, Italian, Norwegian, Portuguese, Scottish, Spanish, and Swedish. Omits certain Dutch, French, and German characters.
ISO-8859-2	Latin-2	ASCII plus most Central European languages, including Czech, English, German, Hungarian, Polish, Romanian, Croatian, Slovak, Slovene, and Serbian.
ISO-8859-3	Latin-3	ASCII plus characters required for English, Esperanto, German, Maltese, and Galician.
ISO-8859-4	Latin-4	ASCII plus most Baltic languages, including Latvian, Lithuanian, German, Greenlandic, and Lappish; now superseded by ISO-Latin-6.
ISO-8859-5		ASCII plus Cyrillic characters for Slavic languages, including Byelorussian, Bulgarian, Macedonian, Russian, Serbian, and Ukrainian.
ISO-8859-6		ASCII plus Arabic characters.
ISO-8859-7		ASCII plus Greek characters.
ISO-8859-8		ASCII plus Hebrew.
ISO-8859-9	Latin-5	Latin-1 except that some Turkish symbols replace Icelandic ones.
ISO-8859-10	Latin-6	ASCII plus most Nordic languages, including Latvian, Lithuanian, Inuit, non-Skolt Sami, and Icelandic.
ISO-8859-11		ASCII plus Thai.
ISO-8859-12	Latin-7	ASCII plus Celtic.
ISO-8859-13	Latin-8	ASCII plus the Baltic Rim characters.
ISO-8859-14	Latin-9	ASCII plus Sami (Finnish).
ISO-8859-15	Latin-10	Variation on Latin-1 that includes Euro currency sign, plus extra accented Finnish and French characters.

Appendix C

Glossary

· ·

absolute: When used to modify pathnames or URLs, a full and complete file specification (as opposed to a relative one). An absolute specification includes a host identifier, a complete volume, and path specification.

anchor: In HTML, an anchor is tagged text or a graphic element that acts as a link to another location inside or outside a given document, or an anchor may be a location in a document that acts as the destination for an incoming link. The latter definition is most commonly how we use it in this book.

animation: A computerized process of creating moving images by rapidly advancing from one still image to the next. In HTML, animated GIFs are typically used to produce this effect.

attribute: A named characteristic associated with a specific HTML element. Some attributes are required, and others are optional. Some attributes also take values (if so, the syntax is `attribute="value"`), depending on the particular element and attribute involved.

bandwidth: Technically, the range of electrical frequencies a device can handle; more often, bandwidth is used as a measure of a communication technology's carrying capacity. The more bandwidth users have on their machines, the more quickly they can access HTML files.

beta testing: When you and a limited group of users test your Web site before you share it with the rest of the world.

bookmark: A reference from a saved list of URLs kept by the Netscape Web browser. Bookmarks allow quick loading of a Web site without retyping the URL. Bookmarks are also known as Favorites in Microsoft Internet Explorer.

browser: A Web access program that can request HTML documents from Web servers and render such documents on a user's display device. See also *client.*

bugs: Issues that sometimes show up in software in the form of major or minor errors, mistakes, and gotchas. Bugs got their name from insects found in antiquated tube-based computers of the late 1950s and early 1960s that were attracted to the glow of the filament in a tube. Bugs that show up in HTML markup can mess up a visitor's attempt to navigate your site.

CGI (Common Gateway Interface): The specification that governs how Web browsers communicate with and request services from Web servers; also the format and syntax for passing information from browsers to servers via HTML forms or document-based queries.

client: The end-user side of the client/server arrangement; typically, client refers to a consumer (rather than a provider) of network services; a Web browser is therefore a client program that talks to Web servers.

client-side image map: The same as a server-side image map, except that the hot-spot definitions are stored within the HTML document on the client side, rather than in a map file stored on the server.

content: The raison d'être for HTML; although form is important, content is why users access Web documents and why they come back for more.

CSS (Cascading Style Sheets): A method of markup that allows users to define how certain HTML, XHTML, or XML structural elements, such as paragraphs and headings, should be displayed using style rules instead of additional markup. The versions of CSS are CSS1 and CSS2. CSS2 is the most recent completed version, and CSS3 is underway.

default: In general computer-speak, a selection made automatically in a program if the user specifies no explicit selection. For HTML, the default is the value assigned to an attribute if none is supplied.

deprecated: The term used to earmark an HTML element or attribute that is to be left for dead by future versions of HTML.

DOCTYPE declaration: HTML markup that tells the processor where to locate the DTD and contains declarations for the particular document. Also called a *document type declaration*.

document: The basic unit of HTML information; a document refers to the entire contents of any single HTML file. Because this definition doesn't always correspond to normal notions of a document, we refer to what can formally be called HTML documents more or less interchangeably with Web pages, which is how browsers render such documents for display.

DTD (Document Type Definition): A formal SGML specification for a document. A DTD lays out the structural elements and markup definitions to be used to create instances of documents.

element: A section of a document defined by a start and end tag or an empty tag.

e-mail: An abbreviation for electronic mail; e-mail is the preferred method for exchanging information between users on the Internet (and other networked systems).

empty tag: An HTML element that does not require the use of a closing tag. In fact, the use of a closing tag in empty tags is forbidden.

entity: A character string that represents another string of characters.

error message: Information delivered by a program to a user, usually to inform him or her that the process hasn't worked properly, if at all. Error messages are an ill-appreciated art form and contain some of the funniest and most opaque language we've ever seen (also, the most tragic for their unfortunate recipients).

event: A user activity, such as moving a mouse pointer over an image, clicking a link, or selecting a drop-down menu.

external style sheet: A style sheet that resides outside a Web document in a separate, external file.

footer: The concluding part of an HTML document, containing contact, version, date, and attribution information to help identify a document and its authors. Most people use the `<address>` element to identify this information.

form handler: A program on the Web server or even possibly a simple `mailto` URL that manages the data a user sends to you via the form.

forms: HTML markup that lets browsers solicit data from users and then deliver that data to specially designated input-handling programs on a Web server. Briefly, forms provide a mechanism to let users interact with servers on the Web.

FTP (File Transfer Protocol): An Internet file transfer service based on the TCP/IP protocols that provides a way to copy files to and from FTP servers elsewhere on a network.

GIF (Graphic Interchange Format): A graphics format commonly used in Web documents because of its relatively small file size and relatively sharp resolution.

graphics: Files in HTML documents that belong to one of a restricted family of types (usually .GIF or .JPG). Graphics are referenced via URLs for inline display on Web pages.

GUI (Graphical User Interface): Pronounced "gooey," GUIs make graphical Web browsers possible; they create a visually oriented interface that makes it easy for users to interact with computerized information of all kinds.

heading: A markup element used to add document structure to HTML documents. Sometimes the term refers to the initial portion of an HTML document between the `<head>` . . . `</head>` tags, where titles and context definitions are commonly supplied.

helper applications: Applications that help a browser deliver Web information to users. Although recent browsers can display multiple graphics files (and sometimes other kinds of data), sometimes they must pass certain files — for instance, motion picture or sound files — over to other applications that know how to render the data they contain.

hexadecimal: A numbering system used to condense binary numbers. The hexadecimal system is composed of six letters and ten numbers. In HTML, hexadecimal numbering is used with elements and their attributes to denote what colors should comprise backgrounds and other elements in a Web page.

HTML (Hypertext Markup Language): The SGML-derived markup language used to create Web pages. Not quite a programming language, HTML nevertheless provides a rich lexicon and syntax for designing and creating useful hypertext documents for the Web.

HTTP (Hypertext Transfer Protocol): The Internet protocol used to manage communication between Web clients (browsers) and servers.

hyperlink: A shorthand term for *hypertext link,* a block of text that a user can activate with a mouse click to navigate to another Web page.

hypermedia: Any of a variety of computer media — including text, graphics, video, sound, and so on — available through hypertext links on the Web.

hypertext: A method of organizing text, graphics, and other kinds of data for computer use that lets individual data elements point to one another; a nonlinear method of organizing information, especially text.

image map: A synonym for *clickable image,* an overlaid collection of pixel coordinates for a graphic that a user can select to activate a related hypertext link for further Web navigation.

inline content: A word or string of words inside a block element.

inline element: Any element that controls presentation on an element-by-element basis, and an inline element does not denote structure. In other words, it's a text element, for example the <b> element is an inline element.

internal style sheet: A style sheet that resides inside the Web document in which you're working and controls how its information appears on-screen.

Internet: A worldwide collection of networks that began with technology and equipment funded by the U.S. Department of Defense in the 1970s. The World Wide Web is just a portion of the Internet. Today, it links users in nearly every country, speaking nearly every known language.

ISP (Internet Service Provider): An organization that provides individuals or other organizations with access to the Internet, usually for a fee. ISPs usually offer a variety of communications options for their customers, ranging from analog telephone lines, to a variety of higher-bandwidth leased lines, to ISDN and other digital communications services.

Java: An object-oriented, platform-independent, secure, and compact programming language designed for Web application deployment. Most system vendors support Java, which was created by Sun Microsystems.

JPEG (or JPG): Joint Photographic Experts' Group; an industry association that defined a highly compressible format for images designed for complex color still images (such as photographs). JPEG files take the extension .JPG or .JPEG. Today, .JPG is one graphics format of choice for Web use, particularly for complex or photographic images.

layout: The overall arrangement of the elements in a document.

link: Also called a *hyperlink.* A pointer in one part of an HTML document that can transport users to another part of the same document, or to another document entirely. This capability puts the *hyper* into hypertext. In other words, a link is a one-to-one relationship/association between two concepts or ideas.

Lynx: A widely used text-based Web browser, useful for checking a Web page before *going live* with it (or using a Web server to host the page on the Web).

maintenance: The process of regularly inspecting, testing, and updating the contents of Web pages; also, an attitude that such activities are both inevitable and advisable.

mark up: To embed special characters (*metacharacters*) within a text file to tell a computer program how to handle the file's contents.

markup language: A formal set of special characters and related capabilities used to define a specific method for handling the display of files that include markup; HTML is a markup language used to design and create Web pages.

metadata: Specially defined elements that describe a document's structure, content, or rendering within the document itself or through external references. (Metadata literally means data about data.)

multimedia: A method of combining text, sound, graphics, and full-motion or animated video within a single compound computer document.

nameservers: Computers on the Internet that translate domain names into the actual Internet location for your computer's browser.

navigation: Refers to the use of hyperlinks to move within or between HTML documents and other Web-accessible resources.

navigation bar: An element on a Web page that arranges a series of hypertext links on a single line to provide a set of navigation controls to help users move through an HTML document or a set of HTML documents.

nesting: One structure that occurs within another; in HTML, nesting happens most commonly with list structures that may be freely nested within one another, regardless of type.

online: A term that indicates information, activity, or communications located on or taking place in, an electronic, networked computing environment (such as the Internet).

operating system: The underlying control program on a computer that makes the hardware run and supports the execution of one or more applications. DOS, Windows, Unix, and OS/2 are all examples of operating systems.

page: The generic term for an HTML document that Web users view on their browsers.

PDF (Portable Document Format): The rich, typographically correct document format of Adobe, used to provide multiplatform document access through its Acrobat software as a more powerful alternative to HTML.

plug-in: Hardware or software added to a system that adds a specific feature such as plug-ins that allow Netscape Navigator to play video.

properties: In CSS, they are the different aspects of the display of text and graphics, such as font size or background color.

relative address: An abbreviated document address that may be combined with the <base> element to create a complete address or is the complete address for a local file found in the same directory.

resource: Any HTML document, capability, or other item or service available via the Web. URLs point to resources.

robot: A special Web-traveling program that wanders widely, following and recording URLs and related titles for future reference in search engines. Also called a *spider.*

script: A set of programming instructions that activate when an event that you define occurs.

scripting language: A special kind of programming language that a computer reads and executes at the same time (which means that the computer figures out what to do with the language when it appears in a document or at the time that it's used. JavaScript is a common scripting language associated with Web use).

search engine: A Web-based application that searches the contents of a database of available Web pages and other resources to provide information that relates to specific topics or keywords, which a user supplies.

search tools: Any of a number of programs that can permit HTML documents to become searchable, using the <isindex> element to inform the browser of the need for a search window, and behind-the-scenes indexing and anchoring schemes to let users locate particular sections of or items within a document.

selector: In CSS, identifies the element to which a style rule applies.

SGML (Standard Generalized Markup Language): An ISO standard document definition, specification, and creation mechanism that makes platform and display differences across multiple computers irrelevant to the delivery and rendering of documents.

shareware: Software, available by various means, that users can run for free for a trial period. After that trial period expires, users must register and purchase the software, or they must discontinue its use.

specification: A formal document that describes the capabilities, functions, and interfaces for a specific piece of software, a markup language, or a communications protocol.

spider: A Web-traversing program that tirelessly investigates Web pages and their links, while storing information about its travels for inclusion in the databases typically used by search engines. Also called *Web spider, Web crawler, search bot,* and *robot.*

style sheet: A file that holds the layout settings for a certain category of a document. Style sheets, like templates, contain settings for headers and footers, tabs, margins, fonts, columns, and more.

syntax: The rules that govern how HTML markup looks and behaves within HTML documents. The real syntax definition for HTML comes from the SGML Document Type Definition (DTD). Markup written with the correct syntax is likelier to run well.

syntax checker: A program that checks a particular HTML document's markup against the rules that govern its use; a recommended part of the testing regimen for all HTML documents.

tag: The formal name for a piece of HTML markup that signals a command of sorts (instructions), usually enclosed in angle brackets ($<$ $>$).

template: Literally, a model to imitate. In HTML terms, a template describes the skeleton of a Web page, including the HTML for its heading and footer, and a consistent layout, and a set of navigation elements.

test plan: The series of steps and elements to follow when conducting a formal test of software or other computerized systems; we strongly recommend that you write — and use — a test plan as a part of your Web-publication process.

thumbnail: A miniature rendering of a graphical image, used as a link to the full-size version.

title: The text supplied to a Web page's title bar when displayed, used as data in many Web search engines.

Unix: The operating system of choice for the Internet community at large and the Web community, too, Unix offers the broadest range of tools, utilities, and programming libraries for Web server use.

URL (Uniform Resource Locator): The primary naming scheme used to identify Web resources. URLs define the protocols to use, the domain name of the Web server where a resource resides, the port address to use for communication, and a directory path to access named Web files or resources.

URL-encoded text: Text encoded specifically for the purpose of passing information requests and URL specifications to Web servers from browsers. URL encoding replaces spaces with plus signs (+) and substitutes special hexadecimal codes for a range of otherwise-irreproducible characters. This method is used to pass document queries from browsers to servers.

user interface: The overall design of your site, including the way it looks, fits together, and works to provide access to information. Abbreviated as *UI.* See also *GUI.*

valid: Markup that follows all the syntax rules defined in a DTD, allowing the document to pass through a validator program with no errors.

validation: The process of comparing a document to a set of document rules, in this context a DTD.

Web: Also called the *World Wide Web, WWW,* or *W3.* The complete collection of all Web servers available on the Internet, which comes as close to containing the "sum of human knowledge" as anything we've yet seen.

Web page: Synonym for an HTML document. In this book, we refer to Web pages as *sets* of related, interlinked HTML documents, usually produced by a single author or organization.

Web server: A computer, usually on the Internet, that hosts HTTP protocols and related Web-service software. See also *Web-hosting provider.*

Web site: An addressed location, usually on the Internet, that provides access to the set of Web pages that correspond to the URL for a given site. A Web site consists of a Web server and a named collection of Web documents, both accessible through a single Web address. See also *URL.*

Web-hosting provider: A company that provides space on Web servers for individuals or companies to host Web sites. See also *ISP.*

well-formed document: An HTML document that adheres to the rules that make it easy for a computer to interpret.

white space: The breathing room on a page — parts of a display or document unoccupied by text or other visual elements. A certain amount of white space is essential to make documents attractive and readable.

WYSIWYG (What You See Is What You Get): A term used to describe text editors or other layout tools (such as HTML authoring tools) that attempt to show on-screen what final, finished documents will look like.

XHTML (Extensible Hypertext Markup Language): The reformulation of HTML 4.0 as an application of XML 1.0.

XML (Extensible Markup Language): A system for defining, validating, and sharing document formats. Its main difference from HTML is that you can create your own elements.

Index

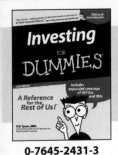

FOR

DUMMIES®

PERSONAL FINANCE & BUSINESS

HOME, GARDEN, FOOD & WINE

FITNESS, SPORTS, HOBBIES & PETS

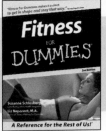

FOR DUMMIES®

A world of resources to help you grow

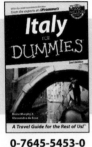

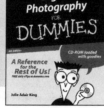

FOR DUMMIES®

Helping you expand your horizons and realize your potential

GRAPHICS & WEB SITE DEVELOPMENT

0-7645-1651-5

Creating Web Pages FOR DUMMIES

0-7645-1643-4

0-7645-0895-4

Also available:

Adobe Acrobat 5 PDF
For Dummies
(0-7645-1652-3)
ASP.NET For Dummies
(0-7645-0866-0)
ColdFusion MX for Dummies
(0-7645-1672-8)
Dreamweaver MX For
Dummies
(0-7645-1630-2)
FrontPage 2002 For Dummies
(0-7645-0821-0)

HTML 4 For Dummies
(0-7645-0723-0)
Illustrator 10 For Dummies
(0-7645-3636-2)
PowerPoint 2002 For
Dummies
(0-7645-0817-2)
Web Design For Dummies
(0-7645-0823-7)

PROGRAMMING & DATABASES

0-7645-0746-X

0-7645-1626-4

0-7645-1657-4

Also available:

Access 2002 For Dummies
(0-7645-0818-0)
Beginning Programming
For Dummies
(0-7645-0835-0)
Crystal Reports 9 For
Dummies
(0-7645-1641-8)
Java & XML For Dummies
(0-7645-1658-2)
Java 2 For Dummies
(0-7645-0765-6)

JavaScript For Dummies
(0-7645-0633-1)
Oracle9i For Dummies
(0-7645-0880-6)
Perl For Dummies
(0-7645-0776-1)
PHP and MySQL For
Dummies
(0-7645-1650-7)
SQL For Dummies
(0-7645-0737-0)
Visual Basic .NET For
Dummies
(0-7645-0867-9)

LINUX, NETWORKING & CERTIFICATION

1545-4

0-7645-1760-0

0-7645-0772-9

Also available:

A+ Certification For Dummies
(0-7645-0812-1)
CCNP All-in-One Certification
For Dummies
(0-7645-1648-5)
Cisco Networking For
Dummies
(0-7645-1668-X)
CISSP For Dummies
(0-7645-1670-1)
CIW Foundations For
Dummies
(0-7645-1635-3)

Firewalls For Dummies
(0-7645-0884-9)
Home Networking For
Dummies
(0-7645-0857-1)
Red Hat Linux All-in-One
Desk Reference For Dummies
(0-7645-2442-9)
UNIX For Dummies
(0-7645-0419-3)

erever books are sold.
dummies.com or call 1-877-762-2974 to order direct